CALIFORNIA MARRIAGE & DIVORCE LAW

By
RALPH WARNER • TONI IHARA • STEPHEN ELIAS

with editorial assistance from
Katherine M. Galvin
Robin Leonard

Important: The information in this book changes rapidly and is subject to differing interpretations. It is up to you to check it thoroughly before relying on it. Neither the author nor publisher of this book makes any guarantees regarding the outcome of the uses to which this material is put.

NOLO PRESS ■ 950 Parker Street, Berkeley, CA 94710

PLEASE READ THIS: Nolo Press is committed to keeping its books up-to-date. Each new printing, whether or not it is called a new edition, has been completely revised to reflect the latest law changes. This book was printed and updated on the last date indicated below. Before you rely on information in it, you might wish to call Nolo Press at (415) 549-1976 to check whether a later printing or edition has been issued.

Printing History

Difference between new *editions* and *printings:*

New *printing* means there have been some minor changes, but usually not enough so that people will need to trade in or discard an earlier printing of the same edition. Obviously, this is a judgment call, and any change, no matter how minor, might affect you.

New *edition* means one or more major--or a number of minor--law changes since the previous edition.

First Printing:	September 1976
Second Edition:	September 1977
Third Edition:	May 1979
Fourth Edition:	January 1981
Fifth Edition:	March 1983
Sixth Edition:	January 1984
Seventh Edition:	March 1985
Eighth Edition:	February 1986
Ninth Edition:	September 1987
Legal Research:	Katherine M. Galvin
	Elizabeth Ryan
	Mary Randolph
	Robin Leonard
Illustrations:	Linda Allison
Book Design:	Keija Kimura
Production:	Stephanie Harolde
	Kate Miller
	Glenn Voloshin
Printing:	Delta Lithograph

ISBN 0-87337-055-4
Library of Congress Catalog Card No.: 80-11750
© Copyright 1976, 1981, 1983, 1985, 1986 and 1987 by Ralph Warner and Toni Ihara

Thank You

Asking a person to review part of a manuscript is always a bit of an edgy thing. One part of you wants them to read it, correct a few commas and say that it's terrific, while another, hopefully stronger part, wants lots of criticisms and suggestions for change. Well, if we were ever worried that our friends would be the passive type critic, we needn't have. Like ecstatic termites, they bored right in, gnawing away at our fragile words as if they were a yummy hunk of maple.

"Don't you think you ought to include something about the right of adopted children to inherit?"

"This section on foreign marriages is confusing."

"If I were you, I would include more hints on how to collect after an auto accident."

"You know that tax stuff on unmarried couples? Well, I don't want to hurt your feelings, but you don't add very well."

By the time our friends were done munching, we sat in a great pile of discarded words--our egos a lot smaller but our book a lot better. Both results were beneficial and we wish to extend our sincerest thanks to all our termite friends for a job well done. Without their creative energy, this would be a far lesser book. Thanks to: David Brown, Mary Randolph, Katherine Galvin, Peter Jan Honigsberg, Jon Johnsen, Ed Sherman, Mary Willis, Harriet Whitman Lee, Tom Andres, Peggy Hill, and Robin Leonard.

Update Service
• Introductory Offer •

Our books are as current as we can make them, but sometimes the laws do change between editions. You can read about law changes which may affect this book in the NOLO NEWS, a 24-page newspaper which we publish quarterly.

In addition to the Update Service, each issue contains comprehensive articles about the growing self-help law movement as well as areas of law that are sure to affect you (regular subscription rate is $7.00).

To receive the next 4 issues of the NOLO NEWS, please send us $2.00:

Name _____

Address_____

_____

Send to: NOLO PRESS, 950 Parker St., Berkeley CA 94710

M&D 9/87

Recycle Your Out-of-Date Books & Get 25%off your next purchase!

Using an old edition can be dangerous if information in it is wrong. Unfortunately, laws and legal procedures change often. To help you keep up to date we extend this offer. If you cut out and deliver to us the title portion of the cover of any old Nolo book we'll give you a 25% discount off the retail price of any new Nolo book. For example, if you have a copy of TENANT'S RIGHTS, 4th edition and want to trade it for the latest CALIFORNIA MARRIAGE AND DIVORCE LAW, send us the TENANT'S RIGHTS cover and a check for the current price of MARRIAGE & DIVORCE, less a 25% discount. Information on current prices and editions is listed in the NOLO NEWS (see above box). Generally speaking, any book more than two years old is of questionable value. Books more than four or five years old are a menace.

OUT OF DATE = DANGEROUS

This offer is to individuals only.

Table of Contents

Introduction

Here is a practical book about the laws that affect marriage and divorce. We discuss marriage requirements, community and separate property, marriage contracts, taking title to a house, laws affecting children and their support, as well as the legal and practical issues of divorce, including property division, spousal support and the divorce process itself. Our aim is to speak plainly, eliminating as much legal gobbledy-gook as possible. Like it or not (and no one does), laws and legal procedures are all around us. After reading what follows, you will be equipped to deal with many of them, or at least know what you need to do to make a start.

This book is not meant to replace lawyers completely. We believe that their role in our society and our lives is grossly out of proportion to what it should be. There are times, however, when it would be wise to consult a lawyer, and we will indicate them as we go along.

Giving birth to any book is a time-consuming, attention-demanding process, but some deliver - ies are rougher than others. This one has been our hardest to date. Problems began with the scope of the book itself. We first planned to compose a book that focused mainly on marriage contracts. But you can't write a sensible marriage contract, or even think about one intelligently, unless you know something about the laws governing marriage. What is community property? Are you mar - ried if one person's divorce turned out not to be final at the time of your ceremony? Who is legally responsible for child support? What last names can a married couple use, or give the kids? What happens if you don't make a will?

Our simple project to show you how to prepare a marriage contract was on the verge of turning into a ponderous encyclopedia that you probably wouldn't read. But what to include and what to leave out? How were we to give you enough information without burying you? Our solution was to include chapters discussing subject areas essential to married couples and to leave out others (landlord/tenant, business law, personal injury, etc.) that were no more likely to affect the married than anyone else. Once this distinction was made, we tried to be consistent, but soon found our -

selves wallowing in our own nit-picking as to what logically should, or shouldn't, be included. Finally, we gave up and, like the parent who suddenly decides that a little order is worth more than a lot of consistency, got downright arbitrary. So you will find information on children, who it is true, often follow marriage, and about taking title to a house, which applies to lots of people who aren't married. Logical? Hell no, but we had to draw the line someplace.

The basic problem involving marriage isn't discussed at all—whether or not to get married in the first place. We have no opinion one way or the other, believing that it's up to each person to answer it individually.

We are often asked such questions as: Is it cheaper to be married as far as taxes are concerned? (For most working couples, tax liability is less if they live together.)[1] Will I lose my social security widow's benefits if I marry again? (No.) Do I get extra property rights if I marry? (See Chapter 4.) These questions are important and we will discuss them in detail, but we don't believe that most people decide to marry or divorce solely (or even mostly) for economic reasons. If you prefer being single or living together, don't give it up because someone told you that you ought to accumulate some community property. We think that good marriages are made in the heart, not the pocketbook.

Once you have decided to get married, however, it's time to pay close attention to the rules. It's all very nice to soar off on a magic carpet, but sooner or later you will have to land and decide who is going to pay at the grocery store. There is nothing hard about the laws and procedures we discuss, yet some overlap a bit and others come wrapped in the needless rigamarole beloved by lawyers. Be prepared to go slowly here and there and to read things several times to be sure that you have them right side up.

In the first two editions of this book, we included no chapters on divorce, believing that it would be negative to mix divorce into a book on marriage. We were obviously naive. Many of the questions and comments that we have received from readers indicate that they were using this material as part of a dissolution, or were at least thinking about the possibility of ending their relationship and were annoyed that we had stopped short of discussing the divorce process in detail. So, as part of a general re-working of the next editions, we have integrated material about ending as well as beginning relationships.

In an age in which marriages in the traditional, "until death do us part" sense are obviously difficult for millions of people to sustain, we believe that a good, caring divorce can go a long way toward retaining or restoring self-respect. We don't advocate divorce, but for those who do decide to separate, we provide solid information aimed at making it as painless a process as pos - sible.

This is just one of our series of books designed to give people ordinary legal information about their lives. Surprisingly, our books (we think of them as tools) have often been controversial. Many, it seems, believe that no one but lawyers should be allowed to fill in blanks on forms and shuffle papers. Happily, however, some progress has been made and recently "do your own" law publications and projects have been sprouting everywhere. These are fragile but hopeful signs that the black robe is slowly being pulled from the legal priesthood and that before long lawyers will be revealed for what they are—a lot of smart, aggressive men and women with a good hussle

---

[1] The so-called "marriage tax" has been reduced by the creation of a tax credit for married couples in situations where both work. Even so, if both members of a couple earn substantial income, it is still considerably cheaper to live together.

(monopoly) which they aren't going to put down without a fight. By reading what follows and making some of your own decisions, you join us in giving the robe a few tugs.

Here and there throughout this book we will refer you to the others in the series, as well as to other helpful reference sources. This is because it is silly for us to repeat information which is already covered in detail. You will find an order form for our books at the end of this one. Nolo Press books are also available at almost every public library in California.

CHAPTER 1

Getting Married

Remember those great old 1930's movies where the boy and girl (virgins both), after over - coming numerous obstacles and almost losing one another through the machinations of a dozen dubious villains, load into a Model A Ford and head off to find a justice of the peace who marries them in his nightshirt with his wife holding the candle and a kindly cow looking on? Well, as you might guess, nothing is that easy these days—even getting married involves a surprising amount of red tape.

In theory, there are many people who aren't supposed to get married at all, or at least not to each other. In legal language this means that they don't have the "capacity" to enter into the mar - riage contract. This is true even though they get a license, go through a ceremony and set up housekeeping together. For example, people who are still married to somebody else (even if they don't know it), can go through a second or even third ceremony with others, but these subsequent marriages are void. Unless all previous marriages of both spouses have been completely dissolved prior to their marriage, it simply doesn't exist.

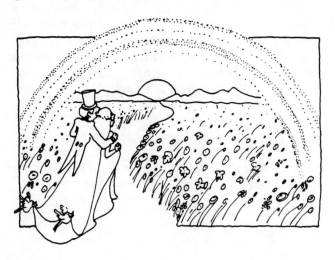

A. California Marriage Requirements[1]

California Civil Code 4100 reads as follows:

Marriage is a personal relation arising out of a civil contract to which the consent of the parties capable of making the contract is necessary. Consent alone will not constitute marriage; it must be followed by the issuance of a license and solemnization as authorized by this code . . .

• **Age of Consent:** California sets 18 as the age for marriage. People below 18 need the consent of a parent or guardian and a Superior Court judge, who may, and probably will, require marriage counseling before giving consent. For more details, see Civil Code 4101.

• **Family Relationship (Incest):** California Civil Code 4400 reads as follows:

Marriages between parents and children, ancestors and descendants of every degree (this means grandparents and grandchildren, etc.), and between brothers and sisters of the half as well as the whole blood, and between uncles and nieces, or aunts and nephews, are incestuous, and void from the beginning, whether the relationship is legitimate or illegitimate.

Although the statute doesn't say so, in-laws are fair game.

Note: In most states, second cousins are known as "kissing cousins" and can marry, while first cousins are covered by the incest statute and can't legally marry. California doesn't have this rule, however, and first cousins are free to do all the kissing and marrying they want.

• **Race:** Unbelievable as it may seem, in California, until 1948, it was illegal for whites to marry "negroes, Mongolians, Malayans or mulattoes." Statutes such as these were common in the U.S., especially in those states that had rebelled against the union to protect the institution of slavery. It was not until 1967, over 100 years after the rebellion was crushed and black people were supposedly liberated, that the U.S. Supreme Court, in the case of *Loving v. Virginia*, held that all remaining state laws regulating marriage on the basis of race were unconstitutional.

• **Mental Capacity:** Insane people (including the severely mentally retarded) don't have the ability to enter into a contract and thus can't marry. Of course, it is very difficult to tell when a person is, or isn't, insane, and courts have held that a person who is experiencing a lucid interval between periods of insanity can enter into a marriage contract. Certainly the fact that a person has been mentally ill in the past is no bar to marriage.

• **Sobriety:** A person who has been drinking or is obviously under the influence of a drug will not be issued a marriage license. There are no blood alcohol tests administered, however. It's up to the discretion of the County Clerk as to whether a person has had too much sauce.

• **Physical Capacity:** The old notion that marriage is a license to have sexual relations aimed at producing children is still with us in law as it is in religion. In theory, each party to a marriage must at least have the physical ability to have intercourse, even though the woman is past child-bearing age. A marriage where a person can't have intercourse, or can't have children, if of child-bearing age, is voidable unless the facts have been completely disclosed to, and understood by, the other person prior to marriage [see Section C(2) below].

---

[1]Requirements (laws) for marriage, divorce, child support, property rights, etc., are set out in California Civil Code Sections 4100-5138. You can find the Civil Code which is indexed as to subject in any county law library and in most public libraries. If you look at the annotated version, excerpts from relevant court decisions will be included after each statute.

• **Prior Marriage in Force:** You can only be married to one person at a time. If either party to a marriage is married to someone else, the subsequent marriage is completely void. Often married people file papers to get a divorce or an annulment and think this means that they can remarry. Not true—you need a final decree of divorce or annulment.[2] Generally, any divorce or annulment decrees obtained in any state will be recognized in any other state for purposes of remarriage. Divorce decrees obtained outside of the U.S. (often the quickie Mexican or Dominican Republic decrees that you hear so much about) will only be recognized if both spouses consented to the jurisdiction of the foreign court. This means that husband and wife must either appear before the court in person, or one must appear in person while the other files a written form consenting to the divorce.

If only one spouse gets the out-of-country divorce, it will probably not stand up if the other challenges it. But what happens if one spouse goes to Mexico and gets a divorce without the consent of the other, but then both spouses carry on their lives as if the divorce was valid? Does this mean that the divorce can't be challenged later? It may mean just that. In many situations, courts will prevent a spouse who did not consent to a foreign divorce at the time it was entered from later contesting it, if that spouse acted as if he (she) believed it to be valid (for example, got remarried). In some situations foreign divorces will be recognized to the extent that they end the marriage, but will not be recognized for purposes of child custody, support, visitation or property division. Obviously this is an extremely tricky area of the law and it would be wise to see a lawyer if you have questions.

_____

[2]It takes at least six months to get a divorce in California, and usually longer. It is necessary to wait for the "final decree" ending the marriage to take effect before you can remarry. Unless one spouse appeals, a final judgment of dissolution automatically takes effect after the hearing, or six months after defendant was served with papers, whichever comes later.

A Little Friendly Advice: Now that the California divorce law has been simplified, we think it very foolish to try to save a few months by going out of the country for a divorce.

There is one minor exception to the rule that a marriage is completely void if either party to it is still married to someone else. It is found in Section 4401(2) of the Civil Code and dates back to the days when men got in ships, sailed over the horizon and sometimes simply never came back. It states that if a former husband or wife is absent and not known to be living for at least five successive years immediately preceding a subsequent marriage, then the second marriage is merely voidable. This means that it is a legal marriage, but can be annulled. Thus, it is theoretically possible to be simultaneously married to two people if "Rip Van Winkle" turns up after a long snooze. Children and property of a voidable marriage are treated just as if a completely regular marriage existed.

• **Marriage Licenses:** California, like all governments, never misses a chance to tax. Marriage is no exception, and of course both people must show up at the County Clerk's office and buy a permission slip (marriage license) to get married. At the time the license is obtained, a physician's certificate, not more than 30 days old, must be presented saying that a test has been performed and that neither person has communicable syphilis. In addition, the woman, unless she is over 50 years of age or surgically sterilized, must present a physician's certificate stating whether or not a test indicates that she is immune to German measles (rubella).

Both people must state their names, ages and places of residence. The clerk is legally prohibited from asking about race, but he or she can inquire into any of the other requirements we have discussed in this section. If either member of the couple is under age, they must also file parental and Superior Court consent forms as outlined above. The marriage license, when issued, is good for ninety days.

• **Confidential Marriages:** Section 4213 of the Civil Code provides that unmarried people who have been living together may marry without complying with the regular licensing and blood test requirements. There are two different ways to take advantage of this law. These are:

• County Clerk Method (more common); and

• Notary Public Method (very rare).

1. The County Clerk Method

When you use this confidential marriage method you must:

a. Personally appear before the county clerk to obtain a confidential marriage license. (You will have to pay the clerk the proper fee, approximately $50.);

b. Use the marriage license (i.e., get married) in the county where it was issued within 90 days of issuance;

c. Deliver the license to the person who is marrying you (judge, priest, rabbi, county clerk);

d. Have the person who performed the marriage 1) file a certificate of confidential marriage with the county clerk within four days after the marriage, and 2) give you a copy of the certificate and an application for a certified copy of your certificate; and

e. Fill out the application, send it to the county clerk and receive back a certified copy of your marriage certificate.

2. The Notary Public Method

To use the notary public method, you must:

a. Locate a notary public who has been specifically licensed by the county clerk to perform confidential marriages (The clerk will have a list of these people--there are very few);

b. Have the notary public perform the marriage;

c. Have the notary public file a certificate of confidential marriage with the county clerk within four days of the ceremony;

d. Obtain a copy of the certificate, and an application for a certified copy, from the notary public; and

e. Send in the completed application and you'll receive back a certified copy of your marriage certificate.

In order to obtain authorization for a confidential marriage you must meet the following requirements:

1. Neither of you is a minor;

2. One of you must be an unmarried man and the other an unmarried woman (i.e., no gay marriages allowed); and

3. You have been "living together" for a length of time. (This length varies among counties.)`

• Ceremony and Certificate of Registry: There must be some formal ceremony to have a marriage. Section 4206 of the Civil Code states:

No particular form for the ceremony of marriage is required, but the parties must declare in the presence of the person solemnizing the marriage that they take each other as husband and wife.

A marriage, whether it is conducted after a license is obtained or under the living together exception (Section 4213), may be solemnized (you're right, that is a silly word, but since it is in the Code we are stuck with it), by any judge or retired judge, commissioner or retired commissioner or assistant commissioner of a court of record or justice court, or by any priest, minister or rabbi of any religious denomination of the age of eighteen or over. Any religion means just that. A minister of the Universal Life Church, or for that matter, the United Evangelical Society of Polar Bear Worshippers, is just as qualified to marry you as is the Roman Catholic Cardinal in charge of the Los Angeles diocese. The person marrying you must fill out a form called the Certificate of Registry of Marriage which will be given you by the County Clerk when you get your marriage license. This form must be filed within four days after the marriage ceremony, along with a completed copy of the marriage license, by returning it to the clerk.

Couples getting married under Section 4213 (people living together and not getting a regular license) need no health certificates prior to marriage, but the person performing the ceremony must also fill out a Certification of Marriage form. This form is obtainable from the County Clerk and must be filled out and returned to the clerk within four days of the marriage.

• Witnesses: California requires one witness to a marriage other than the spouses and the person conducting the ceremony.

B. Common Law Marriages—Are They Legal?

There is a widespread belief that if you live with a person for a certain period of months or years, even though you never got a marriage license or went through a ceremony, you are automatically married. In the great majority of states, including California, this is simply not true. There is one little trick in this area, however. A state that does not provide for a common law marriage within its own boundaries will recognize such a marriage if it was properly formed in a state that does provide for marriages without a formal ceremony. This is so because, under the U.S. Constitution, each state must give "full faith and credit" to the acts of the other states.

Example: Abigail and Amos started living together in San Jose, California, in 1957. They are still together, have never participated in a marriage ceremony and have never moved out of California. Are they married? No. California does not recognize common law marriage.[3]

Example: Wanda and Walter started living together in Colorado in 1965 with the intention of forming a common law marriage and have been living together ever since. In 1971 they moved to Los Angeles. Are they married? Yes. California will recognize the marriage as valid, as Colorado recognizes common law marriage and the marriage took place in Colorado before they came to California. Wanda and Walter would legally be required to get a divorce or annulment before either could marry anyone else.

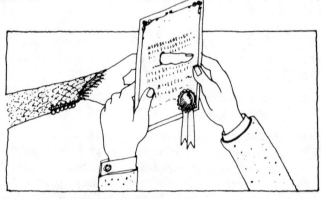

Important: Even in states recognizing common law marriage, living together does not automatically result in marriage. In addition, both parties must intend to enter into the marriage. The length of time people live together is not in itself normally important, but may be considered insofar as it tends to show intent. The length of time people live together is not the best way to show intent, however. Whether both people use the same last name, hold themselves out to the community to be married, file joint tax returns, etc. is probably more important in determining whether a common law marriage exists. Once the common law marriage requirements are met, however, the marriage exists and can't be legally ended short of divorce.

The following list indicates those few states still recognizing common law marriage. If you were living with someone in one of these states and then came to California, it is possible that you may have questions as to the legal status of your relationship. The law that controls is the

---

[3]There is much recent law in the area of unmarried couples living together centering around the Lee Marvin and other legal decisions. We discuss living together in detail in *The Living Together Kit* (see order information at the back of this book).

law in the state from which you came. Any large county law library or law school library will have the laws and case decisions from all states, and you might start by doing a little of your own research. Practically speaking, however, you only have a problem if you and your friend disagree as to whether or not you are married as there are no official records of your marriage.

If you both want to be married to each other, it would be wise to go through a formal ceremony in California, just to avoid the possibility of confusion in the future.

If you both agree that you aren't married and want to split up, simply do it, after making sure that your property and obligations have been fairly divided and you have provided for the kids, if any. In Chapter 9 you will find a sample property settlement agreement which may prove useful. This was designed for people contemplating divorce, but you can use it as a written separation contract.

If you want to stay together, but want to be sure that you aren't married, and that neither one of you will change your mind in the future, it might prove helpful to type out and sign an agreement such as the following.

SAMPLE AGREEMENT

Wanda Walters and Walter Winters agree as follows:

1. That they have been and plan to continue to live together as two free independent beings and that neither has ever intended to enter into any form of marriage, common law or otherwise.

_____   _____
Date   Wanda Walters

_____   _____
Date   Walter Winters

(Notarization is optional)

If one of you believes that a marriage exists and the other doesn't and you are unable to talk the situation out, you may have to see a lawyer. But remember, anyone can get a divorce in California by simply filing a few papers and, in some situations, making an appearance down at the local courthouse, so it would only make sense to insist that a marriage exists and go through a divorce if there were substantial disagreement as to property, support, child custody, etc.

States Recognizing Common Law Marriages

Alabama	Montana
Colorado	Ohio
District of Columbia	Oklahoma
Georgia	Pennsylvania
Idaho	Rhode Island
Iowa	South Carolina
Kansas	Texas

C. What If It Turns Out That Your Marriage Isn't Legal? Void and Voidable Marriages

After the politicians (mostly lawyers, of course) got through making all the neat little rules as to who can or cannot get married, when and how, as discussed in Section A of this chapter, a funny thing happened: Large numbers of people went right on conducting their lives the way they wanted to, paying very little attention to the rules. Marriages, which according to the law were either void from the start, or voidable by the action of one or both parties, have been, and are continuing to be, conducted by the thousands.

Faced with that anti-social (some might say endearing, or even noble) human perversity that doesn't always want to follow rules, you might have thought that the rule makers would give up. This would be a serious misunderstanding of politicians and judges, however. Just as some people love to break rules, these folks dearly love making them. What has happened is that a whole new set of laws has been invented to take care of those who paid so little attention to the first set. The result is that people who don't like rules have simply refused to get married at all. Did you guess? Probably you did—now the rule-making establishment is turning its attention to making rules for couples who refuse to get married.

Be patient and read on and we will outline the most important rules affecting void and voidable marriages. There are important differences between the two, but it's really not hard to follow if you go slowly.

1. Void Marriages

Marriages where either person was still married to someone else at the time the ceremony was performed are void, with the one minor exception discussed in Section A above.[4] This means that they do not legally exist. This is true even if both parties to the second marriage believed in entire (but mistaken) good faith that they were free to marry. At the risk of being overly repetitive, let us state again: To be divorced, there must be a final decree of divorce. It is not enough that a divorce has been filed, or even that a final decree could have been entered if someone took the trouble to do it.

In addition to multiple marriage situations, incestuous marriages are also void. They simply can't legally exist, even though a marriage certificate has been issued and a ceremony held. See Section A above for a definition of incest.

Important: Many, many thousands of people in the above situations have had what they consider to be good marriages. This is true even though they were never legally married under the law of California. People in void marriages don't need a divorce or annulment if they wish to separate—they can simply walk away from one another. There is no legal relationship to end. However, California has made lots of laws affecting the division of property and the support and

---

[4]Being married simultaneously to more than one person is also a crime—bigamy. However, it is almost never prosecuted in a situation where a person simply marries a second, or even third, time without getting a valid divorce, unless the subsequent marriages are part of a scheme to cheat someone. Oh, and it makes no difference what your religion is. You can't beat the bigamy statutes by saying that your religion requires you to have lots of wives (husbands).

custody of children. Basically, both of these areas are treated much the same, whether a void or a valid marriage has been terminated.

People in void marriages who simply want to separate, and have no children and not a lot of property, may wish to write out an agreement such as the following to avoid misunderstandings in the future.

SAMPLE AGREEMENT

Wanda Waters and Walter Winters went through a marriage ceremony on July 8, 19__. In 19__, they learned that Walter was validly married to someone else at the time he married Wanda. Both Wanda and Walter hereby understand and state that they are not married and want none of the legal rights of married people. All property accumulated during the time Wanda and Walter believed they were married has been divided to the mutual satisfaction of both.

_____   _____
Date   Wanda Walters

_____   _____
Date   Walter Winters

(Notarization is optional)

People who have accumulated a lot of property during the course of their non-marriages may or may not have problems dividing it fairly. Again, the property settlement agreement contained in Chapter 9 can be used as a sample contract. It need not be presented to a court as there is, of course, no marriage to dissolve.

2. Voidable Marriages

Certain marriages are voidable. This means that they can be ended by an annulment as well as by a divorce. In the days when divorce was based on fault and was more difficult to obtain, an annulment was often a simpler way to end a marriage. Now, since divorce rules have been eased, annulment is commonly the more complicated of the two. However, there are still a few people who think it is better to have an annulment than a divorce, so we include here a list of types of marriages that can be annulled.[5] Remember, a voidable marriage is valid unless someone initiates an action to end it and the judge agrees. It is not the same as the void marriages discussed above, which are never any good. In most cases, the annulment action must be commenced promptly after the discovery of the grounds for ending the marriage.

The following marriages are voidable by annulment:

• Where the person filing the annulment, or on whose behalf an action is filed by a parent or a guardian, was under age (see Section A above) at the time of the marriage and did not have the permission of parents and court to marry. However, this sort of action won't work if the underage person continues to live in the marriage relationship after coming of age.

Example: Jane married Roger even though she is only 16 by lying about her age. Two weeks later, her parents have the marriage annulled. But if Jane stayed with Roger past the time she turned 18, she could no longer get an annulment.

• Where the first husband or wife of either party, missing for five years or believed dead before the second marriage took place, shows up, the second marriage is voidable;

• Either party is of unsound mind, unless such person, after coming to reason, freely lived with the other as husband and wife. Unsound mind means mentally incapable of consenting to the marriage;

• The consent of either party to the marriage was obtained by fraud, unless such person, after obtaining full knowledge of the facts making up the fraud, continued to live with the other as husband and wife. This is the most common ground for annulment and has been expanded by the courts to allow all sorts of things to constitute fraud. Marriages have been annulled for lack of physical capacity, sterility, refusal to engage in sex, refusal to engage in a religious ceremony subsequent to a civil marriage after promising to do so, a woman being pregnant by somebody else at the time of marriage, etc.

Example: Wanda married Walter, telling him that she wants a large family. A month after the marriage, Wanda confesses that she is sterile and can't have children. Walter could get an annulment, claiming that he wouldn't have married Wanda if she hadn't lied. However, if Walter stays with Wanda for a couple of years after learning the facts of her sterility, it will be too late to get an annulment.

The fraud must go to the basis of the marriage relationship. Things such as bad treatment, failure to support, refusal to move to another location, etc., may be obnoxious, but they don't constitute grounds for annulment. If you want more information on this, go to a law library and see Section 4425 in the annotated California Civil Code. You will find a digest of court decisions as to what constitutes fraud after the code section.

• The consent of either party to the marriage was obtained by force, unless the person coerced freely cohabitated with the other after marriage and after the force or threat of force was withdrawn;

---

[5]In theory, an annulment erases the fact that you were married, while a divorce ends the marriage.

• Either party was, at the time of the marriage, physically incapable of having sex and such incapacity continues and appears to be incurable.[6] In *Stepanek v. Stepanek* (1961) 193 Cal.2d 760, the court held that:

Test of physical capacity as grounds for annulment is ability or inability for copulation, not fruitfulness, and inability need be only for normal copulation, not partial, imperfect, unnatural or painful copulation.

3. Property and Children of Void or Voidable Marriages

a. Property

In most void or voidable marriage situations, one or both of the people involved originally think they are properly married and rely on this fact in conducting their affairs. A common example is where people get married before a prior divorce involving one of them has become final. The second marriage is void as a result, but the couple might live together for years, accumulating a marital estate before they find out the sad truth.

Under California law, fortunately, a good faith belief that a valid marriage exists is enough to confer the status of putative spouse on the person entertaining the belief. Once this title is conferred on a person, the property owned by both parties must be divided in full accordance with principles discussed in Chapter 4, should the people later separate.

b. Children

California has done away with distinctions between "legitimate" and "illegitimate" children. Therefore, it is not significant whether parents were married, living together, or just happened to have a baby, as far as custody and support are concerned once the actual fact of parenthood is established. Parents of children, whether married or not, have the duty to support and care for them, unless the child is adopted by someone else (see Chapter 7). However, if a man tries to deny that he is the father of children, proof of paternity is affected by whether or not he was legally married to and living with the mother when the child was conceived. In Chapter 7, we discuss the important legal rules governing whether or not a man will be viewed as the child's father.

[6]Most judicial decisions involve the physical capacity of men, but there is no reason why a woman who was psychologically incapable of having sex couldn't also be covered by this legal doctrine.

D. Out-of-State and Foreign Marriages

Section 4104 of the Civil Code states that all marriages entered into outside of California which were valid under the laws of the state or country where they were made are valid in California. Thus, even though the marriage requirements of another state or country (age, for example) are different than in California, the marriage will be treated as good here.

However, there is also a legal doctrine that states that this general rule as to the validity of "foreign" marriages does not apply to marriages performed elsewhere that would be "odious" in California. We don't know exactly what odious means any more than you do, but it has been interpreted to include a woman having more than one husband, or a man with more than one wife, a father marrying his daughter, etc.[7] This sort of marriage, even if it were legal in some part of the world where the rules are different than they are in this country, would not be recognized in California. If you are interested in more information on this subject, see *McDonald v. McDonald* (1935), 6 Cal. 2d 457.

E. Breach of Promise and Alienation of Affection

In times past when marriages often consummated family (and sometimes even national) alliances, the decision of one person to back out of the marriage could have serious consequences. Indeed, in some states it is still possible to sue the person who gets cold feet for breach of contract to marry. This has not been possible in California since 1939. However, it is possible to sue for the return of valuable property when property was transferred in contemplation of a marriage that didn't take place.

Alienation of affection is another legal action that can no longer be brought in California. This means that you can't sue a third person who runs off with an intended spouse or even an actual spouse.

---

[7]The dictionary defines it as "hateful," "disgusting," "offensive."

CHAPTER 2

Lifestyles

A. Sex

There was a time when there were lots of legal rules as to who could go to bed together, especially when one or more of the people was married. Recently, however, such crimes as adulterous cohabitation and sodomy have been eliminated in California. Divorce on the grounds of adultery was wiped out several years ago when California adopted the concept of "no-fault divorce."

Today in California anyone can have sex with anyone else in private—or as someone said long before Henry Ford, "it doesn't matter what goes on in the bedroom as long as you don't do it in the street and scare the horses." Does this mean that having a lover, participating in a group marriage, going to an orgy, or what used to be referred to as participating in unnatural acts, is legal? Yes, that's just what it means.

But suppose one member of a couple engages in extra-marital sexual activities and the other doesn't approve? Would the disapproving spouse be entitled to a divorce? Of course he (she) would. Anyone can get a divorce at any time simply by filing a petition and saying that "irreconcilable differences" exist. The judge has no interest in what the reasons for your incompatibility are. It makes no difference whether you want a divorce because your spouse has been sleeping with your best friend, or because he (she) insists on squeezing the toothpaste from the wrong end. Sexual preferences may still be an issue in the area of child custody, however. As we discuss in Chapter 8, child custody in contested situations is awarded on the basis of the best interest of the child.[1] Judges in this situation are given broad latitude in examining parents' lives to determine which is more fit to have custody. Bizarre sexual activity could, if brought to the attention of the judge, influence the decision. For example, a person who had ten lovers simultaneously might have trouble gaining or keeping custody. Does this mean that having a lover will mean that you won't get custody? Absolutely not. This should be no problem. Does it mean that living with someone of the opposite sex will influence a custody decision? No, living together has been pretty well accepted. But what about gay and lesbian couples wishing to live with one another while raising the children of one member of the couple? In 1967, the California Supreme Court ruled that a parent's homosexuality could not in and of itself prohibit that person from being given custody of her or his children. This doesn't mean that every judge grants every lesbian or gay parent custody. In fact, significant numbers of gay parents do not win custody when a contested custody situation is brought before a judge. Remember, judges must look at the best interests of the child when making a custody award and, in doing so, may more or less consciously be influenced by their own negative views about homosexuals raising children. For a thorough discussion of the rights of gay/lesbian parents, see Curry & Clifford, *A Legal Guide For Lesbian and Gay Couples* (order information at the back of this book). If you believe that you will be involved in a contested custody dispute where your homosexuality will be an issue, you probably want to consult an attorney familiar with this issue (see Chapter 12).

B. Temporary Separation

We are often asked whether it is legal to live separately from your spouse and still be married? The answer is yes, and that many couples find it sensible to do so every now and then.

Should you go ahead and eventually get a divorce, all property acquired after permanent separation is treated as separate property, as long as you keep it separate. There is no need (contrary to the belief of many) to get a "legal separation" because you and your spouse want to see a little less of each other for a time. A "legal separation" is a divorce equivalent which is used by people with some religious objection to divorce. It is not normally suitable for people who simply want a little "time out."

---

[1]The great majority of couples don't fight over their kids, so it is unusual that a person's sexual history should be explored in court.

But what about house payments, children, bank accounts, support, etc., while you're separated? Well, what about it? If you're still into continuing your marriage, you will take care of these by communicating and sharing as you always had. If you're not able to do this, you will probably want to get a divorce. See *How To Do Your Own Divorce in California*, Charles Sherman, Nolo Press.

C. Living Together

Living together as an alternative to getting married is far more popular than it was a few years ago. It is legal in California, but not in all states. Where "cohabitation" is a crime, it is rarely prosecuted, however. If you live with someone, it is important to make a written contract covering your belongings as you are not covered by California community property laws. If Lee Marvin and Michelle Marvin, and the tens of thousands of other couples who have been involved in emotionally and financially draining litigation, had taken the time to write out a simple agreement defining property rights, their problems could have been completely avoided.

Unmarried couples also encounter special legal problems when they have children (a paternity statement should be prepared), buy real property, and plan for death (they are not covered by the intestate succession laws that protect married couples who fail to make a will). We do not go into detail here because all of this information, including sample contracts, paternity statements and a sample will, is set out in detail in *The Living Together Kit*, Ihara and Warner, Nolo Press.

D. Group Marriage

There is legally no such thing as group marriage. You can only be married to one person at a time in California, with the exception discussed in Chapter 1(A). Participating in a second "marriage" while still married to someone else constitutes the crime of bigamy. Bigamy is normally not prosecuted in situations where a person goes through a second or even third marriage ceremony unless fraud is involved. Thus, the person who gets "married" again before his divorce is final is a technical criminal (aren't we all), but isn't likely to end up in the calaboose, while a person who uses marriage as a way to fleece the unsuspecting of money or property may well feel the hot breath of the local constabulary.

Most group marriages aren't marriages at all. They consist of a group of people living and perhaps loving together in a situation where the family unit is defined in some way other than a duet. As long as no one runs down to the court house and starts swearing out multiple marriage licenses, this is legal. If a woman (or man) wants to live with ten men and say she (he) is married to all of them, there is nothing to stop her (him) as long as the "marriages" take place privately and aren't recorded.

E. Gay Marriage

Our society says that people with the same style plumbing can't legally marry, while people who are hooked up differently can.[2] That this should be true doesn't make much sense to us, especially in a world that is miserably overcrowded. What does an overcrowded world have to do with it? Well, the traditional legal justification for limiting marriage to men and women has to do with having children. This is supposed to be what marriage is all about. But what if we don't need any more kids? Isn't it time that these marriage traditions were re-examined? Sure, but then traditions wouldn't be traditions if they didn't have a certain tenacious hold on our mass consciousness, and thus it may take a few more years before gay marriages are legal.

In the meantime, gay people can legally conduct their own private ceremony and write their own legally binding contract as to property. This is not enough for many gay people, however, who want to get legally married, or at least want the option available. But there is perhaps one saving grace: people who don't get married never need a divorce.

---

[2]Civil Code Section 4100 says, "Marriage is a personal relation arising out of a civil contract between a man and a woman...."

F. Private Marriages

Many people are finding that it is positively disadvantageous to be married in the eye of the Internal Revenue Service or some other arm of the central government. This has led to a growing movement to have a religious or spiritual ceremony, but not to file any record of the marriage with the county clerk. This is being done by people in a variety of situations, including older couples who worry about savings being needlessly spent to take care of the other spouse's medical bills that would otherwise be paid by Medi-Cal or a similar public insurance program.[3]

The important thing to remember is that in California, if the proper papers are not filed with the county clerk, you are not married. You may take care of your obligation to your God with a religious marriage ceremony, but you are living together as far as California law is concerned, unless the Certificate of Registry of Marriage is filed. Of course, this may be exactly what you want to accomplish. Should a couple who is living together want to really get married later, they can do so without publicity under the provisions of the "secret marriage" law discussed in Chapter 1.

---

[3]The separate property of one spouse is liable for the debts of the other spouse for the "necessaries of life" (Civil Code Sections 5121, 5132).

CHAPTER 3

Names

What's in a name? For most people, a good part of their identity. The unique sound of our own names can't help but influence our lives.

In some parts of the world, family background is still the basic unit of identification and security; nation, state and tribe are secondary. In these places, the family name is all important, the right to use it often spelling the difference between an easy life and a miserable one. For most of us, however, family heritage has become less important—overwhelmed as we are by the sheer numbers of other families, as well as by the expanding state which we have increasingly invented as the guarantor of our health and welfare. What does it mean to be called Jones when there are 200 others in the phone book and the government won't talk to you unless you can give them a social security number? Still, even in our society, there are remnants of an earlier age: Kennedy, Taft, Rockefeller and Rothschild are all family names that come wrapped with a charisma of power that needs no explanation, even when attached to the relatively less successful members of the family.

As the significance of family background has decreased, so too has the value of keeping the name that you were given at birth. The result has been that many people have decided to name themselves—getting up one day and calling themselves Muhammad Ali or Good Morning or perhaps just plain Humphrey Doolittle instead of Humphrey Herbert Doolittle, Jr. The reasons for the name changes are as many as the people making the changes—convenience, self-expression, religious conviction, etc. But whatever the reasons, the fact remains that lots of people are changing lots of names.

Part of the poetry of the twentieth century has to do with groups of people, seemingly similar, finding good reasons to march in different directions to different drummers. Thus, as many are adopting new last names, others, particularly married women, are struggling to hang onto theirs, or in some cases, to regain them. At least since the wedding of Lucy Stone in 1855, when she

demanded and won the right to keep the name she was given at birth, names have been an im -
portant feminist concern, with more and more women coming to feel as Lucy Stone did.

A. What Name Can You Legally Use?

You can legally use any name you wish regardless of what it says on your birth certificate, as
long as you don't invade another's privacy by seeking to gain notoriety through using their name
(thus, you can't legally use Robert Redford, but you can use John Smith or Abner Smallpossum)
and you don't use the name to defraud anyone, such as creditors. In addition, if you want your new
name to be treated as your legal name for all purposes, you must use it consistently.

Amazingly, you need no permission from the government to change your name. While it is
possible (and sometime desirable) to get a court order changing your name, there is no legal re -
quirement that you do so. It is just as legal to simply commence using a new name, dropping the
old one. Women changing their names to that of their husband at marriage are the most common
example of this sort of name change. The advantage of a "court order" name change is that the
government agencies, which increasingly give us licenses to do everything but breathe, will accept
the new name more readily. For example, the Passport Office makes it far simpler to get a pass -
port in a new name if accompanied by a court order. A court-ordered name change can be accom -
plished by simply filing a petition. A court appearance is not necessary unless somebody objects
to your proposed change (an extremely rare event). David Loeb's excellent book, *How To Change
Your Name in California,* Nolo Press, contains all the forms and instructions needed to do a court
name change, as well as detailed instructions on successfully dealing with the bureaucracy should
you prefer to follow the usage method.

But what if you only want to use a second name for limited purposes (acting, writing, etc.),
while continuing to use your existing name in day-to-day affairs? This is legal as long as there is
no intent to defraud. But if you use a name other than your own to operate a business, you must
file a fictitious name application with the California Secretary of State's office.

Caution: In choosing a new name, it is wise to use the traditional two, or three, name for -
mat. We know people who have tried to use one name, only to find that every form they fill out
demands at least two names and that computers are constantly messing them over. There is noth -
ing illegal about using just one name, but it will likely be more trouble than it's worth.

B. Marriage and Names

Married couples are free to keep their own names, adopt the last name of either for use by both,
hyphenate their names, or choose a completely new name. There is nothing written in the law
anyplace that says a woman should or must use her husband's last name.

Whatever name or names you use after marriage will get written into more and more records
(i.e., driver's license, taxes, credit cards, etc.) as time passes. Be sure you are happy with your
choice before this happens. Many women, for example, wish that they never adopted their hus -
band's last name, but after years of usage, feel that it's too much trouble to re-adopt their old one.

Women keeping their own names after marriage should have no difficulty whatsoever. It was almost impossible for married women to get credit in their own names a few years ago, but new laws granting equal credit rights to women, plus a little determination, should take care of any latent male resistance (Cal. Civil Code 1812.30; Federal Equal Credit Opportunity Act).

C. Married Women Re-Adopting Their Own Name

Many women who adopted their husband's name at marriage later decide that, although they want to stay married, they want to return to using their own name. Just as it is perfectly legal to use any name you wish, it is legal to return to your former name. Obviously, it will be more trouble to do this than if you never changed it in the first place. Again, we recommend David Loeb's *How To Change Your Name in California,* which will guide you through all the problems you will face whether you decide to make the change by simply using your former name, or by going to court. If you decide to go to court, you will find that all the forms you need to file are contained in the book.

Women who have been using their husband's last name may run into trouble establishing credit in their own names. They should be prepared to explain that their credit history is filed under a different name than they are now using and to request that creditors and credit bureaus establish a new credit history on the basis of the one previously established by the couple. Women have a legal right to insist that this be done and should particularly insist on it if a divorce occurs. Although there is no legal reason why this should be true, it is easier to convince many people that a name change is valid if you have obtained a court order. Even without a court order, however, you should have little trouble if you get your new identification in order before you apply for credit. Start by getting a driver's license in your own name, then change your voting registration, notify social security and open a new bank account or change your name on the old one. These are all easy to accomplish and will give you a bunch of official looking papers in your new name. Assuming you are credit worthy (have a job or other assets, etc.), you should be able to get credit cards issued in your own name. It is illegal under both state and federal law to discriminate on the basis of sex in granting credit.[1] In California, it is also illegal for a business to refuse to accept a woman's maiden name if she regularly uses it (Code of Civil Procedure 1279.5).

D. Changing Your Name as Part of a Divorce

As part of a final decree of divorce (dissolution) in California, a woman can get the judge to order the return of any name that she has formerly used. This need not be requested in the initial divorce petition, but can simply be ordered by the judge at the court hearing. Women can return to a former married name as well as to the name given them at birth by this method.

There seems to be no legal authority allowing a man to get a court order to return to his former name as part of a divorce action in situations where he has adopted a hyphenated name or a com- pletely new name at the time of the marriage. However, a man in this situation may as well ask the court to make the change and see what happens. At worst, he will be told that he has to file a separate court action to change his name, unless, of course, he wants to follow the usage method, which is always available.

E. Miss, Mrs., Ms., Mr., Master

People may use any prefix that pleases them, regardless of age or marital status as long as there is no intent to defraud. Women who are married can use Miss as well a Mrs. or Ms., if it pleases them. Of course, more and more people are using nothing at all, but if you do use a prefix before your name, you should know that it is just that—a prefix and not part of your name.

---

[1]Federal Equal Credit Opportunity Act; California Civil Code Section 1812.30. Complaints can be made to Federal Trade Commission office nearest you for non-bank related credit problems and to the Federal Reserve Board, Consumer Banking Unit, 400 Sansome St., S.F., Ca. 94111, for those that are bank-related. Complaints can also be made to the California Attorney General's office.

F. Naming Your Children

Commonly we give our children the same last name that we use, combined with a first, and often second, name that pleases us. There is no written law that says we must do it this way—it's just one of those customs of our society that feels right to most of us.[2] By law, we can give our children any last name we wish. At eighteen they can change it, without our consent, to please themselves.

Recently, some people whose names are household words have decided that their children would be better off without the burden of a famous name and have given their children a different last name. More commonly, children are being given hyphenated last names (Smith-Kerensky).[3] This normally happens when the parents each continue to use their own name. All these approaches to naming children are legal. The important thing is to be sure that the birth certificate properly re-flects your choice. Hospital authorities may assume that you want to do things in the traditional way if you aren't firm with them.

1. Changing a Child's Name

A child's name must be changed by the court petition method. Unlike adults, the usage method will not work for people under eighteen, as the new name will not be accepted by school author-ities, etc. If both natural parents petition the court to change their child's name, there is no prob-lem and the judge will almost automatically grant it. If the whole family wishes to change its name, the parents can simply include the child's (children's) name change as part of the same peti-tion. When a child is legally adopted, his (her) name is normally changed to that of the new par-ents as part of the adoption procedure.[4] If both parents are dead, a legal guardian can also have the children's names changed without trouble.

Problems develop, however, where one parent wants a child's name changed, and the other does not. Commonly this happens after the parents separate in situations where the mother has custody of the child. If the mother returns to her former name, or remarries and adopts her new husband's name, she will have a different name than that of her child, assuming that the child bears the last name of the father. In this situation, the mother often wishes to petition the court to change the child's name to conform to her own.

Traditionally, courts ruled that a father had a right to have the child keep his name if he con-tinued to actively perform his parental role. No longer.[5] Now a child's name may be changed by petition to the court whenever it is in the best interest of the child to do so. Among the factors which the courts will consider in determining this are the length of time the father's name has been used, the strength of the mother/child relationship, and the need of the child to identify with his or her new family unit through the use of a common name. Overall, the courts are now re-quired to balance these factors against the importance of the father-child relationship. What this all

---

[2]We have often thought that it would be a nice custom to give children first names only for use during childhood, with the understanding that they would choose their own name later.

[3]In an interesting article entitled "What To Name the Children When He's Kept His Name and You've Kept Yours," by Jeanette Germain, in the Spring 1982 issue of *Co-Evolution Quarterly*, it is suggested that daughters be given their mother's last name and sons their father's.

[4]For details, see *How To Adopt Your Stepchild*, Zagone, Nolo Press (see back of this book).

[5]*Marriage of Schiffman*, 28 Cal.3d 640 (1981).

boils down to is that a child may now be given the last name of either parent, depending on what a judge perceives to be his or her best interest.

Important: Changing the name of a child to the new name of his or her mother when she has remarried and adopted her new husband's last name in no way obligates her husband to support the child. This occurs only if the new husband legally adopts the child (see Chapter 7).

G. Birth Certificates and Names

The name on your birth certificate remains as a record of the name you were born with whether or not you eventually change your name. Neither changing your name by the usage, or court peti - tion method, changes your name on your birth certificate. It is almost impossible to change a name on a birth certificate. But there are a few special circumstances which are listed below where you can get a birth certificate changed by just contacting the State of California, Bureau of Vital Statistics, 410 N. St., Sacramento, Calif. 95814 (only for children born in California).

1. Typographical and other similar errors on the original certificate (John Sixon instead of John Dixon) can be corrected. But you can't change a last name to something entirely different.

2. Where a child is born to an unmarried couple, is given a last name other than the father's, the blank on the birth certificate for the father's name contains his name or has been left blank and the couple later marry, the child's name can be changed on the birth certificate to the father's name. This can also be done if the couple doesn't marry but the father acknowledges paternity. A form for acknowledging paternity will be found in *The Living Together Kit,* Ihara and Warner, Nolo Press.

3. Where a court, as part of a paternity action, finds that a certain man is the father, the child's name on the certificate can be changed to reflect this fact.

4. In legal adoptions, a new birth certificate is issued, if requested.

H. Names and Paternity

Giving the child the name of a man and saying that he is the father doesn't make it so. We dis - cuss what it takes to be a father in detail in Chapter 7, but it won't hurt to repeat a simple truism here. It's a lousy idea to give a child the name of a man who is not the father and to list that per - son as the father on the birth certificate. Once a person is listed as a father, it is difficult, and often impossible, to get him de-listed, even if the mother later states that he is not the father. A man (unless he was married to and living with a child's mother) can always claim that he is not the father. If he does this, he has a right to a court hearing. This could result in his being found not to be the father at the same time that his name is on, and will stay on, the birth certificate.

CHAPTER 4

Acquiring, Managing and Dividing Marital Property[1]

A. Introduction

Since the very beginning of social organization on this planet, systems have existed for dealing with property acquired by the family unit. The community property system which we use in California is rooted in a property scheme devised by the nomadic Visogoths. The Visogoths brought it to Spain when they swept through Southern Europe in the 7th century A.D. It found its way to the New World via the explorers from Spain and eventually spread to those territories in the United States which were originally settled by Mexican colonists.

The community property system is somewhat of an oddity in the American legal tradition, as most of our law follows the English common law scheme. But if it is an oddity, it is a fair one. Among many simple cultures, where the division of labor between husband and wife was substantially equal (usually equally back-breaking), the community property concept arose to reflect the equally shared ownership and possession of property acquired through their joint efforts. It is much more a people's system than the male-dominated property tradition of England. In England, at least among the propertied classes, the wife was viewed as a decoration, a mere chattel (possession) of

---

[1]"Marital property" is a term we use to describe the whole system of rules relating to property belonging to married people. "Community property," as in the "community property system," can also be used this way, but "community property" normally has a much narrower meaning, describing a particular kind of "marital property." This may seem confusing now, but it will become clear as you read on.

the husband, and as such could have no equal claim to his estate.

Unfortunately, community property, which started as a simple system for the people in a simple world, has grown complex and unwieldy to meet the times. Today, there are lots of rules and formulae that must be applied even to find out what community property is. At first glance, many rules appear simple, but often another rule indicating the opposite result could also, arguably, be applied. So the community property rules furnish only a framework from which to argue, rather than a dependable mechanical solution. And not only is the area of marital property law a perversely wishy-washy one, it is also in flux due to new laws and new interpretations of old ones. The times they are a changin' and the law struggles to keep apace.

Unfortunately, people commonly don't take time to learn about their marital property rights or take sensible steps to protect themselves until it is too late. It's often not until a divorce is filed or one spouse dies that an effort is made to figure out which spouse owns what property. Obviously, the time to understand the marital property rules is at the outset of a marriage. With a little knowledge and surprisingly little effort, a couple can order their own affairs by keeping records which indicate their intentions and so avoid the possibility of chaos later on.

We repeat: Most of what we will discuss here is simple and easy to understand, but it can rapidly become complex to people who find themselves in the middle of a divorce with no, or inadequate, records as to property ownership. We will give you a general outline of marital property law, and a step-by-step analysis of how to divide your property, should you find it necessary to terminate your marriage. Nevertheless, there are still times when it will be wise to see a lawyer (see Chapter 12).

B. Acquiring Property

1. What Is 'Property'?

Before we can begin a discussion of the community property system, we must first define what is meant by the word "property." Included in the legal meaning of property are many things which you may not have considered as "property" in the traditional sense. Your property includes your house, land, furnishings, motor vehicles, money, personal belongings, leases, stocks, stock options, securities, promissory notes, life insurance policies, annuities, pension plans, retirement benefits, animals, growing crops, the goodwill of a business, including the practice of a professional (doctor, lawyer), etc.[2] The above is not an exhaustive list, but will serve to give you some idea of the broad nature of the property concept.

Property owned by a husband and wife in California generally falls into one of three basic ownership categories:

- Community property;
- The husband's separate property; or

---

[2] Houses and other buildings which are attached to land, and the land itself, are known as "real property." All other property is "personal property."

• The wife's separate property.[3]

For purposes of abbreviation in the following discussion, H will stand for husband, W for wife, CP for community property and SP for separate property.

2. What Are 'Community' and 'Separate' Property?

Community property is property that is owned by husband and wife together. Each spouse is viewed as owning an undivided one-half interest in community property. Separate property is property that is owned by one or the other spouse by himself or herself. Whether a piece of property is CP or SP is very important, especially at death or divorce. It's the difference between having a dollar (your separate property), sharing the dollar equally with your spouse (community property), and seeing the dollar only when your spouse feels like showing it to you (his or her separate property).

These are the general rules:

• All property acquired by a spouse prior to the marriage is that spouse's separate property;

• All property acquired by either spouse during marriage (with the exceptions of gifts and inheritances to a specific spouse) is community property;

• All property acquired after the couple permanently separates with the ultimate intention of divorcing is separate property;

• All property acquired during a "trial separation" with the hope of getting back together (regardless of whether the couple does in fact reunite), is community property.

Example: Harold and Maude met in 1975 and began living together in 1977. In 1980, they got married. Things got rough after a while, and so in 1987 they tried living apart on a trial basis. After about a year (1988), they decided they're best off permanently apart, and so they obtained a divorce. Their divorce becomes final in 1989. Here's how to characterize their property:

---

[3]A fourth category of property, known as quasi-community property (property acquired by a couple while living outside of California), will also be discussed below.

3. Examples of Property

Virtually anything tangible (and many non-tangible items such as stocks, business interests and patents) constitute property. As we have said, whether a specific item of property is community or separate depends, with some exceptions, on when it was acquired. Let's briefly look at the most common types of property acquired in the course of a marriage.

a. Earnings

Wages earned prior to marriage and after permanent separation are SP; wages earned during marriage and during any trial separation are CP.

b. Pension/Retirement Benefits

Pensions are deferred compensation, i.e., they are benefits paid to an employee after she retires for work done years earlier. With most pensions, the portion earned during marriage is community property and the remainder is the separate property of the employee/spouse. We go into extensive detail in section F(7) below on dividing pensions and will not repeat that discussion here other than to give you the following basic rules:

• **Private Pensions:** The portion of the benefits earned during marriage and prior to permanent separation is CP. The remaining portion is the SP of the earner.

• **State and Local Government Pensions:** The portion of the benefits earned during marriage and prior to permanent separation is CP. The remaining portion is the SP of the earner.

• **Military Pensions:** In the early 1980's, these were considered the separate property of the spouse who was in the armed forces. Today, however, these pensions are considered CP and treated the same way as the pensions above are treated.

• **Social Security and Railroad Retirement Benefits:** Always the separate property of the spouse who earned them. This means that no division is made at divorce. These benefits belong solely to the person who earned them and that's that.

c. Other Employment Benefits (Insurance, Stock Options, Etc.)

The portion earned during marriage and prior to permanent separation is CP. The rest is SP.

d. Copyrights, Patents, Artwork, Etc.

Although difficult to value, these items are CP if created or invented (even if not sold) during marriage and prior to permanent separation. Those created and invented prior to marriage (even if sold during marriage) and after permanent separation are SP.

e. Personal Injury Damages

Personal injury recoveries by H or W from a third party are community property when received during the marriage, but will be treated as separate property during permanent separation and divorce unless the funds were "commingled"[4] with other community property, or the judge decides that fairness requires the non-injured spouse to receive some of the property.

Example: While walking across the street in a crosswalk, Wilma gets hit by a motorist who runs a stop sign. The money that Wilma recovered from the motorist is placed into a bank account she owns jointly with her husband, Herman. As long as Wilma and Herman remain together, this money is considered CP. Thus, if Wilma dies, the most she could give away by her will (or otherwise dispose of) is 1/2, because Herman owns the other 1/2. If Herman and Wilma go their separate ways, however, the money will be assigned to Wilma, unless the court, after taking into account the economic condition and needs of each party and the time that has passed since the recovery of damages, and other relevant factors, determines that the interests of justice require another disposition. If this occurs, community property personal injury damages will be assigned to the parties as the court deems just, except that at least one-half will go to the injured party. A likely scenario where the court would treat the money as CP would be if after Wilma deposited the money into the joint account, she and Herman both deposited other money into the account, took money out, etc., thus making it impossible to determine precisely what money in the account came from the accident and what came from other sources.

Sound confusing? It is. In fact, one court recently noted that personal injury damages are a unique beast under the California community property statutes. If you are involved in a personal injury damages situation, the chances are you will be represented by an attorney. Check with her for further details on this matter.

Note also, that in recent cases, the California Supreme Court has held that Workers' Compensation and Disability pay are to be treated like personal injury damages. That is, they are CP while people are married, but payments to the recipient spouse are considered SP when made after permanent separation.

---

[4]Commingling means that separate property and community property have been mixed together (as in a bank account) in such a way as to make it impossible to tell one from the other. In this situation, what used to be separate property is transformed (transmuted) into community property. We discuss this important concept in Section F below.

Exception: If a disabled spouse has a choice to receive either a retirement plan based on service (CP) or one based on disability (SP when the couple splits up), and he elects to receive disability benefits instead of pension benefits, his spouse will be entitled to the amount she would have received under the pension plan regardless of the fact that the employee/spouse chose disability payments. This is because the courts consider it only fair to force the employee to opt for the program which will benefit the community estate.

In addition, the community is entitled to reimbursement for any medical or other expenses that were paid from CP in connection with an injury.

Reimbursement Note: Reimbursement as it applies to family law is a somewhat confusing, but bear with us as we try to explain by way of an example. Remember Wilma and Herman? Assume that they had a second bank account into which they each deposited their paychecks (CP). Wilma needed medical care as a result of the car accident. Although the negligent motorist's insurance ultimately covered this, a $2500 doctor's bill was paid with money from the second bank account before the insurance company paid off. Because this is a CP account, half of the contents are Wilma's and half are Herman's. When they split up, the damages Wilma got from the accident are her SP, less 1/2 of the $2500 bill paid for out of the community account. (Technically, the CP is reimbursed from Wilma's SP.) We return to the important concept of reimbursement later in this chapter when we discuss dividing property during divorce.

f. Recoveries for Interspousal Injuries

Personal injury damages recovered by one spouse for an injury inflicted by the other spouse are SP of the injured spouse. This is the rule whether the injury occurs prior to marriage, during marriage, prior to permanent separation or after permanent separation.[5]

g. Gifts and Inheritances

Those made specifically to one spouse or the other, no matter when made, are SP. Those made to both spouses (like wedding gifts) are CP.

h. Family Businesses

Businesses existing prior to marriage are SP. The community, however, develops an interest in the business to the extent that community efforts went into running or improving the business during marriage. Those businesses created during marriage are CP, unless created with separate property. (Family businesses are discussed in greater detail in Section F(9) below.)

---

[5]In California, one spouse can sue the other for injuries inflicted deliberately or as the result of negligence, just as if the spouse were a stranger.

I. Life Insurance Proceeds

Those paid out to a spouse during marriage (from for example, a parent, sibling, child, friend) are the SP of the beneficiary spouse. Where one spouse dies during marriage and a life insurance policy had been totally or partially paid for with CP, the portion of the proceeds equal to the percentage of premiums paid with CP are CP. The surviving spouse may claim one-half of the proceeds even if he wasn't named as a beneficiary.

4. How Does Title to Property Affect Ownership?

"Title to property" is the legal way of describing the words which appear on a property deed, stock certificate, car registration, etc. which state who owns a specific item of property.

The following are examples of how a married person or couple normally takes title to property in California:

• John Q. Husband, a married man, as his sole and separate property;

• John Q. Husband and Mary Q. Wife, husband and wife, as community property;

• John Q. Husband and Mary Q.Wife, as joint tenants (or as joint tenants with right of survivorship, in joint tenancy or in joint tenancy with right of survivorship);

• John Q. Husband and Mary Q. Wife, as tenants in common.

Although property is normally held in one of the forms listed above, there are a number of rules which effect title and property ownership:

• Any property acquired during marriage which is held in joint-title form (tenancies in common, joint tenancies, community property and property held as "husband and wife"), will be presumed CP upon divorce, unless it can be specifically shown in a deed, title document or proof of a written agreement that the item is intended to be the SP of one or the other spouse.

• The way title to property is held is not conclusive as to its status as CP or SP. Normally, evidence can be introduced to show that the true ownership intention of the spouses is contrary to the title record. In other words, if title to an asset is taken in the name of H or W alone "as separate property" it can be proven to be CP assuming there is sufficient evidence to do so. Conversely, title can be taken in the name of both spouses "as community property" and yet proven to be the separate property of one spouse.

• If a spouse converts her existing separate property into any joint-title form during the marriage, the property is considered to have been "acquired" by the couple during marriage and thus presumed to be community property.

5. Property of People Who Move to California During Their Marriage

The preceding discussion about community property in California assumes that you and your spouse have lived in California for the duration of your marriage. But what is the legal status of your property if you and your spouse lived in another state prior to moving to California, especially a state that doesn't follow the community property system of property ownership?

As a general rule, all property that would have been CP if the spouses had been living in California when the items or their source were acquired is called quasi-community property and is treated the same as community property.[6]

Example: H earned $10,000 during marriage when domiciled in Florida. If he and his wife move to California and deposit the $10,000 in the bank, the money is considered Quasi-CP, as it would have been CP if H had been living in California when he earned it.

Important: If a spouse keeps property that would be considered Quasi-CP by California out of state during the period of California residence, and then at the time of a divorce leaves California and returns to the state where the assets are located, California courts, as a practical matter, may have trouble claiming jurisdiction over the property (i.e., the courts may not have authority to make an order dividing it).

For inheritance purposes, Quasi-CP is defined by Probate Code 201.5 as covering all personal property wherever located, but only real property located inside California.

Creditor's Exception: There is an important exception to the general rule that Quasi-CP is treated the same as CP. The exception concerns the rights of creditors. Creditors and third party transferees, such as purchasers of property are generally not affected by the concept of Quasi-CP. If the property appears to be the SP of one spouse under the laws of the state where the parties lived when it was acquired, creditors and transferees cannot treat it as community property (see Section C just below for a discussion of marital debts).

C. Acquiring Debts (or Debts Are Property, Too)

While women all over California may have cheered over the enactment of laws giving women equal rights to management of community property, so too did creditors. For, as a general rule, the rights of creditors follow the wielder of management and control of property. Now that women

---

[6]Civil Code Section 4803 states that Quasi-CP is all property both real and personal, wherever located, if it would have been CP had the parties been domiciled in California when it, or its source, was acquired. See Section F below for a full discussion of property division upon divorce.

have been given equal management and control of community property (see Section E(4) below), creditors can much more easily go after the community property to satisfy their debts.

Whether or not a creditor has a right to go after any particular item of property depends on when the debt was incurred and who incurred it. The following are the general rules concerning debts:

• Separate property of one spouse is not liable for debts incurred prior to marriage by the other spouse.

• Separate property of one spouse is not liable for the separate debts of the other incurred during marriage (including up until the date the divorce becomes final) unless the debt is for the "necessaries of life" (e.g., food, clothing, medical care) and there is no separate property of the debtor spouse or community property available to pay the creditor.[7] This exception has prompted many older couples to choose living together as an alternative to marriage. Simply living together doesn't endanger one partner's separate nest egg when the other partner faces the prospect of expensive medical care and would otherwise qualify for state or federal aid.

• Separate property of a spouse is liable for his or her own debts whenever made.[8]

• CP is generally liable for debts made by one spouse prior to marriage except that the share of CP which represents the earnings of the non-debtor spouse are not responsible if:

1. the earnings are kept in a separate "deposit account" to which the debtor spouse does not have withdrawal rights; and

2. the earnings are not mixed with other community property.[9]

Example: When Marie and Pierre married, Marie had student loan debts of $10,000. She had defaulted on 4 payments of $150 each prior to marriage, and has continued to default during marriage. If Pierre keeps his earnings in a separate bank account, they can't be used to satisfy any of Marie's student loan debts.

• To the extent that non-exempt community property (anything other that the non-debtor's spouse's earnings kept in a separate bank account) is used to satisfy prior child or spousal support obligations belonging to the other spouse, the debtor spouse may have to reimburse the community from his or her separate property upon divorce.[10]

Example: When Robert and Rhonda married, Robert had a child from a previous marriage for whom he was paying support. Robert missed a few months payments. If Rhonda's income is kept in a separate bank account, it cannot be used for Robert's child support. If their incomes are combined and then used for Robert's support obligation, Rhonda may be able to recoup 1/2 (her community share) from Robert upon divorce.

---

[7]Civil Code Section 4800(c)(3)(A).

[8]Separate property wouldn't be liable for debts where a creditor agreed in a "security agreement" to look only to CP for reimbursement.

[9]Civil Code Section 4800(c)(3)(A). This rule also applies to child and spousal support obligations that do not arise from the marriage. In other words, if one spouse has a child support obligation in arrears, it is an excellent idea to keep the other spouse's earnings in a separate account.

[10]Civil Code Section 5120.150.

• Community property is liable for the debts of both spouses during marriage,[11] with the minor exception that, if one spouse is held liable for some harm coming to the other, the CP may not be liable (see a lawyer on this one if it affects you).

• Upon dissolution, educational debts are assigned solely to the spouse who incurred them, on the theory that it is unfair to penalize the spouse who not only didn't receive the benefits of the education, but more than likely provided the support for the community during the educational period.

Important: If one spouse takes out a loan, or otherwise obtains credit, and the other signs as part of the security agreement, or co-signs the loan, this means that in addition to the couple's CP, the SP of both spouses is liable for the debt. So don't just put your signature on a credit agreement without thinking. If a wife puts her signature on her husband's credit card agreement, for example, her separate property is liable for any debts he may run up. In other words, money she earned prior to marriage and money she inherited is liable should he charge $1500 on his credit cards before buying a one way ticket to Costa Rica.

Bankruptcy Note: A husband and wife cannot file for bankruptcy as though they were one unit. Each spouse must file as a separate entity and pay a separate fee; the bankruptcy court, however, will make it easier for a husband and wife who both want to file by allowing them to together fill out only one set of the bankruptcy forms. We discuss bankruptcy in *Billpayer's Rights*, Warner and Elias, Nolo Press, and do not repeat that discussion here except to say that your debt problems are often not as bad as you imagine and that there are commonly things you can do to protect yourself, short of bankruptcy.[12] In many instances, if one spouse files bankruptcy, the other one will need to do so, too. This is because the creditors will all close in on the non-bankrupt spouse once the debts of the other are dissolved.

D. Acquiring Property In Marriages That Aren't Quite Marriages

As we discussed in Chapter 1, many people who go through marriage ceremonies aren't in fact married. Often people enter into a marriage in good faith, but later find that due to some technicality, one of them was still married to someone else. At other times, one or both spouses know that they aren't free to marry, but simply do it anyway. People who acted in good faith fall into a category known in legal gobbledygook as "putative spouses," and those who knew darn well they weren't free to marry are said to have a "meretricious relationship." We bother you with these terms because they are important, at least in theory, in deciding property rights.

---

[11]This means that CP is responsible for debts incurred between separation and divorce, since that time is still technically "during marriage." For example, during separation, one spouse could incur a separate debt which might subject the community home to a lien for payment. In such a case, the court would most likely require the spouse incurring the debt to make a contribution to the community estate under principles discussed in Section F below.

[12]Nolo Press also publishes *Bankruptcy: Do It Yourself* and *Chapter 13: The Federal Plan to Repay Your Debts,* both by Janice Kosel in the event you decide that bankruptcy might be appropriate (see back of this book for order information).

1. Putative Marriages

Where both spouses married in good faith, but later find that one or both was still married to someone else at the time of the marriage, or for some other technicality find their marriage invalid, the law provides that acquisitions during the "putative" marriage are treated as if they were community property (the legal term is quasi-marital property).

But what happens if one person married in good faith (was in a "putative" situation), and the other was "meretricious," in the sense that he or she knew that they weren't free to marry?

If the putative marriage is terminated by an annulment or dissolution, the innocent spouse is entitled to the same share of property as if it were a valid marriage (one-half of the quasi-marital property). Also, if there is no quasi-marital property, a putative spouse can recover the "reasonable value of services" during the putative marriage. Here the court implies a contract between the parties so one spouse won't have profited unjustly by the services of the innocent spouse. This applies especially to the person who keeps house while the other works.

In situations where there is a "putative" spouse (from the invalid marriage) and a legal spouse (from the former marriage that was not legally terminated), the legal spouse may file a dissolution proceeding against the other spouse and claim a share of the property accumulated during the "putative" marriage. As we discussed in Section B(3) just above, however, the law in California provides that the earnings and accumulations of either spouse while living apart from the other are separate property. Therefore, the legal spouse has no claim to the property of the putative marriage.

The putative spouse is generally given the same property and support rights on death or dissolution of the marriage as is a legal spouse. Debts are also divided as if a marriage had occurred, which means community debts (except for the education of one spouse) are divided equally. This means that spousal support can be awarded. Also, a putative spouse, in most cases, is entitled to whatever rights are provided by law for "spouses," "widows/widowers," or "surviving spouses" (such as Worker's Compensation, death, pension and retirement benefits).

2. Meretricious Relationships

As we stated just above, a "meretricious relationship" is one where both "spouses" have knowledge of the invalidity of any marriage performed or where they are merely living together, knowing that this does not constitute a "legal" marriage.

The law in this area has traditionally been a mess. On December 27, 1976, however, the California Supreme Court rendered a decision in the case of movie actor Lee Marvin and Michelle Triola, the woman with whom he lived for over six years without marrying, which not only clarifies the judicial response to the living together situation, but profoundly affects all unmarried couples. In *Marvin v. Marvin*, 18 Cal.3d 660, the Court held not only that written contacts between unmarried couples are legal, but also that oral living together agreements, and even agreements "implied" from the conduct of the parties, are enforceable if they can be proved. The Court also specifically stated that a monetary recovery is possible where a person has provided domestic services of a value in excess of support received with an expectation of financial reward.

A later decision held that the pre-marriage agreements of divorcing couples who married after they had been living together are also enforceable.[13]

What these decisions mean in practical terms to the unmarried couple is that they had better articulate their understandings and intentions regarding their property in the form of a written agreement. If they don't, and the relationship ends acrimoniously, a court has the authority to consider other evidence including the testimony of the parties in order to determine whether an oral contract existed in fact or by implication. Obviously, fighting a contested palimony law suit is expensive, unpredictable and best avoided. Fortunately, writing your understandings down as to who owns what is not difficult. Two valuable sources for examples of simple written contracts covering all sorts of property, including boats, cars and real property, as well as personal relationships, such as the situation where one person works and the other takes care of a house and/or children, are *The Living Together Kit*, Ihara & Warner, Nolo Press and *A Legal Guide for Lesbian and Gay Couples*, Curry & Clifford, Nolo Press.

E. Managing Your Property During Marriage

1. When Property Changes Its Character During Marriage

When people get married, they don't usually think about property in terms of "yours versus mine." Mostly, property is referred to as ours regardless of whether it is technically CP or SP under California law. This lumping everything together approach often works fine unless one spouse dies without a will or a divorce occurs. In Section B above, we outlined the basic spousal property ownership rules. In Section F(6) below, we discuss what happens in a divorce when separate and community property have been combined or when spouses have changed separate property into community, or vice versa. Here, we outline the legal rules that apply when ownership of property is transferred from one spouse to the other, from one spouse to both spouses or from both spouses to one spouse.

---

[13]*Watkins v. Watkins*, 143 Cal.App.3d 651 (1983).

2. Changing Title to Property

As we discussed in Section B(4) above, determining how title to property is held is a beginning step in determining the ownership and status of property. It is not, however, conclusive. It is possible to trace the money used to acquire the property and show the true ownership of the property to be other than how it is reflected in the title record.

Therefore, if you want to change the title to your property you should take two steps:

• change the way title is described on the deed or registration certificate (e.g., for a mobile home); and

• make a separate written agreement (contract or gift) reflecting the change.[14]

It is this separate agreement which will eliminate the possibility of ownership being determined by who paid for the property. Here is a sample agreement to be used when changing the title of property.

Sample Agreement

Pauline and Don Chin agree as follows:

1. Since 1970, Don has owned a 1955 Vintage Ford Fairlane.

2. As of the date of this agreement, Don intends to make a gift of one-half of the car to Pauline.

3. Don has written to the Department of Motor Vehicles to request that the car registration be changed from "Don Chin" to "Don and Pauline Chin" as joint tenants, and it is Don's intent that from the date of this agreement forward that Don and Pauline own the Ford Fairlane in joint tenancy.

_____	_____
Date	Don Chin
_____	_____
Date	Pauline Chin

Note: Because Don owns the car, he must sign this document. It is not imperative that Pauline sign, but it's a good idea.

---

[14]Although we provide some basic information here about this subject, we recommend that you obtain a copy of Nolo's *Deeds Book* by Mary Randolph, an indispensible guide for anyone who wishes to transfer or change title to real estate in a family or marriage context. Order information is at the back of the book.

Sample Agreement

I, Frances Miller, hereby give my joint tenancy interest in our family cabin located near Big Bear Lake, in California, to my husband, Thomas Miller, as his separate property.

_____   _____
Date   Frances Miller

Note: As this written statement bears on real property, it should be notarized and recorded at the county recorder's office where the property is located along with a new deed which accurately reflects the ownership change.[15]

3. Changing Ownership of Property Which Doesn't Have 'Title' Documents

Most types of property do not carry with them a deed, registration or title certificate. How, then, do you change community property into separate property and vice versa? You need to draft, date and sign an agreement setting forth the ownership transfer. Here are two examples:

Sample Agreement

We, Judy and Leroy Dubois, hereby agree that from this date forward our earnings and other employment benefits will be the separate property of the spouse who earned them.

_____   _____
Date   Judy Dubois

_____   _____
Date   Leroy Dubois

---

[15]Again, we recommend that you use the Nolo Press *Deeds Book* to help you so this.

Sample Agreement

I, Frances Miller, hereby deposit the $5,000 I inherited as separate property from my Uncle Mickey into the community property bank account number 555-123456, located at the First Bank of St. Thomas, which I own jointly with my husband, Thomas Miller. I intend that this inheritance now be owned by Thomas and me as community property.

_____   _____

Date   Frances Miller

Caution: Agreements between spouses to change title to or ownership of property may later be challenged at dissolution time on the ground that one party didn't adequately understand what was happening and was unfairly influenced to surrender valuable rights to the other. Especially if the property involved in the ownership or title change is extremely valuable and if one spouse has more business sophistication than the other, it may be wise for the spouse who is giving up valuable property to consult briefly with an attorney, just so the agreement will not be vulnerable to this kind of attack.

4. Combining Property

Spouses frequently combine separate and community property without thinking through how this will affect the character of the property. If there is no agreement showing the intent of the spouses, things at divorce time can be a real problem.

Combining usually takes two forms—separate property used to make permanent improvements on something owned by the community (or vice versa), or community and separate (or separate and separate) combined to purchase one item. Here are some sample agreements which will help you get your understandings down on paper.

Sample Agreement

Diane and Danny Huntcol agree as follows:

1. Diane owns a piece of land at 2300 E. 12th St., Oakland, California.

2. Danny and Diane both plan to contribute community property funds and a lot of their own labor to build a house on Diane's land.

3. Danny and Diane will both own the house even though it is situated on Diane's land. This means that if the house is sold, or at death or dissolution of the marriage, Diane is entitled to the value of the land plus the value of one-half of all improvements, and Danny is entitled to one-half the value of all improvements.

4. Title to the property will transfer from Diane to Danny and Diane as tenants in common and a new deed will be recorded.

_____   _____
Date   Danny Huntcol

_____   _____
Date   Diane Huntcol

Note: This agreement and new deed should then be notarized and recorded at the County Recorder's Office, as it concerns real property.

Sample Agreement

Patricia and Zeke Poulos agree as follows:

1. That Patricia owns a 1967 model Chris Craft cruiser valued at $40,000.

2. That the engine in the boat is shot and that Zeke is willing to put $10,000 of his money into the boat to make it seaworthy for a trip.

3. That in exchange for his $10,000 investment, Patricia hereby transfers to Zeke a 1/5 (20 percent) interest in the boat.

4. Should Zeke or Patricia wish to sell their share at any time, they must give the other 90 days notice. During this time, the non-selling spouse may buy the interest of the other for its fair market value, which will be determined by appraisal if the couple can't agree. If, after ninety days, one spouse hasn't bought the other out, the boat will be placed for sale on the open market and the proceeds divided 80 percent to Patricia and 20 percent to Zeke.

5. The title slip to the boat will be changed from Patricia to Patricia and Zeke as tenants in common and the Department of Motor Vehicles will be notified.

_____   _____
Date   Patricia Poulos

_____   _____
Date   Zeke Poulos

Sample Agreement

Jeanne and Wilfred Park agree as follows:

1. That they are buying a 1987 Mercedes Benz automobile using 50 percent community property and 50 percent Jeanne's separate property, which she received from her Aunt Lucy as a gift.

2. That the Mercedes Benz belongs one-fourth to Wilfred and three-fourths to Jeanne, and that, if the car is ever sold, the money received for the sale will be divided following these percentages.

3. That the title slip to the car will indicate that Wilfred and Jeanne own the car as tenants in common.

_____   _____
Date   Jeanne Park

_____   _____
Date   Wilfred Park

Sample Agreement

John and Sandy Kerensky agree as follows:

1. That they're joint owners of a duplex apartment building which they hold as tenants-in-common.

2. That John contributed 80 percent of the money to purchase the building from his SP and that Sandy contributed the remaining 20 percent from their community property.

3. That upon sale of the building, John will be entitled to 90 percent of the money received, and that Sandy will receive 10 percent.

_____   _____
Date   Sandy Kerensky

_____   _____
Date   John Kerensky

Note: Notarize and record this agreement at County Clerk's office along with the deed indicating that John and Sandy own the property as tenants in common. If ownership is in John's name alone, change it.

Synchronicity Anyone?: Just as we finished this section, the phone rang. It was a friend of a friend (let's call him Bill), who told the following story. Two years ago he got married. Soon before the ceremony, he borrowed $10,000 from his mother, signing a note which his future wife (Elaine) didn't sign because she wasn't around that day. The money, which was to buy land, was deposited in the couple's joint bank account. Many deposits and withdrawals were made, and the balance in the account had fluctuated widely. Eventually, land was bought for $8,000 and put in both spouses' names. Soon after this, the couple split up. Elaine filed for divorce and claimed that the $2,000 remaining in the bank, as well as the land, was community property, but that the debt owed Bill's mother was his responsibility. Bill told us that he believes Elaine's characterization of the debt as being his separate property but the land and bank account as CP is unfair. He wants to know if he has a leg to stand on. Although Bill may be able to prove that the debt is CP or that the land is his SP, Bill would be in a far better legal position if either Elaine had signed the original note, or an agreement had been signed recognizing that Bill owned the land as his separate property. Need we say more about the value of doing business in a business-like way?

5. Management and Control of Community Property

Under Civil Code 5125 and 5125.1, a spouse who is managing community property on behalf of the community owes a duty of trust (fiduciary duty) to the other spouse and may be sued during the marriage (or as part of a dissolution action) for breach of this duty. For example, Janis and Tom keep a savings account of community property in Janis' name for the benefit of the community. If Janis uses this money to travel around the world with her lover while Tom believed the money was being saved for a house, upon divorce Tom could sue Janis for breach of the duty of trust.

A spouse who is managing a community business may generally act alone without the other spouse's consent. If all or most of the personal property of the business is disposed of, however, the non-managing spouse must be given prior written notice of the transaction. For example, the spouse running the couple's restaurant may make day-to-day business decisions including buying fixtures and goods for the store, entering into leases, hiring and firing employees, and deciding what to serve, without the other's consent. The spouse-manager cannot, however, sell the restaurant or otherwise dispose of all or most of the assets unless the other consents in writing.

The managing spouse's ability to act alone in respect to CP is also limited when the disposition of CP is in the nature of a gift rather than a sale or trade (discussed below).

6. Transfers of Property to Third Parties

Over the course of a marriage, H or W may want to sell or give away his or her SP or the couple's CP to others. Each spouse can give away his or her own SP property without the other spouse's consent. Conversely, neither spouse has any right to give away the other's spouse's separate property without such consent. If he or she does, the gift is void (invalid and may be set aside).

When it comes to one spouse disposing of community property, however, the rules vary, depending on whether a gift or a sale is contemplated:

a. Gifts of Property

Neither spouse can legally make a gift[16] of any CP without the consent of the other spouse. Written consent is required for any gift of CP furniture and wearing apparel. If the gift is real property, both spouses must join in the transfer by deeding the property to the new purchaser(s).

b. Sales of Property

Here the rules are different, depending on whether the property involved is personal or real.

Personal Property: Either spouse can sell community personal property without the written consent of the other, with the exception of home furnishings and wearing apparel, which do legally require written consent.

Real Property: Neither spouse can sell, mortgage, lease for more than a year, or otherwise transfer any real property which is community property unless the other spouse joins in the execution of the conveyance or gives his written consent (Civil Code 5127).

If a transfer of furniture, clothing or real property has been made without consent, the spouse who did not consent can sue to set aside the transaction. There is a three year statute of limitations on such suits, which means that they have to be brought within three years from the sale (in the case of furniture or clothing) or three years from when the deed is recorded (in the case of real property).

Transfers of community property by one spouse can cause problems, especially if a couple later gets a divorce. When people are a little uptight, it's easy to escalate minor disagreements into something approaching war. The best way to avoid confusion in the future is to make a short agreement when a gift or other transfer of extremely valuable property is made and put it in the file where you keep the important papers relating to your marriage. Oh, we know many of you think that keeping records is too much trouble; it's easier to simply trust your spouse. Well, we have found that in marriage, as in business, trust is the basic building block of a good relationship, but it can erode fast if people don't take sensible steps to protect it. Putting important agreements in writing is one excellent way to do this.

---

[16]Roughly, a gift is any transfer of property without the giver getting something of roughly equivalent value in exchange. For instance, a transfer of title to a house in exchange for $1.00, or $10.00, or even (in most areas) $1,000 would most likely be considered a gift.

F. Dividing Property at Divorce

1. Introduction

If people really got married and lived happily ever after, there would be many more fairy tales and much less need for this section of this chapter. As every marriage runs a high statistical risk of ending short of eternity, however, you should know how the law determines who gets what, when and how if this occurs. We will now, therefore, discuss the principles involved with dividing property. In Chapter 10, we briefly review the actual mechanics of divorce.

A divorce is a bit like the reproduction of a single cell organism. In both instances, one divides into two. The basic problem (with families, not amoebas) is that there is very commonly not enough income to support both new entities in the old manner. Indeed, often the marriage break-up was hastened by the fact that there wasn't enough income to support one family. Obviously, there is no one bit of advice which will apply to every situation, but generally, we believe that when dividing property and arranging for post-marriage support, each person should do his or her best to assure equality of lifestyle and opportunity for all family members after the divorce.

If you and your spouse are arranging your own property settlement as part of a divorce, you are legally entitled to jointly divide your property anyway you like and arrange for any or no spousal support. Child support must be established consistent with the best interests of the child, and a judge will always be interested to see that you have done this fairly (see Chapter 8).

If, however, instead of reaching agreement over your property and support obligation you submit your dispute to the court, a judge will apply California legal rules to your property division. This means broadly speaking that all community property (including your debts) will be divided equally[17] and all separate property will be awarded to the person who rightfully owns it.

---

[17]Of course equal division does not mean everything gets sawed in half. Rather, all the community property is valued and each spouse gets approximately one half its total value. If the community property is worth less than $5,000, and one party to a dissolution can't be located, Civil Code Section 4800 allows it all to be awarded to the other.

Certain rules of reimbursement and credit may apply as well, and we will discuss the fine details for most of the rest of this chapter.

Reminder: It is our strong belief that where justice and fairness prevail between people getting a divorce, their post-marriage relations are likely to be much more constructive. This is especially important where children are involved.

2. An Overview of Property Division Principles

In the rest of this section, we discuss community property division as if a court were making the division and the goal was to arrive at an even split. Even splits aren't always fair in every circumstance, however, and you should realize that as mentioned above, if two informed people voluntarily decide to divide their community property in some other way (e.g., 65-35), a court will accept it.

Warning: Courts do not look fondly on those who cheat by concealing the existence of a community asset. A final divorce can be reopened, even years later, if such a fraud is discovered.[18]

a. Yours, Mine, Ours

Upon divorce, you should start by dividing property into three piles: 1) mine, 2) yours, and 3) ours. (For purposes of this overview, we will assume the role of one party to a divorce with you, the reader, being the other party.) My separate property goes into "my" pile, your separate property goes into "your" pile, and all property belonging to the community goes into the "our" pile. Of course, there will often be a fourth pile consisting of disputed items: ("Aunt Fanny gave that carpet to me—her favorite nephew—as a gift, and it's mine." "Oh no it's not. Remember, it really came from my Uncle Frank.") With a little good will and willingness to compromise on both of our parts, we should be able to agree to distribute this fourth pile among the other three.

When a court is asked to divide marital property, it gives "your" pile to you, and "my" pile to me. When the separate property is safely in "my" pile and "your" pile, the Court will then try as best it can to divide the "ours" pile equally between us. The "ours" pile is called the "community estate."[19] Remember, the basic rule (subject to several special rules to cover particular circumstances) is that the community estate be divided 50-50 as to value.

b. The Source Rule—Or "Rose Is a Rose Is a Rose"

Generally speaking, property takes the character (H's SP, W's SP, CP) of the property used to acquire it. That is, the original source of an item of property is what is responsible for deciding whether it's CP or SP. Using the source rule will help you determine what goes into your pile, my pile and our pile.

---

[18]*In re Marriage of Modnick,* 33 Cal.3d 897 (1983).

[19]If this community estate is worth less than $25,000 and we cannot agree on how to divide it, the Court may require us to have a judge arbitrate the matter under Civil Code Section 4800.9, in order to divide it fairly.

Example: An automobile purchased with H's earnings during marriage (CP) is community property. However, if it is purchased with H's earnings acquired before the marriage (SP), then it is H's separate property.

Caution: Remember that the character of an item of property can be affected by the actions of the spouses so that a SP automobile can become a CP automobile if H and W so agree in writing. (See Section E, above.)

In application, the source rule can get a little complicated. Here is how it works in several common situations:

• **Revenues and Profits from Community Property**

Generally speaking, revenues and profits from community property (e.g., rents, interest) are community property. Likewise, the revenues and profits from separate property are SP, even when received during marriage.

• **Buying, Selling and Trading**

As long as you can trace property to its source, it does not change character because it has been turned into a different kind of property. Thus, if H uses his earnings (CP) to buy an apartment building (CP), which produces rent (CP), which he uses to buy a boat (CP), which he sells and buys stock, or if W uses an inheritance (SP) to buy a car (SP), which she trades for a boat (SP), which she sells, using the money to buy a cocker spaniel (SP) the character of the property as CP or SP does not change. To repeat, it is the character of the source of the property which determines the character of the property unless there are actions by the spouses which will produce a change in the character. (We discuss some of these changes in section 6, below.) This is an important principle to remember when dividing the property into piles.

• **Loans and Credit Transactions**

Generally, money borrowed during marriage is CP. However, if the person who is loaning the money, the creditor, intends at the time the loan is made to secure it with SP, or he is counting exclusively on SP for repayment of the loan, then the loan itself is separate property. This is referred to as the "intention of the creditor" test.

Even when evidence exists, it is sometimes hard to determine the creditor's intention. The courts have, therefore, fashioned several tricky rules to help in deciding whether a debt is SP or CP. If this is a major problem for you, see a lawyer.

• **Insurance**

Income insurance and life insurance policies (both "whole" and "term")[20] are considered property and therefore, under the general rules, if they are acquired with CP funds, they are CP and if acquired with SP, they are SP. Questions concerning life insurance policies usually arise upon death or dissolution.

---

[20]Although "whole" life insurance is unequivocally considered CP when bought with CP, courts are split as to whether "term" insurance is CP when bought with CP funds.

1. Death of the Insured Spouse: The proceeds of a life insurance policy purchased with community property are CP and the surviving spouse has a claim to his or her one-half CP interest. This is true even though another person is named as the beneficiary.[21] There is, however, an exception: The owner of a National Service Life Insurance policy (NSLI, federal government employee insurance) has the right to select anyone he or she pleases as the beneficiary and the surviving spouse has no claim to the proceeds. However, the court, in a dissolution proceeding, can award other community property equal in value to the non-owner spouse in order to arrive at an overall equal division of CP.

2. Divorce: There are two rules which apply in cases of divorce, depending on whether the court divides the policy at the time of the divorce or waits until the insured dies:

• If the court does not divide interests in the life insurance policy upon divorce, then the non-insured spouse retains the interest in the policy and the proceeds when the insured dies. This interest is computed as a fraction. The numerator is one-half the value of the premiums contributed during the marriage and the denominator is equal to the total value of the premiums.

Example: H worked for Acme Illusions, Inc., which provided him with a life insurance policy of $20,000. H started working for Acme in 1970, he married W in 1975, they were divorced in 1985 and he died in 1990. If the value of the premium was $10 per year, then W is entitled to:

1/2 (10 yrs. x $10) divided by (20 yrs. x $10), or 1/2 of 100/200, which is 1/4 or 25% of the policy proceeds.

• If the court divides the policy at the time of divorce, it can be done by giving the non-insured spouse a pro-rata interest in the policy or by ordering the insured spouse to pay the non-insured spouse one-half of the cash value or one-half of the value of CP premiums.

3. Dividing Community Debts

It is unfortunately true that more marriages than not end up with no assets and lots of debts. As discussed above, debts are property (actually negative property), and therefore, when allocating community assets to the community estate category, it is necessary to similarly allocate debts. Such allocation fixes responsibility between the spouses so as to preserve the principle of equal division, but, as mentioned earlier, has no effect on creditors. Thus, even if one spouse agrees to assume all community debts, a creditor would be able to collect against either or both spouses. In this event, the spouse having responsibility for the debts would have to reimburse the other spouse for whatever sums the other spouse was forced to pay.

Where one spouse has a lot of assets or a well-paying job, it often makes sense to assign responsibility for all community debts to that person and balance this unequal assignment with a proportional increase in the community assets distributed to that person. This will help assure the payment of debts without further disagreement between the spouses. In fact, when called on to allocate liability for debts, the court must take into consideration which spouse is most able to pay

---

[21]A portion of the proceeds of a term insurance policy purchased by separate property may also be considered CP if the insured was uninsurable at the time the term policy was purchased with the separate funds but the policy was written because of the prior term paid for by community property funds. *Pritchard v. Logan* (1987).

them and which arrangement will best assure payment of all creditors.

Note: Although debts incurred during the marriage are characterized as community debts, there is one notable exception. A debt incurred which in no way has any benefit on the community should be considered a separate debt of the spouse who incurred it. For example, if two weeks before separating, one spouse treats his or her lover to a trip to Hawaii (while claiming to be on a business trip), the spouse who stayed home can argue that the Hawaii trip is the other spouse's separate debt. When we say "no benefit on the community," we mean no benefit. A bill for books on a subject only one spouse is interested in is a community debt because it enhances that spouse which in turn enhances the community. The same generally can't be said about the Hawaii trip.

4. How a Community Estate Is Divided at Divorce

Courts are entitled to be quite creative in dividing property, so long as each spouse ends up with approximately half of the community estate's assets and burdens according to their value as near to the date of the trial or hearing as possible.[22] Some of the property will be distributed "as is," while other property will be ordered sold and the proceeds split. For example, if one party gets a major community asset like a house, the other party may be given a number of smaller assets, such as a car, boat and pension plan. Or perhaps the person who gets a valuable asset will be ordered to pay debts.

An Overview of Property Distribution Rules

Remember as we discussed in sections A(2), A(3), C, and E above:

• Separate property belongs to its owner;

• Community property is evaluated as near to the date of trial or hearing as possible and distributed so that each spouse receives an equal share of the total value, taking into account their respective liabilities for community debts;

• Where the same property is part separate and part community, the respective shares are apportioned and the community share is divided with the rest of the community estate;

---

[22]Civil Code Section 4800 requires valuing of community property to be done as near to the date of the trial or hearing as possible. There is, however, an exception: any asset which has changed in value since separation because of the substantial efforts of one spouse will be valued as of the date of separation.

• Debts are a form of negative property. Separate debts are assigned to the individual responsible for them and community debts are equitably divided in such a way that is most likely to benefit the creditor, except debts incurred for the education of the spouse which are always assigned to that spouse.

• If both spouses agree, these rules may be deviated from and one spouse may get more or less of the property and assume responsibility for more of less of the community debts.

In order to put these principles in the proper perspective, let's consider an example.

Example: Suppose that upon divorce you and I own the following property:

- Your boat
- My photo equipment
- Our house
- Our vintage Mercedes
- My retirement pension
- Our summer cottage
- Our five rooms of household furniture
- My stamp collection
- My books
- Our phonograph records
- Miscellaneous personal effects (yours and mine)
- Your 26 oil paintings painted during our marriage

The first step would be to make three separate columns and list the property accordingly:

Mine	Community	Yours
Photo equipment	House	Boat
Stamp collection	Mercedes	Personal effects
Books	Cottage	
Pension[23]	Furniture	
Personal effects	Records	
	Pension [23]	
	Oil paintings	

The next step would be to evaluate all property which wholly or partially consists of community property so the court will be able to equally divide it. In this instance, for example, the photo equipment, stamp collection, books, and boat do not need to be evaluated. The items listed as community property and the pension do, however, need to be evaluated.

Evaluation Note: The evaluation of property can be very simple. For example, the two of us may agree as to how much each item of property is worth. If we can't agree, the disputed property should be appraised. In the case of very valuable property, such as a house, we may want more than one appraisal. When a valuable pension plan is involved, an appraisal is essential to arrive at the value. The first step to getting any property appraised is to agree on the person who will do the appraising. This can be anyone from a friend knowledgeable about the particular field to

---

[23]Even though the pension may be mine, if it were earned during our marriage at least a portion would belong to the community estate unless it were a railroad retirement or social security pension (see Section A above).

a professional appraiser (every field has plenty). Which of these appraisers is best? There is no right answer. It depends on a number of factors including the value of the property and the relationship and attitudes of the disputing parties. For example, a good approach might be to hire the real estate agent from whom we bought the house for a couple of hundred dollars to eyeball the house. Or we may choose a different appraiser altogether. If, however, we can't agree on an appraiser, we can each choose one and then to have the two appraisals averaged. Of course, often the easiest, way to arrive at the value of a piece of property is to sell it. The oil paintings are probably the hardest to value. Here again, if we can't agree, an appraisal by one or more art appraisers or knowledgeable dealers, selling the paintings is the best way to arrive at their value.

While valuing property is normally not difficult, it can be tricky in some circumstances. For example, it is not always easy to agree on a fair value for a house, especially if interest rates and other factors are in the state of flux. You agree on an appraiser (or if you can't agree, you each choose one and then take the average) who values the house as near to the trial date as possible. If there is no trial, agree upon a date for the appraisal.

What about other property, such as vintage cars, antique furniture, patents, copyrights, family jewelry or a garage full of oil paintings painted during marriage by an artist whose work is largely undiscovered but who has recently made several significant sales? These are probably situations for appraisers (antique appraisers, jewelers, art appraisers, etc.). In other words, an appraiser isn't only necessary when we can't agree. We also need the help of an appraiser when neither of us has any idea of the value.

Now that we have a better grasp of the concept of evaluation, let's continue with our example. Say we agree (for purposes of the example) on the values listed below. Let's assume also that the interest in the pension was 50 percent earned during the marriage and thus is 50 percent community property. The entire pension is worth $100,000, but only half, or $50,000 worth, is community property.[24]

Community Property Evaluation

House	$100,000
Mercedes	25,000
Cottage	25,000
Furniture	8,000
Records	2,000
Pension	50,000
Paintings	3,000
TOTAL	$213,000

---

[24]Pension evaluations are discussed in Part 8 below.

Okay, we know that our community estate is worth $213,000, assuming no community debts.[25] Now what? There are many ways to divide or distribute the property. Here are a few:

a. Sell everything except the pension and divide the proceeds equally. In addition, you get 25 percent[26] of the pension proceeds when I retire.

b. Sell the house and split the proceeds. You take the Mercedes, I'll take the cottage and furniture. You take 29 percent of the total pension proceeds (worth $29,000) when I retire and I'll take 71 percent, or $71,000. (You got $4,000 more of the pension here than in the first example because I kept all $8,000 worth of furniture.) You take the punk records and I'll take the reggae. We continue to own the paintings jointly and split the proceeds when and if they sell.

c. I'll take the house, you take the Mercedes, cottage, furniture, records and paintings. Because my total is $100,000 and yours is $63,000, we need to make up the difference with the pension. Of the community share, your's take $43,500 and I'd take $6,500. I still, of course, get the other $50,000 as my SP.

To summarize, once you have separated the community property wheat from the separate property chaff, and obtained appraisals where appropriate, list all your community property and its value. Then it's time to start some serious negotiation and distribute the items between yourselves as much as possible (down to the ironing board, raft and chandelier, so to speak). Don't try to do this until you agree on the value of everything. Although you may not believe it at the time, you will almost always be better off by giving way on any issue where the other person feels very strongly, unless it is one involving major financial impact (e.g., a house, pension, etc.). Why? When there is a contest in court, the chances are that attorneys will be involved. If you doubt what this means, consider this from the Cheyenne, Wyoming Leader of January 14, 1888:

"Four sheep, a hog and ten bushels of wheat settled an Iowa breach of promise suit where $25,000 damages were demanded. The lawyers got all but the hog, which died before they could drive it away."

---

[25]In most cases, community debts would figure into this distribution scheme. For example, if we had community debts of $11,000, a total of $202,000 in property would be divided and the debts would be assumed fairly.

[26]Although the pension is 50% CP, you only get 25% of the pension because I get my separate share (50%) and 1/2 of the community share (25%).

5. What If We Can't Determine What's Yours, Mine or Ours?

As we discussed above, married couples rarely think about keeping their property separate during marriage. Often, no matter how the property started out (your inheritance, my income, a gift to you), it's just referred to as "ours."

Problems sometimes arise, then, when we try to divide property where ownership isn't clear. Memories can fade, and if they do, animosities can run high. One spouse may claim that the other spouse made a gift to the community of a SP inheritance. Even where there is no disagreement as to the character (separate or community) of property, if it has been combined, it may be difficult to figure out who gets what (or what percentage).

Here are a few rules from Sections B(4) and E to remember:

• Property held in any joint title (joint tenancy, community property, tenants in common, husband and wife, jointly) is presumed to be community property to be divided 50-50.[27] This presumption can be legally challenged (i.e., rebutted) by showing the source of the money used to obtain the property was something other than what is on the title (e.g., one spouse's $10,000 inheritance was put into a joint bank account containing only $5,000 and then a $10,000 car was purchased with this money, but the registration has both names. The spouse with the the inheritance will be able to show that the car is his).

• A spouse who has made a separate property contribution to any jointly-owned property is entitled to be reimbursed for that contribution unless there is a written agreement showing that the contribution was a gift to the community.[28]

• Where CP and SP are mixed together, the resulting property is generally considered to be CP. There are, however, two methods of overcoming the CP presumption:

a. Direct Tracing

Property bought with commingled funds can be shown to be SP by proving that at the time it was purchased there was an excess of SP income over SP expenses (this must be done by reconstructing each item of separate income and each SP expenditure during the marriage) and then tracing this excess into whatever property was acquired. There must be evidence that the spouse

---

[27]Refer to Section B(4) above.

[28]This rule applies to divorce actions filed after January 1, 1984 and property combined after that same date. If your divorce was filed before that date, the spouse who contributed the separate property is not entitled to be reimbursed unless he or she can prove an agreement (oral or written) showing otherwise. If your divorce was filed after January 1, 1984, but the separate property was mixed with other property before January 1, 1984, you probably need to see a lawyer (Chapter 12). Whether the separate contributor is entitled to be reimbursed is unclear. The California Legislature said yes; the California Supreme Court said the law was unconstitutional. The Legislature passed a new law effective April 10, 1986. The Supreme Court hasn't ruled on it yet, but most family law experts feel the court will say it's unconstitutional; and one lower court already has. (*In re Marriage of Griffs*, 231 Cal.Rptr. 510 (1986).)

intentionally used this excess to purchase the item in question rather than simply showing that an excess existed.

b. Family Living Expenses

This method is based on the presumption that family living expenses are paid from community funds. For example, if W has earnings (CP) and income from SP as well, it will be presumed that the family living expenses were paid entirely from CP to the extent available. If there is no excess of CP over living expenses, it will therefore be presumed that any remaining assets or accumulations are W's SP.

If you face a contested law suit with a spouse or former spouse, you will want to consult a lawyer (see Chapter 12). Remember, however, that you and your spouse can always sit down and make a written statement as to which property is separate and which community. Many people, even when divorcing, find that a willingness to compromise can at the very least save a bundle in legal fees.

To avoid problems in the event you and your spouse divorce, we recommend that separate property be kept separate, using separate bank accounts, safe deposit boxes, etc. If you and your spouse buy valuable property together, using SP and CP, you will be wise to make a simple written agreement. Obviously, the time to do this is when you don't think you will ever need it. It's easy to agree when times are good. By the time the storm signals are in the air, memories of past conversations tend to blur and it may not be so easy to agree. If you never have occasion to rely on your written agreements, you haven't lost much, but if you do go through a rocky time with your spouse, you will be very glad that you wrote some things down.

• Any agreement made after January 1, 1985 to change the character of property must be in writing to be valid. If an agreement was made before January 1, 1985, whether it needs to be in writing depends on what property will be changed. Changes in property are called transmutations and the law applied is shown in the chart below.

Example: H has a run-down SP boat. He decides to rebuild it so that he and W can enjoy their summer vacations sailing. He uses CP funds to do the work. Unless W indicates in writing that she regards the CP contributions to the boat to be H's SP, she retains her CP interest in them. Of course, if H never told her he was using CP funds, W can't be considered as having given consent to it being his SP. In all dealings with CP, H and W owe a "fiduciary duty" to each other. This means that they must deal fairly with each other and disclose all important facts surrounding any transaction.

TRANSMUTATION PROPERTY CHART

	SP contributing to CP	One's SP contributing to other's SP	CP contributing to own SP	CP contributing to other's SP	CP changed to SP	SP changed to CP	SP changed to SP
Pre 1/84	Contribution presumed gift to community unless written agreement to contrary	Contribution presumed no gift unless written agreement to contrary	Contribution presumed no gift unless written agreement to contrary	Contribution presumed gift unless written agreement to contrary	Change may be shown by written or oral agreement	Change may be shown by written or oral agreement	Change may be shown by written agreement only
1/84 to 1/85	Contribution presumed no gift unless written agreement to contrary	Contribution presumed no gift unless written agreement to contrary	Contribution presumed no gift unless written agreement to contrary	Contribution presumed gift unless written agreement to contrary	Change may be shown by written or oral agreement	Change may be shown by written or oral agreement	Change may be shown by written agreement only
Post 1/85	Contribution presumed no gift unless written agreement to contrary	Contribution presumed no gift unless written agreement to contrary	Contribution presumed no gift unless written agreement to contrary	Contribution presumed no gift unless written agreement to contrary	Change may be shown by written agreement only	Change may be shown by written agreement only	Change may be shown by written agreement only

6. Dividing a Family House

Although the general discussion above applies in dividing a home, as well as other types of property, we'd like to focus in more detail on situations when a divorcing couple owns a house. If the house is 100 percent community property, as it would be if it were purchased during marriage with community assets or is held as community property, the steps necessary to divide it are relatively easy:

Step 1: Obtain the fair market value of the house (this will require an appraiser if you cannot agree);

Step 2: Subtract the amount of any loans and any liens against the property;[29]

Step 3: Divide what's left by selling the house and splitting the take, having one spouse transfer his or her share to the other in exchange for getting clear title to other CP assets of equal value or having one spouse "buy out" the other's share.

a. Separate Property Contributions to a Community Property Home

It is not uncommon for a community property house to be purchased and/or improved with a combination of separate and community property funds. For example:

• One spouse's separate property is used as the down payment, while the mortgage loan is taken out as a community property obligation and title of the house is in community property;

• The house is purchased during the marriage with a community property down payment and mortgage loan, but one spouse's separate property is used to make some or all of the subsequent mortgage payments;

---

[29]The difference between the fair market value and the indebtedness on the property is called "equity."

• The house is purchased during the marriage as a joint tenancy (therefore presumed to be community property in case of a divorce). Both spouses use their separate property for the down payment, for improvements, and for payments on the mortgage principle.

If you are in these or similar situations, here is how the court is required to divide the property in a dissolution proceeding:

Step 1: Determine the fair market value of the property;

Step 2: Determine how much is owed on the property;

Step 3: Compute the separate property contributions to the property. Contributions are down payments, improvements, and payments on a mortgage principle loan. Payments of interest, insurance and taxes are not contributions;

Step 4: Determine if one or both spouse's separate property contributions were gifts to the community. Unless the separate property owner has made a written gift of the separate property to the community, he or she is entitled to be reimbursed for all separate property contributions.[30]

Step 5: After the separate property reimbursement is calculated, the rest of the equity in the property is divisible 50-50 as community property. Or, put another way, the separate property owner is not entitled to any more of the increase in the value of the property (once his or her separate property contribution is subtracted) than is the other spouse.

Example: Suppose that in 1976 Paul and Mary (husband and wife) bought a house costing $50,000. The down payment of $10,000 was made with Paul's separate property. Paul and Mary assumed a 30-year mortgage for the balance as a community property obligation and took title as husband and wife. In 1985, Paul invested an additional $25,000 of his separate property in the house for various improvements. In 1988, Paul and Mary dissolved their marriage. The house has gone up in value and has a fair market value of $200,000. Paul and Mary own an equity of $170,000 ($30,000 is left on the mortgage). Despite the fact that the major portion of the house was paid for out of Paul's separate property, Paul is only entitled to a dollar for dollar reimbursement of his separate property, or $35,000. The additional $135,000 (which includes the appreciated value of the home) is divided 50-50 as community property.

b. Community Contributions to Separate Property Home

Where a house is owned by one spouse before marriage and improved with community property funds after marriage, it can get a little difficult to figure out who owns what. While the basic house can be said to be the owner's separate property because it was owned prior to marriage, the community estate will be entitled to an allocation (termed reimbursement[31]) for the amount of funds contributed to the improvements, unless there was a specific agreement to the contrary. If an outstanding separate property mortgage is paid with community funds after marriage, the community share of the house will be large. Add to this problem the question of appreciation in value both before and after the marriage and you get a most complex situation.

As difficult as this may seem, however, it becomes easier to compute if you take it step-by-step. Let's give it a try.

---

[30]Remember, however, footnote 28.

[31]See Section B(3)(e) above.

Example: Assume Irene bought a house in 1976 as her separate property for $25,000, putting $5,000 down and taking a second deed of trust (mortgage) for the $20,000 balance. In 1982 Irene married Ben. At the time, the house had a fair market value of $55,000 and the loan was down to $15,000.[32] Between 1982 and 1986, the remainder of the loan was paid off with community property funds. In 1984, Ben and Irene borrowed $25,000 against the house and spent it on travel and other pleasure items too diverse and numerous to mention. In 1987, Ben and Irene separated; they filed their divorce action in 1988, and the property has increased to a fair market value of $125,000. The $25,000 loan was paid off by Ben from his separate funds. Throughout their marriage, Irene and Ben had always agreed that if they split up, each would be entitled to be reimbursed for his or her SP contributions.

Confused? Bear with us a little longer and it will become clearer (we hope). First, a couple of general principles that should now be familiar:

• The value of the down payment and the original loan are originally the separate property of Irene;

• The increase in value prior to the marriage in 1982 is also the separate property of Irene because prior to 1982, the house was solely her separate property.

• The increase in value between 1982 and 1988 is partially the separate property of Irene because the house is basically her SP.

Remember, the house is valued at $125,000. That amount needs to be divided between Ben and Irene.

Step 1: Determine how much of the $50,000 (the value at the time of marriage in 1982) Irene is entitled to. Because the house increased in value from date of purchase to date of marriage from $25,000 to $50,00, Irene is entitled to the $25,000 increase outright.[33]

Step 2: Apportion between Ben and Irene the $25,000 purchase price ($5,000 down, $20,000 loan) which was paid partially by Irene before she married Ben and partially by the community between 1982 and 1986.

At the time Irene and Ben married, the loan totaled $15,000. That was paid by the community. Thus, of the $25,000 total purchase price, 60% ($15,000 divided by $25,000) is community and 40% ($10,000 divided by $25,000) is Irene's separate property.

Remember, the house is worth $125,000. $25,000 of that is Irene's outright because it represents the increased equity prior to marriage. So, of the $100,000 remaining, Irene's separate share is $40,000. (40% x $100,000). The remaining interest in the house is $60,000.

Step 3: Reimburse Ben the $25,000 loan he paid off with his separate property from the remaining $60,000.

Step 4: Split in half the remaining $35,000.

---

[32]How do you know what an estate such as a house was worth at some time in the past? You don't, and no expert can really tell you. Your best bet is to arrive at a compromise figure and accept it. If you hassle the matter in court, it will be compromised eventually anyway and it's liable to be one of the most expensive compromises you ever made.

[33]This is required by the case *Marriage of Marsden,* 130 Cal.App.3d 426 (1982).

Therefore, Irene gets $82,500 ($25,000 + $40,000 + $17,500) and Ben gets $42,500 ($25,000 + $17,500). Look at the tables below:

1. $50,000   value in 1982
   -25,000   original purchase price (partially unpaid in 1982)
   $25,000   increased equity from 1976 to 1982; all to Irene

2. $125,000   value in 1988
   -25,000   Irene's equity from Step 1
   $100,000   amount to be apportioned

3. $25,000   original purchase price
   -10,000   amount paid by Irene ($5,000 down and $5,000 on loan)
   $15,000   amount paid by community between 1982 and 1986

4. Those percentages:
   $10,000/$25,000   =   40% Irene's SP percentage
   $15,000/$25,000   =   60% CP percentage

5.   40% (Irene's SP percentage) x $100,000 (amount to be apportioned from Step 2) = $40,000 (Irene's SP portion)
   $100,000 - $40,000 = $60,000 (CP portion)

6. $60,000   CP portion
   -25,000   Ben's SP loan to be reimbursed
   $35,000   CP portion to be divided in half

7. $35,000   divided by 2
   $17,500   each spouse's CP share

Irene		Ben	
Step 1	$25,000	Step 6	$25,000
Step 5	$40,000	Step 7	$17,500
Step 7	$17,500		
	$82,500		$42,500

If the house was sold, the proceeds would be distributed with Irene getting $82,500 and Ben getting $42,500, less any closing costs which would be divided equally. If the house was kept, the community estate would be credited with $35,000.

Note: You may have wondered why the house wasn't evaluated when the parties separated instead of when they sought a divorce. This is because, as we have mentioned, property is to be evaluated as close as possible to the time a dissolution goes to court unless justice dictates otherwise. In this situation, there was nothing to suggest that evaluation at separation would have been more fair. If Irene had put a lot of labor into fixing the house up between separation and divorce (for example, if she put on a new roof, repaved the driveway, repainted the entire house and added a deck), however, a good argument could be made to move the evaluation up to the time of separation in order to give Irene the benefit of her work.

Warning: If you are faced with a situation like this, it would be a good idea to get your figures checked by an accountant or an attorney. Especially if your situation is somewhat different, you will want to be sure you have calculated correctly. Also, remember that no law requires you to follow exactly the sort of division approach a court would use. We give it to you as a general framework to guide your thinking, not as a straitjacket from which you're forbidden to escape.

In some cases, the court may delay the sale of a family home and award it to a spouse with custody of minor children for her/his temporary use. See Section G(1) below.

7. Dividing Pensions

Pensions and other retirement benefits, with the exception of social security and railroad retirement benefits, are a type of property subject to division at divorce. For divorce purposes, pensions are simply considered as current employment benefits which happen to be deferred until time of retirement or permanent disability, whichever comes first. Put simply, an employer says to the worker: "If you work for 20 years, I will agree to pay you an amount of money each month for the rest of your life when you retire." In other words, the pension is additional compensation for loyalty to the company.

Pensions are considered community property, at least the proportion of the pension which was earned during the marriage. But pensions are different form other wages in a couple of fundamental ways. First, you are not entitled to the pension unless you meet the eligibility requirement—i.e., longevity on the job. Second, you usually don't know exactly how much your pension will be worth until payments begin. This is because the amount of your pension will depend on several variables, among them being how many years you work.[34]

Nevertheless, courts have ruled that:

• Pension interests are property subject to division at divorce even before the worker becomes eligible to receive them, and

---

[34]Pensions, and your right to receive them, are discussed in more detail in *Social Security, Medicare & Pensions: A Sourcebook for Older Americans,* Matthews, Nolo Press (see back of this book for order information).

• The future worth of pensions can be evaluated through actuarial analysis.

In other words, one spouse may be awarded a piece of his or her spouse's pension even if the pension might never be paid. Determining how much a future pension is worth now is beyond the scope of these materials, but here are some general guidelines about pensions to help you understand the basic principles and to determine how best to proceed in your situation.

a. Vesting and Maturing

When an employee begins working and accruing an interest in a pension, she has no guarantee that she'll ever collect any of the pension benefits. Most companies require an employee to work a number of years (usually 20, 25, or 30) before becoming eligible to receive her pension. Once the employee has worked those years, the pension is said to have vested. (A few companies may base vesting on a point system, rather than a time system, such as in sales where points are awarded for numbers of sales or amount of commissions and then the pension vests after the accrual of a certain number of points.)

What does it mean to you to have your rights in a pension "vest?" It means that the benefits are yours (whatever they may end up being) and cannot be taken away. You may be fired the next morning or quit in two months, but the pension is yours.[35]

Even though a pension has vested, an employee is not necessarily eligible to receive payments at that time. Most pensions require that a worker reach a certain age (often 65) before collecting. When the employee reaches the age, the pension is said to have "matured" and the employee may retire and receive payments immediately. As an alternative, the employee may choose to work longer and postpone receiving the benefits.

b. Determining the Community Property Portion of a Pension

In order to determine each spouse's share of the pension, you must determine the percent of the pension that is separate property and the percent that is community property. The non-employee spouse is entitled to one-half of the community percent.

To determine the community portion, use the following formula. (This formula is written for pensions based on years worked; if yours is a "point pension," substitute "points" wherever you see "years.")

$$\frac{\text{Number of years worked during marriage}}{\text{Number of years required for pension to vest}} \times 100$$

Example: Tricia and Steve married in 1976. In 1983 when she was 23, Tricia left her job as a waitress and began working for ABC Company, where she is eligible for a pension. 25 years are needed for Tricia's pension to vest (the year 2008). In 1988, Tricia and Steve divorce. The community interest in Tricia's pension is (5 divided by 25) x 100 = 20%. Five is the number of years Tricia worked at ABC during marriage (1983-1988) and 25 is the number of years needed for the

---

[35]There are laws which protect employees form being fired right before their pension is to vest (wrongful discharge laws). If this happens to you, you will want to consult a lawyer.

pension to vest. Steve is entitled to one-half of the 20% CP portion or 10% of the total value of the pension.

The next question is 10% of what? After all, Tricia still must work many years before the pension vests and even a longer time must pass before she can receive it at age 65. To determine how much the possible future interest in a pension is worth now normally takes the skill of an actuary (lawyers and accountants don't usually know how). The figure is based on the employee's estimated remaining life span, the amount the pension is likely to pay over that period, and other factors such as the likelihood that the employee will keep working for the employer.

c. How to Divide the Pension Plan

You have a number of options concerning how to divide a pension plan as part of the divorce. Here are the common ones:

• **Waiver**

If the community interest isn't worth much (as would be the case in a short term marriage such as the example of Tricia and Steve given above), then the non-employee spouse can simply waive (give up) all interest in it just to have the matter settled. The waiver should be part of a written agreement and should say something like: "I, _____, am fully aware that there is or may be a community interest in my spouses' retirement benefits derived form employment with _____. I hereby waive any and all right which I may have to these retirement benefits." Considering the fact that it costs approximately $500 to have an actuary determine the value of a pension plan, where there has been a short marriage or little time on the job, it may be economically most efficient to waive any interest.

• **Trade-Off**

The employee gets both halves of the community interest in his or her own retirement benefits, and in exchange the non-employee spouse gets some other community property of equal value. This could be an interest in other retirement benefits, or an interest in the family home, but it could also be a promissory note.[36]

• **Pay-Off**

If the pension benefits are being paid currently as is common if older people divorce, the recipient can be ordered to pay the other spouse a sum equal to one-half the community share as each payment is received. If the right to benefits has matured but the benefits are not yet being paid (because the employee has chosen not to retire)[37] the other spouse can demand to be paid an equivalent amount, or wait until the employee does retire, when benefits will probably be worth

---

[36]Promissory notes, as well as number of other useful contracts, are covered in *Make Your Own Contract,* Elias, Nolo Press. Order Information is at the back of the book.

[37]A worker, however, may not refuse to retire as a way of frustrating his or her ex-spouse's interest in the pension.

more. By not waiting, you give up the chance for increased benefits, but if you wait, the employee could die or lose rights and you may get nothing.

• In-Kind Division

When a pension has not yet vested, and the non-employee spouse doesn't' want to waive an interest or trade off the interest in another asset, the non-employee spouse can ask the court to "reserve jurisdiction" to supervise the payments when the pension matures. If this is done, the eventual payments would be made pro rata to the two spouses based on their shares. This avoids the necessity of a complex and expensive valuation (you need only determine the community interest and when the pension vests and matures). The non-employee spouse, however, does run the risk of the pension not vesting (the employee spouse dying or changing jobs). This option works best with a long-term marriage and employment or where the employee's pension has already vested or is to vest in the near future.

Note: If you chose a pay-off or an in-kind division, you will need to notify (actually, join in as a party to your divorce case) the pension plan administrator. This is because your marital settlement agreement is not sufficient to require a pension administrator to pay you. To join the plan, you need to file several forms[38] ("Request for Joinder of Employee Pension Benefit Plan and Order," and "Pleading on Joinder-Employee Pension Benefit Plan") with the County Clerk. You then must have the sheriff or a disinterested adult over 18 (i.e. anyone over 18 who is not a party to the divorce action) deliver these forms along with a "summons" (completed by the court clerk) and a blank "Notice of Appearance" to the pension plan trustee, administrator or agent for service of process. Your spouse-employee, if requested by you in writing, must give you within 30 days the name, title and address of the plan administrator, trustee or agent. See *How to Do Your Own Divorce in California*, Sherman, Nolo Press which tells you how to do this.

---

[38]These forms are available at the Superior Court Clerk's office in your county.

d. Survivability of Benefits

If your former spouse (the employee) has a vested pension and dies before you've received all you're entitled to, your interest doesn't die too. At the time of your divorce, the court is required to protect your interest in the pension by for example, ordering your ex to name you for any survivors' benefits.

e. Military and Federal Pensions

Spouses of marriages that last through ten years or more of active military service gain advantages in the enforcement of pension awards. Spouses of marriages that lasted through at least twenty years of active military service are also entitled to commissary and PX benefits. Don't be hasty in getting a divorce if you are approaching a 10 or 20 year deadline. For example, if your marriage has lasted nineteen years, you will probably want to delay your divorce for a year.

Also, a spouse retiring from the military can be bound to a written agreement to designate a former spouse as beneficiary under a Survivor Benefit Plan (SBP) if the agreement is incorporated, ratified, or approved in a dissolution judgment, and if the Secretary concerned receives a request form the former spouse along with the agreement and court order.

In addition, it's now easier than it was a few years ago for a spouse to go back and obtain a portion of his or her ex-spouse's military pension if this wasn't done in the original dissolution proceeding. Our advice is, if your ex-spouse has military pension rights or benefits which weren't divided as a community asset in your divorce action, see a lawyer about reopening the case.

Virtually all pensions in this country are covered by the Employee Retirement Income Security Act (ERISA), a federal law which governs how employers administer pensions. Under ERISA, California courts can divide any pension as CP (except for those identified in Section B(3) above), as long as there is a QDRO (a "qualified domestic relations order") which:

• is a court order relating to payment of pension benefits;

• identifies the non-employee spouse as being entitled to receive benefits;

• names the specific pension plan (e.g., MBI Corporation Pension Plan);

• includes your and your ex's names and addresses;

• states the amount or percent the non-employee spouse is entitle to receive (or the method to calculate the amount or percentage; and

• states the number of payments or length of time of the payment.

Final Note: As we warned at the outset of this discussion, dividing pensions is not easy. If there is a substantial interest in a pension as part of your marriage (particularly if one spouse worked at a covered job for more than 10 years), we strongly recommend that you check your plan to divide the pension with an expert (Chapter 12).

8. Dividing a Family Business

As is true with real estate, dividing a family business along SP and CP lines can become problematical. Such questions as who should receive the benefits of an increase in the business value, what types of property were put into the business over the years, and who should receive the business all must be addressed. When discussing these issues it helps to divide family businesses into the following two types:

- Businesses already existing when the marriage began; and

- Businesses created during the marriage.

a. Businesses Already Existing When the Marriage Began

We learned above that revenues and profits derived from SP are also SP.[39] We also learned that the earnings of both spouses during the marriage are CP, absent an agreement to the contrary. But what happens when a spouse works for his own or for his wife's SP business which grows into a more valuable business? The answer is often that, if the business grows, the profits are partly attributable to the original capital (SP) and partly to the spouse's labor (CP).[40]

In this kind of a situation, it often becomes difficult to figure out just what portion of the business is separate property and which portion community. Over the years, the courts have come up with a formula for allocating the interests, called the "apportionment by reimbursement" approach.

The key to this method is whether or not the profits of the business are attributable to H or W's unique skills or, instead, to the natural growth of a business. If you have this sort of problem, you should see an attorney, but here is an introduction to what's involved.

Example: Suppose at the time of the marriage, Wendy owned a store valued at about $300,000. Since the marriage, Wendy has continued to manage and direct its operation. An

---

[39]Section F(2)(b) above.

[40]This discussion assumes an actual business of the retail, wholesale, or manufacturing type which has come down through the family or has existed for a significant period of time prior to the marriage. Businesses which arise from professional degrees are virtually always considered CP during the marriage because profits come from the spouse's labor.

appraiser states that the business is now worth $600,000. To what extent is the $300,000 increase Wendy's SP and to what extent is it CP?

If the greater factor in creating the increase was Wendy's personal service (a community property asset), the profits are CP. Wendy's SP, however, is entitled to reimbursement for the amount of interest that could have been earned on the value of the separate estate (in this example, $300,000), if invested in a long-term, well-secured investment.

If Wendy's personal services, however, were not the greater factor in creating the increase in value (in other words, it would have increased without Wendy working in the business), then the increase is deemed to flow from the business itself and would therefore be Wendy's SP. In this situation, community property is only entitled to reimbursement for the reasonable value of Wendy's services (less anything which may have been taken out in salary).

b. Businesses Created During Marriage

Often after the spouses marry, one (or both) will begin a business. This is especially true if one earns a professional degree (doctor, social worker, art therapist, lawyer, etc.) and then opens her own office. Sometimes the spouse goes into business for herself alone; other times with partners or other business associates. This business is CP if the spouse works alone; if she has a partner, then her share of the business is CP.

Example: Julie and Carl married the summer after Julie finished her medical residency. That fall she and Carl borrowed $50,000 for her to start her medical practice (in partnership with another young doctor (Pat), each partner owning one-half of the business) and for Carl to open a silk-screening business. After 10 years of marriage (and the loan paid off), Julie and Carl part ways.

While both Julie and Carl would undoubtedly keep their own businesses upon divorce, if Julie and Pat's practice was worth $150,000 (thus Julie's share $75,000) and Carl's business worth $25,000, Carl, would be entitled to $25,000 (one-half of the $50,000 difference) in additional CP to make up the difference.

When a family business started during marriage is run by both parties, an obvious problem arises on divorce: who gets the business. We know one couple who divided all their CP but the family business and continue to work together. This, of course, requires that the parties get along sufficiently to continue a working relationship. More common is for one spouse to "buy out" (that is purchase) the other spouse's interest. Usually, the spouse with more money and/or more dedication to the business buys the other spouse's interest. Where spouses cannot agree or cannot afford a buy-out, a court may force the business to be sold and the revenue to be split.[41]

Good Will Note: The evaluation of assets of any business should include the value of good will. Good will is a slightly mystical concept. If refers to the ability of the business to make money because of factors like customer respect for the name, market leverage, or the probability of future contracts or patronage. For example, businesses such as IBM, Time Inc., or Otis Elevator clearly have value over and above the current balance sheet of the particular business. Almost every ongoing business, whether a neighborhood termite exterminator or your favorite candy shop, has

---

[41]To avoid this drastic possibility, spouses who start a business together might be well advised to execute a partnership agreement at the outset which addresses a number of contingencies, including divorce.

some good will. If a couple cannot agree on the value of their business' good will, an experienced small business appraiser will usually be required.

9. Dividing Bank Accounts

The reason we discuss bank accounts separately is that unlike most tangible property, they give rise to special problems. Why? Because money is fungible (one dollar bill looks much like the next) and once community property and separate property dollars are mixed together in an account, it's impossible to figure out which is which. It's a bit like mixing your ten bushels of wheat with my hundred bushels and then trying to give you back just the wheat you started with.

A common practice among married people is to have a joint account where all the family money is deposited (and from which it usually disappears in a frighteningly short period of time). These kinds of accounts are usually considered to be community property even though some of the funds may have come from separate property. For example, supposing your grandmother gives you a gift of $50 for your birthday. Although you might go out and treat yourself to a separate property dinner, you will more than likely deposit it in your joint account from which you pay monthly bills. Remember, where separate property is mixed together with community property, it is said to be "commingled." Commingled property is community property and by placing your $50 in the account with your undisputed community funds, you would lose your separate property claim to it forever.[42]

A similar problem arises when an object (say a camera) is purchased with funds from a joint account. While property purchased with separate funds is separate property, it will usually be impossible to tell in retrospect whether your separate property deposit of $50.00 was the same $50.00 used to buy the camera. In order to overcome the commingling principle, it is necessary to keep separate property scrupulously separate (see Chapter 5) or to keep detailed records for a joint account, showing the separate ebb and flow of community and separate funds. Most people think of doing these things only when it's too late.

As a general rule, therefore, when dividing funds in joint bank accounts, you should consider all funds as community property unless you have an adequate accounting to justify another conclusion. Also, even funds in one person's separate account may be counted as community property if they came from community funds. One common example is where a spouse secretly establishes a separate account to save a small portion of the weekly paycheck against a rainy day, only to find that since the money came from a community source and there is no agreement to make it separate, it is still community property. (See Chapter 5 for sample agreements to keep property separate.)

---

[42]Sometimes it's possible to show that separate property mixed with community property was not commingled. For example, if you can show that between the time you deposited the $50.00 and the time you decided to claim it as separate property (say at divorce), no other withdrawals or deposits had been made, you might be successful in defeating the commingling monster.

10. What If One Spouse Put the Other Spouse Through School?

It frequently happens in the course of a marriage that one spouse goes to school while the other spouse works. In this situation, if a divorce occurs, the educated spouse probably has an enhanced earning ability, while the working spouse has gained little.

The law provides two methods for evening things up at divorce time. First, the working spouse, with some exceptions, will be entitled to reimbursement in the amount of one-half of his or her earnings (or any other community property) that went for the other spouse's education or training, assuming the education or training substantially enhanced such spouse's earning capacity. This, of course, means such common types of education and training as college degrees, graduate school, technical training colleges, real estate license courses, professional schools, trade licenses and insurance training courses.

Second, the court may impose additional spousal support obligations on the educated spouse when necessary to make up for the economic and educational sacrifices by the other spouse. In this section, we will discuss the reimbursement scheme, and in Chapter 9, we cover the spousal support remedy.

The way the reimbursement portion of the law works is relatively simple. The spouse who receives the training or education is required to pay back (reimburse) the community estate for all payments toward the education that came from community property. "Payments toward the education" means both the education itself (tuition, books, fees, etc.) and any money spent in supporting the student (rent, food, etc.). The working spouse will get up to half of his or her contribution back at divorce time, along with interest at the going legal rate, which is currently 10%. If the community, however, benefited from the education (i.e., the community estate increased because of increased income resulting from the education), the level of required reimbursement may be reduced accordingly. Such community benefit will be presumed if the education or training occurred more than ten years before the commencement of the dissolution proceeding. Otherwise, the spouse who wishes community benefit to be taken into account must prove it. Also, if each spouse received some education or training at community expense, the community contributions can offset each other. Finally, if a spouse's education or training has reduced his or her need for spousal support, reimbursement may be reduced or waived.

Example: Glen and Pauline marry when both are seniors in college. After they graduate, Glen takes a job in an insurance company, while Pauline attends graduate school. The total cost for

Pauline's graduate course is $60,000, paid for out of Glen's earnings. Five years later, a year after Pauline obtains her Ph.D., Glen files for a dissolution. Since a doctorate degree substantially increased Pauline's earning capacity, she would have to reimburse the community for the full cost of the education (plus interest) unless she can fit within one of the grounds for reduction. The reimbursement would result in Pauline receiving $30,000 less of the rest of the community property and Glen receiving $30,000 more.

G. Miscellaneous Considerations

The above general discussion applies to all types of property. Because unique problems arise in certain situations, we address two of these situations below.

1. Dividing the Family Home When There Are Minor Children or Adult Disabled Children

Whenever there are minor (or adult disabled) children and a family home, a difficult problem usually arises. The home may be the lion's share of the community estate and, because former spouses seldom continue to live together, if it is not sold one spouse will get "everything" and the other spouse "nothing." But if the house is sold, the minor children will lose their home.

When minor or adult-disabled children are involved, the court must thoroughly investigate the situation (including the impact on the children and the economic detriment to the non-custodial parent) before ordering the family house to be sold. There is an understandable desire to allow the children to remain in their home so as to minimize the economic, emotional and social impact of the divorce on their lives. This means that the spouse having physical custody of the minor children (or with whom adult disabled children will be living) will have temporary use of the house, subject to the discretion of the court. The court may terminate or modify such temporary use order at any time (absent written agreement of the parties to the contrary).

What happens to the other spouse's community property share in the equity of the house? There are generally two solutions. The first is to defer the receipt of that parent's community property share of the house until the house is sold or the youngest child reaches 18, whichever happens first.[43]

The second is to require the parent in possession of the house to execute a promissory note in favor of the parent out of possession to cover that person's half of the house's equity. The payment terms for the note, interest, etc., would be determined by both market conditions and the ability of the person in the house to pay. Either way, the parent out of possession may get "nothing" immediately and may also have to pay spousal and child support in the bargain, depending on the situation.[44]

---

[43]This period may possibly be extended when adult disabled children are living in the home. Civil Code Section 4800.7.

[44]The parent given possession of the house may be required to maintain insurance on the house naming the other parent as co-insured. Also, When a family home is awarded to one parent, title

If the party with temporary use of the family home remarries, or if there is any other change in circumstances affecting the economic status of the parents or children, the court will presume that a delay in selling the home is no longer required to protect the custodial spouse and children. This presumption, however, can be overcome if the custodial spouse makes a showing to the contrary (Civil Code Section 4800.7).

2. Spousal Support as It Relates to Property Division

Spousal support used to be known as "alimony" in legal jargon. Many people still call it that, but lawyers themselves have invented a new term, perhaps just to confuse us. Whichever term you use, the idea is the same—to support a spouse whose contributions to the home during marriage resulted in a failure to develop easily marketable skills. In the not too-distant past, a woman would typically forgo career development in favor of working in the home, while a man would be steadily increasing his earning power. Upon divorce, the man would have his career, but the woman would have no way to earn a living.[45] Spousal support was designed to take care of this gap. While spousal support is not nearly as large a factor in divorces as it used to be, it is still important in many instances. We raise the subject here specifically as it relates to property division. Spousal support in general is discussed in detail in Chapter 10.

How does spousal support relate to property division? Simply put, because both are economic assets, it sometimes makes sense to trade one for the other. To take but one example, it may make sense for a primary earning spouse to keep a greater share of the community property in order to continue bringing home the bacon (e.g., a family-owned business) in exchange for paying a larger spousal support amount than would otherwise be called for. In other words, the distribution of community property and the awarding of spousal support are often intimately related.

H. Reducing Your Property Agreement to Writing

Once you have agreed on the division of the community property, it is necessary to take some steps to carry it out. If you have a small amount of property, the simplest thing to do is to go ahead and divide the property before filing any papers in court. This way the petitioner can simply state that there is no community property to be divided.

However, if you have a lot of property it will probably be wise to have your agreement reduced to writing and approved by the judge. The primary way of doing this is the Marital Settlement Agreement. We reproduce the one contained in *How To Do Your Own Divorce in California*, Sherman (Nolo Press) to give you an idea of what's involved. We strongly advise you to use that book if you are contemplating doing your own divorce.

---

in the home should be changed from joint tenancy (community property or husband and wife) to tenancy in common. *Marriage of Stallworth*, 87 C.D.O.S. 1606 (1987).

[45]We don't mean to imply that this arrangement no longer occurs. Men are still statistically in a much more advantageous position upon divorce than are women.

Note: If you and your spouse have a lot of property or are confused about the status of certain property, you should consult an attorney to review your efforts at drawing up your settlement agreement. You very likely only need to consult an attorney rather than hire one to handle your entire divorce (see Chapter 12). If you are confused about the status of any property, you may want to look at the chart on the next page before consulting a lawyer.

Warning: (See V(B), below.) Sometimes these agreements contain "magic words" which may greatly affect the results. In this one, the magic words are "The parties intend that this amount may/may not be modified by court action in the future." Generally, unless modification of spousal support is expressly disallowed, it will be permitted. *Marriage of Forcum,* 145 Cal.App.3d 599 (1983).

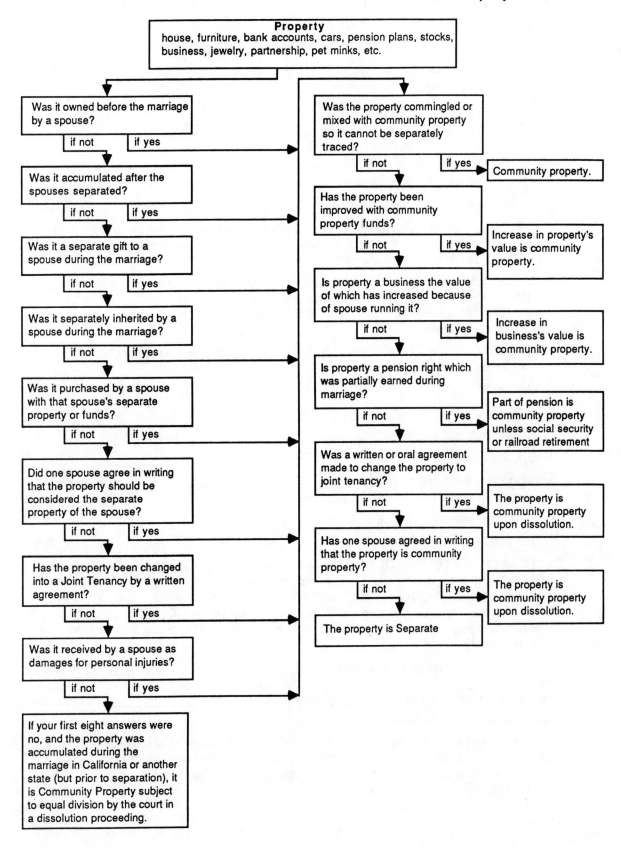

Property
house, furniture, bank accounts, cars, pension plans, stocks, business, jewelry, partnership, pet minks, etc.

Was it owned before the marriage by a spouse?
if not | if yes

Was it accumulated after the spouses separated?
if not | if yes

Was it a separate gift to a spouse during the marriage?
if not | if yes

Was it separately inherited by a spouse during the marriage?
if not | if yes

Was it purchased by a spouse with that spouse's separate property or funds?
if not | if yes

Did one spouse agree in writing that the property should be considered the separate property of the spouse?
if not | if yes

Has the property been changed into a Joint Tenancy by a written agreement?
if not | if yes

Was it received by a spouse as damages for personal injuries?
if not | if yes

If your first eight answers were no, and the property was accumulated during the marriage in California or another state (but prior to separation), it is Community Property subject to equal division by the court in a dissolution proceeding.

Was the property commingled or mixed with community property so it cannot be separately traced?
if not | if yes

Community property.

Has the property been improved with community property funds?
if not | if yes

Increase in property's value is community property.

Is property a business the value of which has increased because of spouse running it?
if not | if yes

Increase in business's value is community property.

Is property a pension right which was partially earned during marriage?
if not | if yes

Part of pension is community property unless social security or railroad retirement

Was a written or oral agreement made to change the property to joint tenancy?
if not | if yes

The property is community property upon dissolution.

Has one spouse agreed in writing that the property is community property?
if not | if yes

The property is community property upon dissolution.

The property is Separate

Marriage Settlement Agreement

I, _____, Husband, and I, _____, Wife, agree as follows:

I. **GENERALLY:** We are now husband and wife. We were married on _____, 19__, and separated on _____, 19__. We make this agreement with reference to the following facts:

A. **Children:** There are (choose 1 or 2)

1. No minor children.

2. The following minor children (list by full name and give birth date of each).

B. Unhappy and irreconcilable differences have arisen between us which have caused the irremediable breakdown of our marriage. We now desire and agree to completely settle all of our mutual rights and duties by this agreement.

II. **SEPARATION:** We agree to live separately and apart, and, except for the duties and obligations imposed and assumed under this agreement, each shall be free from interference and control of the other as fully as if he or she were single. We each agree not to molest, interfere with, or harass the other.

III. **CUSTODY OF CHILDREN** (exclude this section if there are no minor children; otherwise choose A, B, C or D.)

A. Wife

B. Husband

C. Wife and Husband, jointly[46]

D. Other (specify)

shall have the care, custody, and control of the minor child(ren) of the parties, subject to the right of the other spouse to visit the child(ren) (choose 1 or 2)

1. At reasonable times and places

2. As follows: (give the details)

IV. **SUPPORT OF CHILDREN:** We agree that we have read and understand the Minimum Child Support Information booklet. We make this agreement freely without threat or duress. The needs of our child(ren) will be adequately met under this agreement. The right to support has not been assigned to any county. No application for public assistance is pending. (This paragraph is required when support is lower than the minimum (see Chapter 8). The booklet referred to is available from Clerk's Office.)

Subject to the court's power of modification, _____ shall pay to _____, as and for child support, the sum of $_____ per month per child, a total of $_____ per month, payable on the _____ day of each

---

[46]Under the California joint custody law, it is possible to have join physical and legal custody in both parents, joint physical custody but sole legal custody in one parent (rare), and joint legal custody but sole physical custody to one parent (very common). You should specify your intention clearly, rather than just say "jointly."

month, beginning on the _____ day of _____, 19___ and continuing for each child until said child dies, marries, becomes self-supporting, or reaches the age _____, whichever occurs first.[47]

Recommended Option: As additional child support (Husband/Wife) shall obtain and maintain in force a policy of insurance providing major medical (and dental) coverage for each child for the duration of the support obligation. (Wife/Husband) shall pay all medical and dental expenses which are not covered by this insurance, including the amounts deductible under the terms of the policy, and expenses in excess of coverage.

OTHER OPTIONS—any of the following: In addition, during the term of the support obligation for each child, (Husband/Wife) shall

A. Pay the entire cost of (books, tuition, incidental fees, living expenses) for each child who attends an accredited college or university (or private school, or other), up to a maximum of $_____ per year (per child). Such obligation shall end for each child either upon completion of four years of post-secondary schooling or at age 25, whichever comes first.

B. Pay for said child's required/extraordinary medical and dental expenses (to the extent of his ability to do so);

C. Carry and maintain a policy of life insurance in the amount of $_____, and shall name as beneficiaries (Husband/Wife/Said Minor Children) and shall not borrow, assign or otherwise encumber said policy.

Other provisions for children: Sometimes spouses agree that the child(ren) will keep the father's surname and not take on the mother's maiden name or name of any new spouse, at least until the child is old enough (state the age) to make that decision. Some spouses want an agreement about the child(ren)'s religious upbringing and education.

V. PAYMENTS TO SPOUSE: (choose A or B)

A. **Waiver of Right to Support:** In consideration of the other terms of this agreement, both parties waive all right or claim which they may now or may at any future time have to receive support or maintenance from the other [see Chapter 9]. This waiver shall be made a part of any dissolution judgment.

B. In consideration of the other terms of this marital settlement agreement, _____ agrees to pay the sum of $_____ per month, payable on the _____ day of each month, beginning 19___, and continuing until (any or all of the following—some certain date, the death of either party, remarriage of the recipient, some precise condition), whichever shall occur first to _____. The parties intend that this amount (may/may not) be modified by court action in the future.

---

[47]In some counties you will have to handle child support in a separate document (available from the Clerk) called "Stipulation to Establish or Modify Child Support." Modifications of existing child support orders are covered in *How to Modify and Collect Child Support In California*, by Matthews, Siegel and Willis, Nolo Press.

[**Note:** Also remember that Civil Code Section 4801.5 creates a presumption of decreased need for spousal support when the recipient begins cohabitating. If you want cohabitation to terminate the support, you must specify that here.][48]

[**Insurance Note:** A marital settlement agreement in which the spouses make a final disposition of all marital property operates to remove a spouse as beneficiary of a life insurance policy, absent express evidence to the contrary. Thus, if a divorcing spouse owning a life insurance policy intends for the other spouse to remain as a beneficiary of the policy after divorce, he or she must include an option in this agreement naming the supported spouse as sole irrevocable beneficiary. See Option C under child support, above.]

VI. CONFIRMATION OF SEPARATE PROPERTY:

A. The following property was and is the separate property of Wife, and Husband confirms it to her and waives any claim to or interest in it: list—**describe clearly.**

B. The following property was and is the separate property of Husband, and Wife confirms it to him and waives any claim to or interest in it: list—**describe clearly.**

VII. DIVISION OF COMMUNITY PROPERTY: The property itemized under this section is a complete list of all the community (and quasi-community) property of the parties.

A. Husband transfers and quitclaims to Wife all his right, title, and interest in the following items: (list and indicate value of each item. Give legal description of any real estate).

B. Wife transfers and quitclaims to Husband all her right, title, and interest in the following items: (list and indicate value of each item. Give legal description of any real estate).

[**Note About a Family House Where There Are Minor or Disabled Children:** If you decide that the parent with the primary responsibility to provide a home for minor or adult disabled children should remain in the family home, which is a community property asset that would otherwise be divided, use the following to accomplish this:]

Family House: ____(husband or wife)____ and the minor children (or state the name of the adult disabled children) are entitled to the sole occupation and use of the house located at until (choose any or all of the following)

1. The support obligation for all children has terminated,

2. Husband/Wife dies or remarries,

3. Husband/Wife no longer has custody of any child of the parties,

4. Husband/Wife and children cease to reside in the home,

5. Husband/Wife becomes 60 days delinquent in any payment set forth in this paragraph.

On termination of Husband/Wife's right to occupy the house, it shall be sold and the proceeds,

---

[48]If the agreement as to spousal support provides for its own modification, the court can not only modify the amount of support (the first option), but can also extend the support beyond any termination date that you provide [*In re Marriage of Vomacka,* 36 Cal.3d 459 (1984)]. Accordingly, if you wish to provide for modification as to amount but not as to duration, use the following language: "The parties intend that this amount may be modified by court action in the future but that the termination date for spousal support payments may not be extended beyond the termination date fixed in this agreement."

after deducting costs of the sale, shall be distributed according to their percentage of ownership. Husband/Wife shall be responsible to make all payments on existing encumbrances, together with taxes, insurance and other assessments, without right to reimbursement, such payments being considered fair value for occupancy. Capital expenditures for improvements may be made when agreed by the parties, and the cost divided equally between them. Individual outlays for $500 or less shall be deemed maintenance.

Note About Pension Plans: If there is a community interest in a pension plan, be sure to deal with it clearly in this agreement. If it is to be given entirely to the employee spouse, list it in Item VI or Item VII. If one spouse wishes to waive his or her interest in the other's plan, put it in here, using the language suggested in Chapter B(3)(c) of *How To Do Your Own Divorce in California* as your guide. If the matter is to be reserved for the future, put that in here like this:

B. Pension Plan: The parties intend that the community interest in the pension plan of (husband/wife) , (full identification of plan) , will be valued and divided when the employee-spouse first becomes eligible to receive payments under the plan. To this end, the parties agree to keep each other notified of changes in address and of any changes in pension plan provisions. (employee spouse) specifically agrees not to apply for or accept benefits under said plan without prior written notice to (other spouse) and application to a court for determination and division of community property rights in the plan.

Alternative Method To Divide Property (for cases with little or no significant property:)

Husband and Wife agree that their community property is minimal and that they have already divided it to their mutual satisfaction. Each hereby transfers and quitclaims to the other any and all interest in any property in the possession of the other, and agrees that whatever property the other may possess is now the sole and separate property of the other.

VIII. DEBTS:

A. Husband shall pay the following debts, and indemnify and hold Wife harmless therefrom: (list—identify clearly, give value of each item).

B. Wife shall pay the following debts, and indemnify and hold Husband harmless therefrom: (list—identify clearly, give value of each item).

C. Husband and Wife each promise the other that they shall not incur any debt or obligation for which the other may be liable, and each agrees that if any claim be brought seeking to hold one liable for the subsequent debts of the other, or for any act or omission of the other, then each will hold the other harmless, and defend such claim.

[Alternative when little or no debts and little or no community property: Add the phrase "and debts" to the "Alternative method to Divide property" above to the first sentence following the words "their community property"]

IX. **TAXES:**[49]

A. Any tax refunds for the current fiscal year shall be distributed a follows: (specify).

B. Any tax deficiencies for the current year shall be paid as follows: (specify).

C. (Husband/Wife) may claim the tax exemption for (name of children). Optional: ...for any year in which support payments for said child are not over 45 days in arrears.

X. **EXECUTION OF INSTRUMENTS:** Each agrees to execute and deliver any documents, make all endorsements, and do all acts which are necessary or convenient to carry out the terms of this agreement.

XI. **PRESENTATION TO COURT:** This agreement shall be presented to the court for incorporation and merger into the Judgment in any dissolution proceeding between the parties.

XII. **DISCLOSURES:** Each party has made a full and honest disclosure to the other of all current finances and assets, and each enters into this agreement in reliance thereon.

XIII. **BINDING EFFECT:** This agreement, and each provision thereof, is expressly made binding upon the heirs, assigns, executors, administrators, representatives, and successors in interest of each party.

_____
Date

_____
Husband

_____
Date

_____
Wife

---

[49]Property division upon divorce can be handled in a number of different ways and the tax consequences vary greatly, depending upon which alternative is chosen. For example, the right to spousal support can be taken in periodic payments over time or exchanged for property at the time of dissolution or at a future time. Each choice has a different tax liability, which can be considerable. We especially advise you to consult an accountant or tax lawyer to understand the consequences, if spousal support is to exceed $15,000 for any one year.

CHAPTER 5

Marriage Contracts

A. Marriage Is a Contract

When you are growing up, marriage is the happy ending to countless variations of the beauti-
ful princess, worthy prince story, complete with the scent of orange blossoms, an exchange of
vows pledging eternal love, and a rosy fade-out into the sunset. With the coming of age and acqui-
sition of just a little practical experience in the nature of human relationships, a more pragmatic,
more sharply focused image usually emerges. However, an essential aspect of the marriage venture
still escapes many prospective partners, and that is that marriage, at its core, is a contract. Indeed,
California statute defines marriage as a "civil contract" (California Civil Code Section 4100).

When you enter into this contract by purchasing a license and saying "I do," you are subscrib-
ing to a whole system of rights and responsibilities. Unlike most other contracts, however, you
never get the chance to read the terms or the fine print because the provisions are unwritten and the
penalties for breach unspecified.[1] In few other legal areas are contracting parties so in the dark.
Indeed, there's more bargaining power and more options surrounding a contract made with a fast-
talking door-to-door salesperson than when it comes to getting married. If all men and women
were required to read the "marriage contract" and consider the rights and obligations contained in it
prior to marriage, it would be interesting to see how many would still be willing to say, "I do."

This chapter and the previous one do two things:

---

[1]Some of the rights and obligations of the marriage contract can be found in the massive volumes
containing California laws, but many appear only in the decisions of lawsuits. Others are bound
up with the practices and procedures of courts and judges and don't appear anywhere.

• Explain the basic provisions and assumptions of state law (the traditional marriage contract);

• Discuss ways in which you can make legal alterations in the traditional marriage contract[2] to fit your lifestyle more comfortably.

1. The State's Marriage Contract

The traditional marriage contract fixed the role of the husband as head of the household and made him solely responsible for financial support, while the wife was responsible for domestic services and child care (barefoot, pregnant and in the kitchen). The wife was basically regarded as the alter-ego of the husband, dependent and inferior, who lost her separate identity upon marriage. The state also assumed a monogamous, heterosexual, "until death do us part" union.

As in many other areas, the law lags more than a bit behind the social reality. Although laws that relate to marriage have changed greatly in recent years, the ghosts of centuries of traditional marriage ideas are still with us and are likely to stick around a while. The slowness with which laws governing marriage respond to changing values and ideas about families means that many couples will want to understand the ways in which they can legally write their own marriage contract.[3]

2. Modifying the State Marriage Contract

Under the old English common law, husband and wife became one person upon marriage. Contracts between husband and wife were thus void—you need two parties to have a contract. In the 19th century, the Married Women's Property Acts granted married women the power to con - tract, and eventually antenuptial (pre-marriage) and postnuptial (after marriage) contracts became accepted.

Marriage contracts have been around for a long time. Many early feminists, like Mary Woll - stonecraft in the 18th century and the famous Lucy Stone in the 19th, abhorred the inequities of traditional marriage and drew up their own contracts, which started with the provision that the wife was to be treated as an equal human being.

Courts, however, have always been suspicious of contracts that alter too greatly the traditional concept of marriage, which since the beginning of our cultural history has been viewed (usually by male commentators) as one of the main foundations upon which our civilization is built. Thus, the state's interest in promoting the good of society by preserving and regulating the family unit has been consistently upheld by judges who wax poetic upon the need for benevolent state protection:

Marriage is an institution in the maintenance of which in its purity the public is deeply interested for it is the foundation of the family and of society without which there would be neither civilization or progress.[4]

---

[2]In this chapter, we use the term "marriage contract" to refer to prenuptial contracts (those made before marriage) and contracts made during marriage.

[3]Contracts made between people living together without getting married are covered in depth in *The Living Together Kit*, Ihara and Warner (Nolo Press).

[4]*Maynard v. Hill*, 125 U.S. 190, 211 (1888).

Courts have generally looked with favor on, and accorded recognition to, marriage contracts entered into by couples which deviate from the provisions of the official state contract as to property ownership and division. Changing other areas of the marital relationship (e.g., those affecting children or support) by contract has not met with equal favor. As we discussed more particularly in Section C of this chapter, provisions trying to establish spousal support, child support, child custody or child visitations will not be enforced unless the judge who examines them happens to agree that they are fair.

B. Who Needs a Marriage Contract?

The most common marital contracts in California are those which deviate from California community property law. Especially when money marries money and the result is more merger than marriage, a contract setting out the spouses' rights to the marital property often accompanies the ceremony.[5] An example is the legendary contract between Jackie Kennedy and the late Aristotle Onassis, which supposedly contained 170 clauses, including a provision for a $600,000 a year allowance for Kennedy to "shelter her from want." Most folks own considerably less than Kennedy and Onassis, but regardless of size, a married person's property in California is governed by the community property laws set out in Chapter 4, unless there exists an agreement to the contrary.

There are many reasons why a couple might contemplate a property agreement. Most often, a couple will simply want to run their own financial affairs and not be subject to California's community property rules. For example:

• A prospective wife who expects large earnings or an interest in a business or professional practice might want the assurance that they will remain her separate property after the marriage.

• A prospective husband who has large holdings of property may want to provide that this property and its proceeds will remain separate after marriage regardless of the amount of com - munity time and effort expended in its management.

---

[5]Normally marriage contracts are entered into prior to marriage to take effect on the date of the marriage. However, it is both legal—and not uncommon—to enter into them after a marriage has commenced.

• A couple whose members have been through a nasty divorce where lots of property which had been mixed together was laboriously and expensively separated may want a contract so that the same thing can never happen again.

• A husband or a wife might want to convert part or all of his or her separate property into community property.

• A wealthy, older man who intends to marry a younger, poorer woman may want to assure her (or she may want to be assured) of adequate provision for her and any children of the marriage.

• Or, most commonly, couples who marry at a time when either or both already have children may wish to keep their property separate so as to better protect the inheritance rights of their natural children from claims by the other spouse.

C. What Goes Into a Marriage Contract

1. Enforceable Provisions

An individualized marriage contract can, in theory, cover any aspect of the marriage relationship, including the division of housework, child care, finances, sexual rights, birth control, children, and who feeds the canary. However, because the clauses that deal with most "lifestyle" subjects are not enforced by courts (in fact, the inclusion of sexual rights may nullify the entire agreement), we do not deal with them here. As discussed above, however, more often, a couple will want to draw up an agreement not to regulate every detail of domestic life, but to settle a few major and potentially troublesome issues of property ownership. Most such agreements present no enforceability problems. Generally speaking, a court will enforce a properly drawn contract concerning property (including income, debts, and division of property if there is a dissolution) but will not enforce agreements attempting to regulate social conduct (who does the dishes or takes care of the kids).

Below is a list of some topics to consider when drawing up a marriage contract. All of these provisions can be enforced in a court of law. California law [Civil Code Section 5312] also authorizes agreements on any other matter not in violation of "public policy" (see Section C(2) below) or a criminal statute.

a. Property

A couple may want to make an agreement concerning all property acquired by either spouse before or after the date of the marriage or the date of the contract (for property owned before marriage, including a signed list in the contract is a good way to do this). Property should be designated as separate property or community property. Also, it may be wise to agree on who should have management and control of the property.

b. Provisions for Wills and Inheritances

Provisions can be made for estates and the creation of trusts or the drafting of specific or mutual wills. Inheritance provisions can be agreed to for children of the marriage, or of a former marriage. This sort of agreement is particularly important for older people who already have families by former marriages when they marry.

c. Income

An agreement can be made as to the ownership and control of wages, and other types of income, such as capital gains interest or insurance or pension benefits. If there is only one earning partner, the couple might want it to be considered community property with joint management and control (this is the case under law, unchanged by agreement), but if there are two earning parties, they each may want to consider their own income as separate property and retain separate management and control over it. In this context, the California Supreme Court has upheld a premarital agreement that provided that the husband's earnings would remain his separate property during marriage [*In re Marriage of Dawley,* 17 Cal.3d 342 (1976)].

d. Debts

A definition and allocation of responsibility for separate and community debts can be included. Different types of debts might well be treated differently. Of course, this agreement would have no effect on rights of creditors that independently exist under California law. See Chapter 4.

e. Support and Living Expenses

If a man or woman has children from a former marriage, the couple may want to decide whether expenses of child support are to be taken care of jointly or separately. Even if there are no children, if the couple is to share some expenses and pay others separately, mutual living expenses should be identified. A list could be made of items which will be considered community living expenses, such as rent, utilities, food, telephone, automobile, medical/dental, recreation, etc., along with a provision that indicates the financial responsibility of each spouse for these expenses. There are many alternatives: If both spouses are working, they could pool their incomes and pay shares proportional to their incomes, or husband and wife could each pay half of the expenses and keep what is left of their earnings as separate property, or they could allocate responsibility for separate items, e.g., husband takes care of rent and utilities, while wife is responsible for food and clothing.

Important: However you decide to share or allocate expenses, under California Civil Code 5100 you cannot contract away the basic duty to support your spouse for the necessaries of life, which include clothing, food, shelter and medical expenses.

f. Increased Earning Capacity From Education

If one spouse goes to school and increases his ability to earn, the other spouse apparently has no community property interest in this increased earning capacity [Civil Code Section 4800.3(d)], although the community (the couple) is entitled to reimbursement for the contributions of community funds toward the spouse's education at dissolution. Because there is some uncertainty on this point, many couples opt to cover it in their own agreement.

g. Pension Plans

This is an increasingly popular area of premarital contracting because court decisions holding that pension plans are community property have made many divorces far more complicated and expensive. With a marriage contract, a spouse can keep this asset (except Social Security and Railroad Retirement Pensions) as her separate property from the start. One reason to do this is that the actual value of pension rights is difficult and often expensive to assess at divorce (see Chapter 4).

As noted, few people will want to include all of these topics. The important thing to remember is that each couple's situation is unique, and the specific areas of concern in a relationship vary widely. To illustrate some ways contracts can be used, we include at the end of the chapter several hypothetical contracts tailored to fit different lifestyles. We also provide some sample agreements that can be filled in.

2. Unenforceable Provisions

The basic rule is that courts will not enforce contracts that alter the "essential elements" of the marital relationship or that are made in promotion of divorce, such as an agreement which gives a spouse a definite financial reward upon divorce.

The Uniform Premarital Agreements Act, which has been adopted in part by California[6] also prohibits enforcement of a prenuptial agreement (the Act does not cover contracts made during marriage) that is unconscionable (grossly unfair) when it was made if one spouse did not fairly disclose the extent and nature of her property holdings to the other spouse. This provision doesn't actually provide much special protection for contracting spouses, given the fact that unconscion- ability is grounds for voiding any kind of contract. The statute just spells out one factor (lack of disclosure) for a court to consider when ruling on unconscionability of a premarital contract.[7]

a. Contracts That Alter the "Essential Elements" of Marriage

"Public policy" is the reason courts give when refusing to enforce contracts that alter the basic obligations and responsibilities of marriage. As a federal judge stated:

If [married persons could] . . . contract as to the allowance the husband or wife may receive, the number of dresses she may have, the places where they will spend their evenings and vacations, and innumerable other aspects of their personal relationship . . . [it] would open endless field for controversy and bickering and would destroy the element of flexibility needed in making adjustments to new conditions arising in marital life. There is no reason, of course, why the wife cannot voluntarily pay her husband a monthly sum or the husband, by mutual understanding, quit his job and travel with his wife. The objection is to putting such conduct into a binding contract,

---

[6]Civil Code Sections 5200 et seq. It applies to contracts made after January 1, 1986.
[7]The other spouse may, however, waive in writing his or her right to disclosure.

tying the parties' hands in the future and inviting controversy and litigation between them. [Graham v. Graham, 33 F.Supp. 936, 939 (E.D. Mich. 1940).]

But what are the essential obligations of marriage that can't be changed by contract? They include:

1. Sexual Relations: Courts have refused to enforce contracts in which spouses agree to refrain from sexual intercourse or agree not to have any children (see Chapter 8).

2. Spousal Support Duty: According to California Civil Code Section 5100, there exists between spouses a mutual obligation of respect, fidelity and support. The duty to support your spouse during marriage is an obligation that cannot be contracted away. What this means, prac - tically, is that if there is no available community property, separate property must be used to support the spouses while they are living together. This means that each spouse is liable (if he or she has the ability to pay) for the debts contracted by the other for "necessaries" of life—such essentials as medical expenses, food, clothing, and shelter.

When it comes to the duty to pay spousal support after marriage, the law is not so clear. The California legislature specifically rejected the part of the Uniform Premarital Agreements Act that allows couples to contract on the issue of spousal support. However, while courts do not consider premarital contracts to pay a set amount of (or no) spousal support binding[8], they often volun - tarily follow reasonable premarital agreements having to do with spousal support (see Chapter 10 for more on spousal support generally).

3. Child Support Duty: By statute the state (court) reserves the right to regulate and control child support (see Chapter 8).

4. Personal Services: Contracts that included an agreement to reimburse a spouse for per - sonal services (usually housework and domestic services) have been voided by courts on the theory that an implied term of the marriage contract was that these duties are to be performed by a spouse without compensation. This is an area where ideas are changing, however, and we expect that it won't be long before such contracts are honored.

b. Contracts Promoting Divorce

It used to be that contracts made in the mere contemplation of divorce were voided on the grounds of public policy. The state has been in the business of discouraging divorces for so long it has taken the courts a long time to adjust to the fact that divorces and short-term marriages are here to stay and for many people may be desirable. However, California courts now enforce agree - ments as long as they do not work to promote the dissolution of marriage. If two people plan realistically for the future and fairly and freely enter into an agreement for the disposition of their property should their marriage ever be dissolved, that agreement does not violate public policy and will be enforced. What won't be enforced is an agreement that gives one spouse a powerful incen - tive to end the marriage. If, for example, one spouse will get a huge amount of property only upon divorce, the agreement will probably not be enforced.[9]

Note: A financial separation agreement made by spouses when they have already decided to separate is enforceable. However, the agreement must not be interpreted by the court to have

---

[8]*In re Marriage of Dawley*, 17 Cal. 3d 342 (1976).
[9]*In re Marriage of Noghrey*, 169 Cal. App. 3d 326 (1985) (promise by husband to give wife substantial amount of money and property only upon divorce held unenforceable).

induced the separation.

D. Drawing Up The Contract

Before you draw up your agreement, we strongly recommend that you read this entire book carefully. Until you understand what your rights and responsibilities are under the state's marriage contract, you can't make intelligent decisions about what elements you want to change by contract. You should also:

• Make sure both parties have disclosed all assets and liabilities. If you don't and a court decides the agreement was unfair when it was signed, it won't be enforced (Civil Code Section 5315).

• Draw up and sign the agreement together, under normal circumstances. Any contract can be challenged if it appears that one party didn't really understand or have any choice about the terms of the contract. An agreement handed to a prospective spouse minutes before the wedding, or given with a take-it-or-leave-it ultimatum, is not likely to be enforced.

• Get the advice of a tax specialist on the tax consequences of changing the status of large amounts of property.

• See separate lawyers if one party is experienced in business affairs and the other is not. Contracts have been set aside if a court decides someone with business sophistication seems to have put something over on someone more naive.

• Have a lawyer check the contract if it is complex or if a lot of property (either now or potentially) is involved.

California statutes require that pre-marital agreements be put in writing. In addition, if the agreement includes a clause concerning real property, have the signatures notarized and record it at the county recorder's office of the county where the land is situated. If you don't record it, the change in property ownership is not valid as to third parties (creditors, for example) who had no way of knowing ownership changed.

If you want to make any changes in the agreement after it's signed, you must follow the same formalities required of the original contract—that is, the change or revocation must be in writing and, if real property is involved, must also be notarized and recorded.

E. Sample Marriage Contracts

1. Agreements Before Marriage

Below is a sample contract that contains clauses to take care of several common concerns of couples who plan to marry. Following it are two examples of premarital contracts.

Sample Clause for Agreements Prior to Marriage

1. This agreement is entered into on _____19_____between
_____(name of future wife)_____ and _____(name of future husband)_____.

2. We will be married on or before _____.

3. Each clause of this agreement is separate and divisible from the others, and should a court refuse to enforce one or more clause(s) of this agreement, the others are still valid and in full force.

4. In consideration of the promises of the other, _____(name of future husband)_____
and _____(name of future wife)_____ agree as follows:

[If the parties want to provide that all property of each party, no matter how acquired, will be separate, this clause can be used:]

a) _____(name of future wife)_____ agrees that all property (real or personal) wherever located, including, but not limited to, earnings and income resulting from personal services, skill and work, including any interest in a pension plan arising from work, belonging to _____(name of future husband)_____ at the time of the marriage or acquired during the marriage, shall be his separate property and shall be subject to his disposition as his separate property.

b) _____(name of future husband)_____ agrees that all property (real or personal) wherever located, including but not limited to earnings and income resulting from personal services, skill and work, including any interest in a pension plan arising from work, belonging to _____(name of future wife)_____ at the time of the marriage or acquired during the marriage, shall be her separate property.

[In many cases, the parties may want to provide only that all of their property shall be community property. If so, the following clause can be used.]

_____(name of future wife)_____ and _____(name of future husband)_____
do hereby declare that all the property of any kind or nature, now owned or held by them or by either of them and all property that either of them may acquire hereafter, from whatever source,

including inheritance and gift, shall upon their contemplated marriage be their community property.

[A husband may want to support stepchildren that he has no legal duty to support. He can agree to do so in a provision like the following:]

During the marriage of the parties, _____(name of future husband_____ agrees to provide a home for _____(name of future stepchild)_____ and to furnish reasonable support for him/her. In the event of the death of _____(name of future wife)_____ during the marriage, _____(name of future husband)_____ shall pay to or for the benefit of said child the sum of $_____ per month for support until he/she reaches the age of 18.

[In the case where one spouse wants to assure the other of inclusion in a will, the following provision can be made:]

[This is an example of a husband providing for a wife]

In the event of the death of _____(name of future husband)_____ during the continuance of his marriage to _____(name of future wife)_____ and at a time when he and ____(wife)____ are living together as husband and wife, there shall be paid to _____(name of wife)_____ from the estate of _____(name of husband)_____ the sum of $_____ free of all estate and inheritance taxes.*

Dated: _____

  Signature of future husband

Dated: _____

  Signature of future wife

---

*You could substitute for a specific dollar amount, "all the community property interest of _____(name of husband)_____ " or "all community and separate property belonging to _____(name of husband)_____."

State of California   )
) ss
County of _____)

On _____ 19_____ before me, the undersigned, a Notary Public in and for said State, personally appeared _____

_____

_____ and _____

_____

personally known to me (or proved on the basis of satisfactory evidence) to be the persons whose names are subscribed to this instrument, and severally acknowledged to me that they executed the same.

Witness my hand and official seal.

_____
Notary Public in and for said State

Elvira and John

Elvira is a widow of 67 and John a widower of 70. They both have grown children from former marriages, comfortable nest eggs, and fair monthly incomes from freelance activities (Elvira is a paste-up artist and John contributes regularly to a library journal). They want to share the rest of their lives together but feel it unnecessary to embrace the community property system of California.

Sample Marriage Contract

ELVIRA REDWING and JOHN FLEETFOOT agree as follows:

1. That they will get married on or before_____, 19____;

2. That during the course of their marriage, they will conduct their affairs under the terms of this agreement;

3. That each clause and sub-clause of this agreement is separate and divisible from the others, and that should a court refuse to enforce one or more clause or sub-clause, the others are still valid and in full force;

4. That the promises of each party are consideration for the promises of the other;

5. That each has fully disclosed his assets and liabilities to the other and each waives any right to further disclosure.

6. That as of the day this contract is signed, both John and Elvira own various property and that this property and all earnings and accumulations which accrue to this property shall be kept as separate property. To help accomplish this goal, Elvira's separate property is listed in Schedule A of this contract, which is hereby incorporated in and made a part of this agreement, and John's separate property is listed in Schedule B of this contract, which is hereby incorporated in and made a part of this agreement. These lists will be kept up to date as property is sold, transferred and accumulated;

7. That all property (real or personal) acquired after marriage by Elvira and John specifically including, but not limited to, income from personal services and all monies from pension and retirement plans, shall at all times be kept as separate property except as specifically provided in clause 8 and that John and Elvira will maintain separate bank and credit accounts;

8. That the monthly living expenses of Elvira and John while they are living together, including food, utilities, housekeeping, and gardening expenses, shall be shared equally;

9. That if in the future John and Elvira desire to jointly purchase any real or personal property of a value of $1,000 or more, a separate written agreement shall be executed;

10. a) That John is aware that the bulk of Elvira's separate property stems from the estate of her deceased husband and that Elvira feels this property should descend to her children by her former husband upon her death. John respects Elvira's viewpoint and will not assert any rights as husband he might acquire in such separate property;

b) Elvira likewise understands that should John predecease her, he plans to leave his separate property to his children by the use of will, trust and joint ownership investments. Elvira agrees to respect his plan and will likewise not assert whatever rights as wife that she might have in the estate of John after his death.

Ronaldo and Betty

Ronaldo is a 35-year-old salesman who was married and divorced in his twenties. The divorce was drawn-out, nasty and expensive. When it was finally over, he swore he would never go through that again, even if it meant not remarrying. He has a child from his first marriage who lives with his former wife.

Betty and a partner run a small restaurant. After several years of barely scraping by, they have lately begun to make good profits as the restaurant's reputation has spread and it has become a popular spot.

Ronaldo and Betty decide that because they each can support themselves and they don't plan to have children, the easiest way to handle money is to keep all their property separate. This also eliminates the potential problem of assessing Ronaldo's community property interest in Betty's business.

Sample Marriage Contract

Ronaldo Meza and Betty Chen agree as follows:

1. They will get married on or before_____, 19____.

2. During the course of their marriage, they will conduct their affairs under the terms of this agreement.

3. Each clause and sub-clause of this agreement is separate and divisible from the others, and should a court refuse to enforce one or more clause or sub-clause, the others are still valid and in full force.

4. The promises of each are made in consideration of the promises of the other.

5. Each has fully disclosed his assets and liabilities to the other and each waives any right to further disclosure.

6. Ronaldo Meza agrees that all real or personal property acquired by Betty Chen after their marriage will be her separate property. All property means just that, and includes (but is not limited to) profits from her business, any increase in her ability to earn as a result of future education or increase in value of her business interests.

7. Betty Chen agrees that all real or personal property acquired by Ronaldo Meza after their marriage will be his separate property. All property means just that, and includes (but is not limited to) his pension plan, any increase in his ability to earn as a result of future education, and earnings.

8. Betty Chen will not have any responsibility for child support payments to Ronaldo's daughter, Theresa.

9. Betty Chen and Ronaldo Meza will maintain separate checking accounts, own and pay for their own motor vehicles, and will not commingle their separate property in any way.

10. Betty Chen and Ronaldo Meza will each pay one-half of all household expenses, including rent.

11. Should Betty Chen and Ronaldo Meza ever decide to buy a house or other real property together, each will contribute one-half the purchase price and title will be taken in joint tenancy. Each agrees to sign an agreement at that time that the joint tenancy property shall be separate, not community, property.

12. Should Betty Chen and Ronaldo Meza ever dissolve their marriage, neither will have any obligation to pay the other spousal support. [**Note:** This provision is not enforceable. See Section C(2) above.]

2. Agreements Made During Marriage

Any of the topics in a premarital agreement can be covered in a contract entered into after the marriage has taken place. Again, the most common area of concern is property ownership. Below are some short sample agreements that can be used to clarify or change the status of the parties' property.

An Agreement Defining Separate Property and Community Property

1. We, _____(name of husband)_____ and _____(name of wife)_____, husband and wife, make this agreement on _____ 19____.

2. We have been married since _____ 19____.

3. Each of us makes the promises, herein, in consideration for the promises of the other.

4. Should a court refuse to enforce any clause or sub-clause of this agreement, the others remain in full force and effect.

5. We both have certain separate property and our interest in community property. We intend to define such property by this agreement.

6. I, _____, hereby acknowledge that the following described property* is the sole and separate property of my wife and that I have no right, title or interest whatsoever in the property:

(Itemization and description of property)

7. I, _____, hereby acknowledge that the following described property* is the sole and separate property of my husband and that I have no right, title or interest whatsoever in the property:

(Itemization and description of property)

---

*Don't forget to deal with pensions.

8. We declare that except for the property described in 6 and 7 above, all the property of whatever kind now owned by us or standing in the names of either of us, is and shall remain our community property. (An itemization could be included if thought necessary).

_____
Signature of wife

_____
Signature of husband

[Notarization of contracts after marriage is optional, but is an excellent idea. Contracts involving real property should be recorded. This information applies to all the following sample agreements.]

An Agreement Making Existing Property Community Property

1. We, _____(name of husband)_____ and _____(name of wife)_____, husband and wife, make this agreement on _____, 19___.

2. We have been married since _____, 19___.

3. We hereby declare that all the property of whatever kind now owned by us and standing in the record name of either of us on this date is our community property.

4. This agreement isn't intended to affect the ownership of property acquired by either of us after the date of this agreement.

_____
Signature of wife

_____
Signature of husband

An Agreement Making All Property Community

1. We, _____, and _____, husband and wife, make this agreement on _____, 19___.

2. We have been married since _____, 19___.

3. We do hereby declare that all property of whatever kind now held by us and all property that shall hereafter be acquired by either of us from whatever source shall be our community property.

_____
Signature of wife

_____
Signature of husband

An Agreement Changing Specific Community Property to Separate Property

1. We, ____(name of husband)____ and ____(name of wife)____, husband and wife, make this agreement on _____, 19___.

2. We have been married since, _____, 19___.

3. We own the following described community property. It is our desire to divide such property equally between us:

(Description of property)

4. We therefore agree that from this date on, half of the property (include a description of the portion of the property) shall be the separate property of _____(name of husband)_____ and one-half of the property (include a description of the portion of property) shall be the separate property of _____(name of wife)_____.

_____
Signature of wife

_____
Signature of husband

An Agreement Changing All Community Property to Separate Property

1. We _____(name of husband)_____ and _____(name of wife)_____, husband and wife, make this agreement on _____, 19___.

2. We have been married since _____, 19___.

3. We have the following described community property:

(Description of property*)

4. We desire to make a settlement of all of our property rights so that each of us will own approximately one-half of the property as his or her separate property. We agree that from this date the following property will be the separate property of _____(name of husband)_____:

(Description of property)

We also agree that the following property will be the separate property of _____(name of wife)_____:

(Description of property)

5. We agree that all property hereafter acquired by either of us including earnings shall be the separate property of the one so acquiring it.

6. We understand that but for this agreement the earnings and income from the personal services of the other spouse would be community property, but that by this agreement such earnings are made separate.

_____
Signature of wife

_____
Signature of husband

---

*Again, don't forget pension plans.

CHAPTER 6

Buying a House

A. Introduction

Until recent times, a newly married couple could expect to rent for the first couple of years and then purchase a house which would begin them on their way to a settled life. These first houses were referred to in the trade as "starter" houses.

The comfortable vision of each American family comfortably occupying a six or seven room house is rapidly vanishing from our landscape thanks to a number of long term trends in the hous - ing market, including inadequate supply, exhorbitant prices, and out-of-sight interest rates. These trends, of course, are intimately related and greatly affect one another.

To cope with the prices and interest rates connected with single family dwellings, many new types of financing (called "creative financing") have sprung up. A number of books have been published to keep you, the potential housebuyer, abreast of these developments, and rather than reinvent the wheel, we suggest that you visit your library. Be sure you find recently published material, however, as this field is changing fast.

Now, before we go on to the the area of our expertise and discuss the legalities of assuming home ownership, once you have dealt with the financing we want to remind you of several important things:

• Realtors want to sell houses at the greatest possible price since their commissions depend on it. Therefore, they often do not have the buyer's best interest at heart.

• No matter how good a deal looks, you never get something for nothing. If it sounds too good to be true, it probably is.

• Make sure you have a reasonable possibility of meeting all future mortgage payments con -
tained in your creative financing package. This doesn't mean that you can barely squeak out the
payments, but that you have enough in reserve to handle the mortgage even if your most optimis -
tic financial projections fall short.

B. Taking Title to the House

Once you decide to buy a house and have arranged your financing, you must go through the
formal title transfer procedure. The word that is most commonly attached to this procedure is
"escrow." This is real estate jargon for the buyer and seller delivering the necessary money and
documents to a third party (escrow agent), who then exchanges them.[1] This will be handled for
you by the real estate people, bank and title company unless you decide to handle your own
purchase or sale. This is not a book on how to buy and sell your home, but there are several
adequate paperbacks available if you need help in this area.

Even if you handle the transformation yourself, you will have to pay for a title search by a
professional title company and title insurance (to guard against a mistake in the title search). You
may ask, why can't I search the title myself down at the County Recorder's office? You can, but
no one will accept your finding. Because of a complicated system of interrelationships between
real estate people, home builders, bankers and lawyers, you simply will not be able to buy and
finance a house without buying title insurance.[2]

But once you have grit your teeth and agreed to be taken by the title insurance racket, how
should you actually take title to the house? You have several options:

In One Person's Name Only: This would be appropriate if one spouse was buying the
house with separate property, and wanted to keep the house separate.

Joint Tenancy: Taking title to a piece of real property "as joint tenants" means that legal -
ly the joint tenants share in property ownership and each has the right to use the entire property. If
one joint tenant dies, the others automatically take the deceased person's share without the neces -
sity of any probate proceedings. Indeed, when one joint tenant dies, the property can go only to
the surviving joint tenant(s), even if there is a will to the contrary. If one joint tenant sells his or
her portion to a third party, this ends the joint tenancy.[3] The third party and the original joint ten -
ant become "tenants-in-common" (see below).

---

[1]The escrow agent also computes such things as property taxes, insurance premiums, etc., so that
buyer and seller each pay only for that portion of the year during which they occupied the house.
[2]We do not mean to suggest that title insurance is unnecessary given our present land records
system, but that our system is a bad one. In other countries, more enlightened land records systems
are used which make title insurance unnecessary. We feel that it's past time that our legislatures
take a close look at the whole area.
[3]A joint tenancy can also be terminated at any time if one joint tenant unilaterally conveys his or
her interest to him or herself as a tenant-in-common.

It often happens that one spouse puts a piece of separate property real estate into joint tenancy with the other spouse, often at the behest of a lending institution when the house is refinanced. Unless the two spouses sign a written agreement that the property is to remain separate property, it will be considered community property should they divorce. The original owner will be entitled to reimbursement for the value of the property at the time it was placed into joint tenancy, but the other spouse will be entitled to one-half of the appreciation in value that may have subsequently occurred. Simply put, the recipient spouse may be in for a windfall in the event of a divorce. See Chapter 4 for how this works and some sample agreements to carry out your intentions.

Tenancy-in-Common: Tenants-in-common are also each entitled to equal use of the property, but if one party dies, the other party does not take his (her) share unless this has been specified in the deceased person's will. Tenancy-in-common is normally more appropriate to bus - iness partners than to spouses. Spouses who don't want an automatic right of survivorship as in "joint tenancy" should consider the community property alternative below.

However, spouses who own property in unequal shares, or people who have separated and wish to continue to own real property together will find that tenancy-in-common makes sense. We dis - cuss owning property in unequal shares in more detail just below.

As Community Property: With the recent partial reform of the probate law, property held "as community property" can go to the surviving spouse (at the first spouse's death) without going through formal probate as long as a will indicates that this should happen and a petition is filed. This change does away with many of the reasons for joint tenancy ownership, as one reason for the use of joint tenancy has traditionally been to avoid probate, at the same time that it allows you to will your half of the community property to someone other than your spouse if you wish. In some situations, there also may be tax advantages to holding property "as community prop - erty." Most couples buying a house together with community property funds will find that this designation best fits their needs.

C. Contracts Between People Buying Houses

It is all very well to list the common ways of taking title to a house. But how does this help you deal with a situation where one spouse already owns a house and the other moves in, or a situation where one spouse has more money to contribute to the purchase of a house than the other? Because these situations occur more commonly to unmarried couples than they do to mar - ried ones, we go into much more detail in *The Living Together Kit* than we have space for here. We refer you to this book, which will be available at your local library.

Here is a brief outline of the possibilities open to you, with a couple of sample contracts which we have adapted from *The Living Together Kit* . If you are creating your own contract, it will be wise to do the drafting yourself and then have your work checked by a lawyer (see Chapter 12). Find out the fee in advance. Since you have done most of the work, it shouldn't be expensive.

1. One Person Invests More Money in the House than the Other

Let's assume that Wanda has $10,000 of her separate property to invest in a house and Walter has $20,000. They decide that they want to own the property in shares proportional to their respective investments. What should they do? They would probably decide to take title to the house as "tenants-in-common" and then prepare a contract setting out their respective ownership shares. The contract should be notarized and recorded, but you should be aware that once recorded it may be difficult to clear title for a subsequent sale unless both people will sign a quit-claim deed. Tak - ing title to a house as "joint tenants" or as "community property" would not be appropriate, as those methods of ownership only apply where the shares are equal. The sample contract we give you here is only one of many ways to solve the problem. *The Living Together Kit* contains several other alternatives.

Sample Contract

WANDA WALTERS and WALTER WINTERS agree as follows:

1. That Wanda and Walter will purchase the house at 1639 Carolina St., Van Nuys, California. Their initial investment (down payment and closing costs) will be $30,000, of which Walter will contribute $20,000 and Wanda $10,000. Title to the house will be recorded as "Wanda Waters and Walter Winters as Tenants-in-Common."

2. Wanda and Walter will each make one-half of the monthly mortgage, tax and homeowners insurance payments.

3. Wanda has skills as a carpenter and decorator. She will contribute labor to remodel and redecorate the home according to plans that will be agreed to by both Wanda and Walter. Her labor will be valued at $10.00 per hour and any materials she purchases will be valued at cost.

4. A notebook entitled "Exhibit A—'Homeowner's Record' for 1639 Carolina Street" will be maintained and is hereby incorporated into, and made a part of, this contract as Exhibit A. Walter and Wanda shall record the following information in their "Homeowner's Record":[4]

   a. The $20,000 initial contribution made to purchase the house by Walter;

   b. The $10,000 initial contribution made to purchase the house by Wanda;

   c. All money Wanda contributes for house payments, real property taxes and homeowners insurance;

   d. Wanda's labor on agreed upon home improvements valued at $10.00 per hour;

   e. The dollar amount that Wanda pays for supplies and materials necessary for home improvements;

---

[4]The system we set out here is simple and reasonably fair. It credits both parties with all contributions made (not only those which go to equity). It allocates any natural increase in the value of the home along the lines of total contribution and ignores the fact that Walter made a large portion of his contribution before Wanda. If you want to work out a more exactly accurate (and complicated) system, see a computer. Several of our friends are using this sort of system and find that it works well.

f. All money that Walter contributes for house payments, real property taxes and homeowners insurance.

5. The proportion of the house owned by Wanda and Walter respectively as of any particular date shall be computed as follows:

a. The total dollar amount of the contributions by both Wanda and Walter as set out in paragraph 4 shall be separately totaled.

b. The total equity interest in the house shall be computed by subtracting the amount of all mortgages and encumbrances from the fair market value of the house as of the date the computation is made. If Wanda and Walter can't agree on the fair market value, they shall have the house appraised. This shall be done by each of them designating a licensed real estate broker or salesperson who is familiar with the neighborhood to do an appraisal. The average of the two appraisals will be the fair market value of the house;

c. The total dollar value of the contributions of the person making the larger contributions arrived at in Section 5a of this contract shall be placed above the total value of both people's contributions arrived at in Section 5a to form a fraction. This fraction represents the share of the total joint equity interest in the house owned by the person with the larger share. The remainder of the total joint equity interest belongs to the person with the smaller share.

[Editor's Note: If after living together for five years, Walter's contribution totals $30,000 and Wanda's $20,000, Walter would be entitled to 30,000/50,000 or 3/5 of the value of the total equity in the house. Assuming that the fair market value of the house was $125,000 and all mortgages and other encumbrances total $50,000, this would mean that Walter would be entitled to 3/5 of $75,000 or $45,000.]

6. Either Walter or Wanda can terminate this agreement at any time. If this occurs, it is under - stood that the person with the larger equity interest in the house as computed under the terms of paragraph 5 above shall have first choice as to whether he or she wishes to stay living in the house.

7. Should separation occur and a decision be made under the terms of paragraph 6 of this contract concerning who is to stay in the house, the person leaving is entitled to receive at least one-half of his or her share as computed under paragraph 5 of this contract in cash within ninety days of the decision to separate. In addition, the person staying shall give the person leaving a three-year mortgage for the remaining portion of his or her share not paid in cash. This mortgage will be recorded at the County Recorder's office and is payable in 36 equal monthly installments at 9 percent interest. If the person who wishes to stay in the house is unable to meet the terms of this paragraph, the house shall be sold and the proceeds divided according to the shares established under paragraph 5a of this contract.

————	————————————
Date	Walter Winters

————	————————————
Date	Wanda Walters

2. One Person Moves Into a House Already Owned by the Other

We are commonly asked questions by couples trying to figure out how to deal with the thicket of legal, practical and emotional problems that can pop up when one person moves into another's house. Sometimes it seems that even the most relaxed people have problems when one invades another's turf. Let's look at a typical situation.

Alan and Faye marry. They make a decision to keep their earnings and other property separate and sign an agreement such as discussed in Chapter 5.[5] Faye already owns a house and Alan plans to move in. Faye asks Alan to share equally in the monthly house payments, real property taxes, fire insurance, etc. Alan's response to this request is to say, "Okay, but only if I somehow get to own a part of the house."

As it turns out, the house Faye lives in is worth about $75,000, the existing mortgage is $50,000, and her equity is $25,000. Faye agrees with Alan that if he pays one-half of the pay - ments, he should get some interest in the house, but she raises two good points. The first is that since she already has a big investment in the house, Alan can't hope to get much of a share by paying one-half of the monthly payments. Her second point is in the form of a question. Assum - ing that it was decided to give Alan an equity (ownership) interest in the house, how could it be fairly done?

a. The simplest solution would be for Alan to forget buying a share of the house and have him pay Faye a monthly amount for rent. Of course, this should in fairness be considerably less than one-half of the mortgage, tax and insurance costs. Why? Because Faye is buying the house and Alan is not. We suggest that if this approach were adopted, Faye and Alan should check the a - mounts paid by other people sharing houses in their neighborhood to arrive at a fair rent.

b. Another simple solution would be for Alan to pay Faye an amount equal to one-half the val - ue of her equity in exchange for her deeding the house to both of them either as "joint tenants" or as "community property." In this situation, as the equity is $25,000, this would mean that Alan would need to pay Faye $12,500. Alan and Faye might still want to make a contract to deal with questions such as who keeps the house if they break up, etc.

c. A third possible way to resolve Alan and Faye's problem is less simple. Alan and Faye could sign a contract under which Alan agrees to pay one-half (or all, or any other fraction) of the monthly expenses in exchange for a percentage of the total equity equal to the proportion his pay - ments bear to the total amount of money invested in the house by both parties. Here is a way they might do this.

[5]In the following discussion, we are assuming that each person is contributing separate property. If community property is used, the agreement would have to be written, and the figures computed, differently. See an attorney (Chapter 12).

Sample Contract

ALAN MARTINEAU and FAYE SALINER agree as follows:

1. That Faye owns the house at 57 Primrose Path, Oakland, California subject to a mortgage with the Treeland National Bank in the amount of $50,000;

2. That Alan and Faye agree that the house has a fair market value of $75,000 as of the date this contract is signed and that Faye's equity interest is $25,000;

3. That commencing on the date that this contract is signed, Alan shall pay all monthly expenses for property taxes, homeowners insurance, mortgage payments including interest, and necessary repairs, and shall continue to do so until his total payments equal $50,000, or until the parties separate;[6]

4. When Alan makes payments in the amount of $50,000 as set out in paragraph 3, Faye shall deed the house to "Faye Saliner and Alan Martineau" as "community property."[7] From this date on, the house shall be owned equally by Alan and Faye and all expenses for taxes, mortgage, insurance and repairs shall be shared equally;

5. Should Alan and Faye separate prior to the time that Alan contributes $50,000, the house shall continue to belong to Faye, and Alan will be required to leave within thirty days of the decision to separate, but Alan shall be entitled to his share of the equity (see paragraph 7). Alan's share of the total equity value of the house shall be figured at the rate of one-half of one percent for every month that he pays all of the expenses as set out in paragraph 3 above. For example, if Alan pays all the expenses for two years, his interest in the house equity shall be twelve percent (12%);

6. Once Alan contributes $50,000 and Faye deeds the house to both of them "as community property," Alan shall have an equal opportunity to stay in the house if a separation occurs. If the couple cannot agree amicably on who is to stay and who to go after the deed is changed to the community property designation, they shall have a friend flip a coin, with the winner getting to purchase the share of the other and remain in the house;

7. If a separation occurs either before or after the deed is changed to the community property designation, the person leaving shall be entitled to receive his or her share of the equity within ninety days of moving out. If there is a dispute about the fair market value of the house, Faye and Alan shall each select a licensed real estate person to make an appraisal. The two appraisals shall be averaged to determine the fair market value. If it proves impossible for the person who wins the coin flip to pay off the person leaving within ninety days, the other person (the coin flip loser) shall have an additional ninety days to raise the cash to buy out the other person. If neither person is willing or able to buy out the other, the house shall be sold and the proceeds divided under the terms of this agreement.

_____   _____
Date   Faye Saliner

_____   _____
Date   Alan Martineau

---

[6]This contract would be particularly suitable in a situation where Faye wanted freedom from monthly payments for a period of time. Alan is required to pay $50,000 to get a one-half share, even though Faye has only put in $25,000, because the house will probably go up in value during the years that Alan is putting in his share. How much it will go up in value can only be a guess, of course.

[7]Alan and Faye could have chosen "joint tenancy," but normally "community property" achieves the same result, with more flexibility. See Section B of this chapter.

D. Homesteading the House

If you own (or are buying) the place you live in, you can protect a portion of its value from present and future creditors by filing a simple form called a "Homestead." It's not hard to do, and it gains you great protections and security.

Filing a "homestead declaration," which has nothing to do with the old federal land law allow - ing people to claim free land, means that with the exception of certain specific dollar limitations on your protection (discussed below), your home cannot be forcibly sold to satisfy most types of common debts. Once you have filed your homestead, then for the most part no matter what debts you accumulate and no matter for what reason—accident, misfortune, mismanagement or even plain stupidity—your home cannot be taken. In short, your homestead will drive the wolf (in the guise of a hungry creditor) from your door both now and forever after.[8] Debts that are not covered include taxes (naturally), certain types of contractors' liens, and, of course, the money you owe on the house itself.

The amount of equity that will be protected by a homestead is not unlimited. The legislature adjusts it upwards from time to time (now is another good time to do it), but as of the writing of this book, the protection is as follows:

If You Are:	Then Your Equity is Protected in Amounts Up To:
A single person	$30,000
A married couple	$45,000
A single person who qualifies as head of household	$45,000
Anyone over 65 or disabled	$60,000

Homestead Your House , by Warner, Sherman and Ihara, contains all the forms necessary to homestead your house or condominium. Lawyers commonly charge $75-$150, but there is no reason not to do it yourself.

Note: If you fail to homestead your home before judgment liens are filed against you, you can still get much the same protection under a law that automatically provides homeowners an exemption from having their home sold to satisfy debts. This protection isn't quite as broad as homestead protection, but it is very valuable. There are also protections for people living in houseboats, house trailers and mobile homes. All this is discussed in *Homestead Your House* (order information at the back of this book).

---

[8]Usually, a homeowner's equity does not significantly exceed the homestead limits listed, and thus the home is protected from sale. However, if your equity is significantly above such amounts, then a creditor is entitled to force a sale to recover the debt from the difference between the homestead limit and your equity.

E. Refinancing and Second Deeds of Trust

1. Refinancing

Ten years ago, Steven bought a $80,000 home, $20,000 down and a $60,000 "deed of trust" payable over 25 years. He has paid off $30,000 to date. Today he is in debt and needs money. To get it, he can "refinance" his home. He could take a new deed of trust (probably for more than $60,000, as the house will have gone up in value) on his home, use it to pay off what is left on his present mortgage ($30,000) and pocket the difference.

Turning in your equity on your home for cash is sometimes a good idea. But if you intend to do it, consider the following:

a. It will extend the time period in which you have to pay off the deed of trust and make it harder for you to ever own your home "free and clear."

b. If interest rates are high, it will cost you more to pay off your home than if you continued paying at the rate you got at the time you took the original deed of trust.

c. Always go to a bank or credit union first. Be sure to check with the people who have the original deed of trust and find out how much of a pre-payment penalty you incur by paying off the deed of trust ahead of time. Shop around for the best terms.

d. If the equity in your home is climbing above the dollar value of the homestead exemption, you can refinance your home and bring that equity down, so your creditors will not have anything to attach.

2. Second Deeds of Trust

In our above example, Steven could also go to a second mortgage company (they often have the word "plan" as part of their name), borrow $10,000 and pledge his house as security for the loan. This would be a second deed of trust. This type of second deed of trust should not be con-fused with that mentioned in the section on buying the house. When you buy the house, you are normally getting (if you need it) a second deed of trust from the seller at interest rates that are the same or very slightly above the prevailing rate. When you deal with a company specializing in second deeds of trust, you are playing an entirely different game—a game in which you stand a good chance of getting soundly whipped.

People often take second deeds of trust rather than refinance their home. Sometimes they do this in response to a TV ad or some other sales pitch. Usually they are making a bad choice. Whenever possible, you should refinance. It will save you a lot of headaches and possible misery.

Here's how second mortgage companies operate:

Most real estate "loans" which offer second deeds of trust are nothing more than "mortgage brokers" who use the money of wealthy people who want to invest in high interest paying loans. The brokers rarely invest their own money.

The interest rate is extremely high and there are a number of additional charges, like "finder's fees" or commissions, title insurance, credit investigations, and escrow and recording fees. This can total up to a whopping 29 percent of the loan.

On loans for three years or more, many of these companies provide for the final installment payment to be much greater than the preceding installment payments. This final payment is called a "balloon payment." Often people are unable to make this payment and so are forced to refinance and again pay all those costs, commissions, expenses, etc. So, watch out.

These groups advertise that they are not interested in your credit. They will lend you the money no matter how bad your credit. Sounds attractive. But it isn't. Remember, you put up your home as security. And if you miss a payment—zoom—they swoop down and take it from you. They often hope that people will not repay. They can make big profits in foreclosing on your home and milking all the equity you have in it.

Some collection agencies are in cohoots with these "plans." When you owe collection agencies money, they may suggest you take a second mortgage with a "plan" which they name. Watch out. They may have a kickback deal going with the plan. Don't take the "friendly" advice of the collection agency. They are not your friends. Check for the best refinancing or second deed of trust deal on your own.

Checking Out a "Plan": If your bank or credit union will not refinance your home and you need to go to one of these "plans" to get a second mortgage, call the Better Business Bureau. Ask them on which second mortgage "plans" they have received complaints. Don't go to these. Some brokers are more reputable than others. Check around.

F. Making a Complaint

If you have any trouble with people in any way connected to the real estate or real estate financing business, contact the California Department of Real Estate office that covers your area (let the person who has done you dirt know that you are complaining). These offices are located in Sacramento, San Francisco, Fresno, Los Angeles, and San Diego. The addresses and phone numbers are listed in the phone book. It is also wise to send a copy of your complaint letter to your state senator and assemblyperson, as this often causes the Department of Real Estate to take you more seriously. If you are out any considerable sum of money, see a lawyer. California provides a client recovery fund which will reimburse a person for money he has lost as a result of some fraudulent act by a licensed real estate broker. However, you must first get a judgment against the broker and be unable to collect on the judgment. Contact the Department of Real Estate or an attorney for assistance.

CHAPTER 7

Children

"Love and marriage go together like a horse and carriage." So goes the song which seemed to be written indelibly across the psyche of the nation a generation or two ago. Looking back on those years, the only change we might suggest is to add the word "baby" before "carriage." Certainly, marriage and babies seemed to be inseparable as the population of the United States jumped from 122 million in 1930 to over twice that today. More recently, as the world has been getting increasingly overcrowded and opportunities for a sane life have decreased, the rate of population increase has slowed. Still, birth control or not, there are lots more of us every day. Hence, this chapter.

Note: Child custody, visitation and support during and after divorce are discussed in Chapter 8. Marriage contracts involving children are discussed in Chapter 5. Making provisions for your children at your death is discussed in *Planning Your Estate*, by Denis Clifford (Nolo Press).

A. Whose Kid Is That?

Hallelujah, California has gotten rid of the words "legitimate" and "illegitimate" when it comes to describing children.[1] It's about time, too. What nonsense to put people into an "illegitimate" category because their parents didn't get around to finding a justice of the peace before doing what comes naturally.

---

[1]Civil Code Section 7001 now states "the parent and child relationship extends equally to every child and to every parent, regardless of the marital status of the parents."

Even though concepts of "legitimacy" and "illegitimacy" are mostly out the window, it is still important legally to know who a child's natural parents are. In inheritance, child support, custody, adoption and many other areas of the law, the rights and duties of parents are clearly marked out. While it's normally not the most difficult thing in the world to figure out who a child's mother is, identifying fathers can be more difficult. California has adopted the Uniform Parentage Act, which provides rules to establish whether a parent-child relationship exists. (California Civil Code Section 7000 et seq.) These rules are somewhat complicated, but in broad outline provide that a man is *presumed* to be the father of a child if he comes under any one of the following circumstances:

Circumstance 1: If he is married to the mother at the time the child is born, or was married to her within 300 days of the birth of the child. This means that if the man dies, or there is a divorce while the mother is pregnant, he is still presumed to be the father;

Circumstance 2: If he and the mother, before the birth of the child, attempted to get married, in the sense that they got a license, had a ceremony, etc., even though the marriage wasn't valid for some reason, such as one of the parties being still married to someone else (this is the void and voidable marriage situation that we discuss in Chapter 1);

and

The child was born during the attempted marriage or within 300 days after its termination, whether by court order, death or simple separation;

Circumstance 3: After the child's birth he and the natural mother have married (or gone through a ceremony in apparent compliance with law) although the marriage could later be annulled for some reason;

and

a. With his consent, he is named the child's father on the birth certificate, *or*

b. He is obliged to support the child under a written, voluntary promise, or by court order;

Circumstance 4: He receives the child into his home and openly holds out the child as his natural child.[2]

You will note if you reread these rules that we are dealing with presumptions. This normally means in law that a certain fact situation will be presumed to produce a certain legal conclusion unless rebutted by stronger evidence. As we saw in Section A4 just above, if a man takes a child into his home and says that he is the father, even though he was never married to the child's mother, he is legally presumed to be the father. This doesn't mean that he *is* the father—he might still be able to rebut the presumption—that is, prove that even though he received a child into his home and told his friends and family that he was the father, in fact, he was not.

Until relatively recently, in the area of paternity there was one exception to this rule that presumptions can be rebutted. The legislature stated that in one particular fact situation a man

---

[2]We are not concerned in this book with the problems of unmarried couples and the status of their children. See *The Living Together Kit,* Ihara & Warner, Nolo Press, for a full discussion of this area, including a sample paternity agreement for the father to sign to protect himself and the children.

would be legally presumed to be the father even if there was detailed evidence that this wasn't true. Thus Evidence Code Section 621 reads:

Notwithstanding any other provision of law, the issue of a wife cohabiting with her husband who is not impotent or sterile, is conclusively presumed to be a child of the marriage.

The non-rebuttable presumption has produced some bizarre cases, including a number where the racial characteristics of the child were obviously different from those of the mother's husband. Finally, in 1981, the legislature modified this presumption somewhat to say that a husband can raise the question of paternity within two years after the birth of a child, and if all experts concur that on the basis of blood tests he is not the father, the question of paternity will be resolved accordingly.[3] If the issue is not raised within the two-year period, however, the presumption can no longer be rebutted.[4] If the man claiming to be the father attempts to prove it by way of a blood test while the mother is married to someone else, the man claiming to be the father may be out of luck and the mother's husband declared the father.[5]

Legislative hearings are expected to take place before long with an eye to completely restructuring the law in the entire paternity-blood test area so as to more closely fit with current medical and scientific knowledge.

Note on Artificial Insemination: When a married woman has a child by artificial insemination, and was impregnated with semen from someone other than her husband, her husband is nevertheless irrebuttably presumed to be the father and the donor has no rights. The law

---

[3]Recent advances in blood testing make it a great deal easier to prove or disprove paternity than it was even a few years ago. In some situations, tests can indicate that a man is the father with a certainty of over 98 percent.

[4]*Michelle Marie W. v. Ronald W.,* 39 Cal.3d 354 (1985).

[5]Michael H. v. Gerald D., 87 Daily Jour. C.A.R. 2153 (1987) where the lover of the child's mother proved with 98% that he was the father of the child and the court rejected his claim because the mother was married to another man at the time and the court felt the "integrity of the matrimonial family" outweighed any claim to fatherhood by the lover.

"intact" families and does not want the donor to come along and disrupt things, nor wants the husband to fail to support the children.[6]

B. Deciding to Have a Child (or Abortion)

A father recently came to us and asked if he had to support his child in the following circumstances. He and his wife had decided before getting married not to have children. They lived together for two years after marriage, and both agreed that they didn't want children. They then decided to separate and get a divorce. A day or two before they parted, the wife (by her own admission) ceased using her diaphragm without telling her husband, in an attempt to get pregnant. She succeeded, although the fact that she was pregnant wasn't known until six weeks after the separation. *Yes,* the father does have a duty to support.

Courts are not interested in people's private motives, whether they decide to have children by contract, by throwing the I Ching, checking the location of the planets, or just letting it happen. If a child arrives, there is a duty to support. But is this fair to the man in the above situation? Perhaps not, but we aren't writing a book about fairness, only about law the way it is. Do we think that sometime in the future contracts between people to have, or not to have, children will be enforceable? Probably they will be, but it isn't going to happen tomorrow.

What about abortion? That's simple. A woman who is pregnant can get an abortion without the consent of the father whether or not she is married. According to the United States Supreme Court case *Roe v. Wade,* 410 U.S. 133 (1973), an adult woman's decision can be regulated by the state only in the following manner:[7]

1. Prior to the end of the first trimester (3 months) of pregnancy, the state may not interfere with or regulate the physician's decision reached in consultation with his patient, that the pregnancy should be terminated.

2. From the end of the first trimester (3 months) of pregnancy until the fetus becomes viable (is capable of living outside the mother), the state may regulate the abortion procedure only to the extent that such regulation relates to the preservation and protection of the health of the mother.

---

[6]For a very thorough discussion of having children by artificial insemination, see *A Legal Guide for Lesbian and Gay Couples,* Curry and Clifford, Nolo Press. Although that discussion is written for lesbians and gay men desiring children, the information is of a general nature. You are obviously aware of the New Jersey *Baby M* surrogate motherhood case and the various issues that situation raises. If you are considering having a child by surrogate motherhood, you are best to consult an attorney to help you determine the state of the law in California and to draft an agreement. Be aware, however, that the law in this area is minimal, and what little there is is new and mostly untested. Thus, a lawyer may not be able to tell you much more than what you've read in the papers.

[7]In the case of *Belloti v. Baird,* 428 U.S. 132 (1975), the United States Supreme Court struck down a Massachusetts statute which gave parents veto power over a minor's decision to have an abortion. On the other hand, in *H.L.V. Matheson,* 450 U.S. 398 (1981), the Court upheld the constitutionality of a Utah law requiring a doctor to notify parents before performing an abortion on a minor.

3. After the fetus becomes viable, the state may prohibit abortion altogether, except in those cases necessary to preserve the life or health of the mother.

4. The state may make abortions unlawful when performed by persons other than physicians licensed by the state.

The practical aspects of this case for a woman is that if you suspect you are pregnant and want an abortion, you should contact a physician as early as possible for verification, and you should compare prices before you select the physician or clinic that will perform the abortion; the field is competitive[8]. The practical aspect for a man is that there is nothing legally he can do to influence the woman's decision, even if they are married and he desperately wants the child.

What about "Right to Life" groups[9] and their fight to pass a constitutional amendment banning abortion? We are against it. While abortion makes us as queasy as the next person, we believe women must have legal freedom to make the choice. We have seen too many seventeen-year-olds, pregnant and miserable, for whom motherhood would be a disaster, to think otherwise. Passage of a constitutional amendment will simply drive tens of thousands of women out of hospitals and back to the rusty knives of the side alley butchers. Of course, no woman should be coerced through the welfare or prison system, or in any other way, to have an abortion that she doesn't want, but equally, no one should be required to have a child to salve someone else's conscience.

What about the rights of the father? Doesn't it seem somehow unfair to leave all the decision-making to the mother? If she decides to have the child, he has to support it, but if she wants an abortion, he has nothing to say. Although this appears to be unfair, the alternative is unaccept-able. No woman, for emotional, physical, financial, or any reasons should be forced to bear an unwanted child. One legislative change advocated by Berkeley Consumer Group Legal Services director Mary Willis is to require a mother who has the means to do so to support a child born in a situation where both members of the couple agreed not to have children, and the woman then went ahead anyway. As long as the woman has the financial ability to support the child by herself, why should the unwilling father be burdened, Willis argues. Certainly, if the legal responsibilities of parents to care for and support their children are to survive in anything like the form in which we know them, both parents must have some say in deciding when, and when not, to have children.

---

[8]In *Committee To Defend Reproductive Rights v. Myers*, 29 Cal.3d 252 (1981), the California Supreme Court held that the state Medi-Cal program must pay for abortions in the case of women eligible for Medi-Cal benefits. This case was decided under the California Constitution and only applies to California, since the U.S. Supreme Court has ruled that the Federal Constitution does not require the funding of abortions with federal money (*Harris v. McRae*, 448 U.S. 297 (1980).

[9]We put "Right to Life" in quotation marks because we believe it to be a misnomer and a disservice to pro-abortion groups who are very concerned with the life of mothers and the quality of life of their children.

C. The Legal Duty to Support Children

California, as does all states, imposes a civil duty on parents to support their children (Civil Code 206) and also makes non-support a crime (Penal Code 270, 271a). The primary method of enforcing the child support duty is through lawsuits brought by the parent whose child needs support, or by the district attorney on behalf of the welfare department in the event a child is receiving AFDC benefits.

Since failure to support one's children is also a crime, it is also possible for the non-supporting parent to punished by a jail sentence (up to one year) and $1000 fine. In this regard, Penal Code Section 270 reads as follows:

If a parent of a minor child willfully omits, without lawful excuse, to furnish necessary clothing, food, shelter or medical attendance, or other remedial care for his or her child, he or she is guilty of a misdemeanor punishable by a fine not exceeding one thousand dollars ($1,000), or by imprisonment in the county jail not exceeding one year, or by both such fine and imprisonment. If a court of competent jurisdiction has made a final adjudication in either a civil or a criminal action, that a person is the parent of a minor child and the person has notice of such adjudication and he or she then willfully omits, without lawful excuse, to furnish necessary clothing, food, shelter, medical attendance or other remedial care for his or her child, this conduct is punishable by imprisonment in the county jail not exceeding one year or in a state prison not exceeding one year and one day, or by a fine not exceeding one thousand dollars ($1,000), or by both such fine and imprisonment. This statute shall not be construed so as to relieve such parent from the criminal liability defined herein for such ommission merely because the other parent of such child is legally entitled to the custody of such child nor because the other parent of such child or any other person or organization voluntarily or involuntarily furnishes such necessary food, clothing, shelter, or medical attendance or other remedial care for such child or undertakes to do so.... The court, in determining the ability of the parent to support his or her child, shall consider all income, including social insurance benefits and gifts.

The provisions of this section are applicable whether the parents of such child are or were ever married or divorced, and regardless of any decree made in any divorce action relative to alimony or to the support of the child. A child conceived but not yet born is to be deemed an existing person insofar as this section is concerned....

While historically, the duty to support has fallen primarily on the father, since 1971, the law states that both *father* and *mother* have this duty. If either willfully fails to fulfill it, he or she is very likely to be prosecuted by the local district attorney's office under the above Penal Code Section.[10] It makes no difference whether the child's father and mother were ever married as far as the duty to support is concerned; however, if there has been a specific court order under a divorce or paternity proceeding telling one or the other parent to support, this must be followed. Any specific court order takes pre-cedence over the general legal duty that both parents have.

In addition, Penal Code Section 270.5 makes it a misdemeanor for a parent to refuse, without legal excuse, to accept their child into their home, or to provide alternative shelter for the child, when required to do so by a child protective agency. Thus, it is illegal to abandon or desert your child when ordered not to by a governmental agency.

Example: Walter and Wanda marry. They have two children. They split up and live separately for a year, sharing custody of the children. In this situation, both have a legal duty to support. Eventually there is a divorce action and the judge orders joint custody, with the details of who is to have actual physical custody of the children at any time to be worked out by Wanda and Walter. Because Wanda makes three times as much money as a pilot as Walter does as a flight attendant, she agrees and is ordered by a judge to support the children during the months that she has custody and to pay Walter $100 per month per child for the months that he takes care of the children. This order now takes precedence over the general duty to support and should be followed unless circumstances change, in which case the judge would be likely to make a different order if so requested.

Parents who have no income or savings (i.e., are disabled, can't find work, etc.) are not guilty of a crime for failing to support. This is because the law says that it is only a crime to "willfully" fail to support your child. The law does not punish those who can't support for some reason beyond their control. However, a court, in determining the ability of parents to support, will consider *all* of their income, including social security, unemployment, pensions, welfare, gifts, etc., in deciding whether there is enough money to take care of the kids.[11]

Example: Suppose Richard is the sole support of his wife and children. After their separation he quits his job as a cop and goes back to school to be a social worker. Suddenly there is no money for support and his wife and children must apply for welfare. Could Richard be prosecuted under the non-support section? Yes, and he well might be. A judge might be sympathetic to his desire to change careers, but would still want to know why he wasn't supporting. The judge would surely inquire as to why Richard didn't borrow money or go to school part-time while continuing to work. It is likely that the judge would approve a reduction in support, but unlikely that he (she) would waive it altogether.

---

[10]This chapter is not primarily written to cover the problems of non-supporting fathers. That information is provided in Chapter 17 of *Billpayers' Rights*, Warner and Elias, Nolo Press.

[11]Further, a non-supporting parent may be ordered at the request of the custodial parent to submit to a vocational examination for the purpose of determining his or her ability to work.

Warning: The county jails are populated by many fathers (and a few mothers) who have failed to support their families. Also, under recent law, parents who fail to support for two or more months are subject to having their paychecks intercepted directly from their employer.

D. Duty of Care—Neglected & Delinquent Children

Supporting a child isn't enough. California also requires that parents take proper care of their children. Child abuse and child neglect are crimes. Practically speaking, civil authorities (county, state, city) give broad latitude to parents to raise their children as they see fit and won't interfere with the parent-child relationship unless they receive a complaint from a reputable source that the relationship is being abused (i.e., a teacher notices that a child is always hungry or has been beaten). Of course, some children are brought to the attention of the authorities in a more direct way, such as when a cop catches your daughter tossing a brick through the bicycle shop window. Even where parental abuse occurs, however, it is not normal that the parent is prosecuted under available criminal statutes unless the abuse is malicious or has resulted in real physical harm or death. Most commonly, the authorities are more concerned with the welfare of the child than with the punishment of a confused parent who probably needs help as much as the child. When abuse is suspected, a petition is filed in juvenile court to authorize supervision of the home by the Welfare Department or to remove the child from the parents' home and to place him or her in better environment.[12]

If you, or your child, is charged with violating any sections of the Penal or Welfare and Institutions Code, we strongly suggest that you see someone with experience with this type problem. This is normally an attorney. Let us repeat that even though most matters involving children are considered in the relatively less formal Juvenile Court, competent advice is essential

---

[12]Section 202 of Welfare and Institutions Code states that when a child is removed from his or her home, the state owes a duty to give the child a home as good as that which should be provided by the natural parents. Sad to say, standards of care in some foster homes, children's shelters and children's prisons in California are miserable. We have seen many situations where a child is taken out of an admittedly bad home and then placed in a worse one.

(see Chapter 12). If you have no money, you have the right to assistance by the Public Defender or Legal Aid Society. Ask for this help at the Juvenile Court and refuse to proceed without it.

In some situations parent and child won't be viewed as having the same interest in the proceeding and should have separate attorneys. This could occur for a number of reasons, including the simple fact that parent and child aren't communicating well with one another. Where the facts alleged in the Social Services or Probation Department's petition would form the basis for a criminal prosecution against the parent (i.e., child beating), the County Counsel's office automatically represents the child.[13]

Important: We should also mention that the Juvenile Court has the authority to exercise informal probation in cases where it seems that a child is headed for trouble. This will only be done with the full cooperation of the parent and child. The probation officer will attempt to help the parent and the child relate to their problems in a positive way, perhaps by getting them involved in community programs. The time to take advantage of this program, which bypasses all the court hearings, lawyers, formal reports, etc., is before, not after, real trouble develops and a formal petition is filed.

We don't have the space here to repeat all the statutes and court rules relating to juveniles. They are available to you at all county law libraries (these are open to the public) and at most main public libraries. Look in the West or Deerings Annotated Welfare and Institutions Code under Sections 300 and following for neglected children and under Sections 600 and following for out-of-control and delinquent children. Also, Rules of Court Sections 1300 and following govern certain Juvenile Court procedures in more detail than is found in the Code. The librarian will be pleased to help you locate these materials and you may even wish to consult *Legal Research: How To Find and Understand the Law*, Elias, Nolo Press, to help you find your way around the law library and decipher what you read.

E. Adoptions of Children

This is a court procedure whereby an adult or adults assume(s) a parent-child relationship with the natural child of another.[14] The adopting parent(s) assume(s) full legal responsibility for the child, including the legal duty to support. The natural parent(s), assuming that they are alive, are legally eliminated from any relationship with the child.[15] When married people are involved, both husband and wife must consent to the adoption; one can't do it without the other.[16]

---

[13]Depending on county organization, juvenile matters fall under the jurisdiction of either the Social Services (Welfare) or Probation Department.

[14]Adoption of one adult by another is also possible, but is not discussed here.

[15]This means that an adopted child inherits under the intestate succession law from his or her adoptive parents and their family just as if he or she was a natural child, but does not stand to get anything should his or her natural parents die without a will.

[16]Single parent adoptions are legally possible but not common. Adoptions by gay couples are extremely rare, although we are aware of two such adoptions.

Adoption is a heavy step to take. It legally binds you to another being to an even greater degree than does marriage. Unless you are absolutely sure that you want to raise and support the child or children in question, it is better to put off adoption. You can divorce a spouse, but it's not possible to divorce a kid. Adoption can be very beneficial for a child in that it sets up the legal basis for a stable parent-child relationship. However, for many people who are taking care of someone else's child and simply want some legal recognition of their status, guardianship makes more sense than adoption. Guardianship is reasonably easy to terminate and doesn't carry with it the heavy requirement to support (see Section F below).

People often ask questions such as the following:

"I will be 45 years old next month; am I too old to adopt?"

"I have a juvenile arrest; does this mean I can't adopt?"

"My wife is deaf; will they hold that against us?"

"Ten years ago I placed my own child up for adoption; does this disqualify me from adopting?"

The answer to all these questions is a qualified "No." We say qualified because this sort of information and lots more about you will be considered in an effort to decide whether or not it is in the best interests of the particular child that you want to adopt to let you do it. No one fact will either qualify you or disqualify you. But read on.

Adoptions of children fall into four broad categories. They are somewhat different and we will review each briefly. If you wish more legal information on adoption procedure, go to your county law library and see *Cal. Practice Volume 11*.

1. Stepparent Adoptions

This is the most common form of adoption. It is covered in detail in *How To Adopt Your Stepchild,* Zagone, Nolo Press, a book which includes all forms and instructions necessary to do it yourself. Stepparent adoption occurs when the parent with custody of a child (children) marries a new spouse and that person wants to adopt the child (children). Without an adoption, the new spouse, who we will call the stepparent, has no legal responsibility for the child, even though he or she may lovingly and competently perform all the parental duties that a natural parent would normally perform.

If the stepparent wishes to adopt, and both the parent with custody and the child (if he or she is old enough to have an opinion) agree, the next thing to do is to inquire as to the feelings of the non-custodial parent. This is often, but not always, the father. In some situations, where the children's mother was never married to the father, there may be a question as to whether the children have a male parent recognized as such by the law. If there is no such parent, or that parent is deceased, no consent is necessary to the adoption.[17] We discuss whether a man is legally viewed as a father in Part A of this chapter.

---

[17]Where a parent is deceased, a child may be adopted and still keep any social security benefits stemming from the account of the deceased parent. A California case—*Adoption of Rebecca B* . (68 Cal.App.3d 193 (1977)—states that even where a natural parent has not married the mother, or done anything to take care of the child, he must be notified of the adoption.

Assuming, however, that a legally recognized non-custodial parent of a child exists, one of two things must happen before an adoption can take place:

a. The non-custodial parent must consent to the adoption and be willing to sign a consent form in the presence of a county clerk or a probation worker if in California, or a notary, if outside California.

or

b. The non-custodial parent must have abandoned the child. This means that the non-custodial parent has willfully failed to communicate with the child *and* has failed to pay for the care, support and education of the child or children in question, when able to do so, for a period of one year or more.[18]

When an adoption petition is filed with the county clerk in a stepparent adoption case, it will be referred to the County Social Services or Juvenile Probation Department for review prior to being considered by a judge.[19] The county agency will make a full report and recommendation to the court. Before doing this, a county employee may talk with all the people concerned, including the child or children if they are old enough. Normally the Probation or Social Services Department will start with a bias in favor of the adoption—they like to see kids have a secure home. You need not worry that they will be hostile. Even so, social work sometimes tends to attract people who are a bit nosy (they would argue that that's what we pay them for) and like to pry into people's lives more than often seems reasonable. This can be frustrating at times, but you will just have to put up with it, as a judge is not likely to approve an adoption if the county submits a negative report. However, the county need not visit your home as part of its reporting process, and probably won't, unless someone requests the court to order it.

Important: Every family has some problem or problems. None of us is perfect, even though we often waste a lot of energy trying to convince our neighbors that we are. If you have some incident in your life that you think may weigh against you in an adoption, such as a bad conduct discharge from the military, a past drinking or credit problem, etc., it is usually best to be frank with the deputy. He or she will probably learn of your skeletons anyway and we have found that old bones don't rattle as much if you bring them out of the closet yourself. After all, in a stepparent adoption, you are already living with the child and probably exercising parental authority, so the department has little motive to be hostile to your petition.

Assuming that the probation department report is favorable to the adoption, the next step is to go to court and have the judge grant his (her) approval. This is pretty much a formality, with handshakes all around, and the adoptive parents assuring the judge that they will assume full legal responsibility for the child as well as providing the love and care so necessary to all growing things. If the child is over twelve years old, he or she must also consent to the adoption.

---

[18]It is possible to establish abandonment if either lack of communication or lack of care is established. However, this involves a different adoption procedure. This is a tricky area of law which is well-covered in *How To Adopt Your Stepchild*, by Frank Zagone (see back of this book for order information).

[19]It is unwise to file for a stepparent adoption immediately after marriage. The county will want to be sure the new marriage looks solid, and in most cases won't approve stepparent adoptions until the new spouses have been married at least a year.

As part of an adoption proceeding, the child may be given a new name (often the last name of the adopting father). This is not a requirement, however, and the child may wish to keep his or her name. Also, upon submission to the state of the Certificate of Adoption signed by the judge, the state will issue a new birth certificate, with the new name if desired. When a child was born outside of California, it is normally possible to get the other state to issue a new birth certificate. When the child was born outside the United States, however, it is usually impossible.

2. Agency Adoptions

This sort of adoption occurs when a licensed adoption agency places a child in the home of an adopting parent or parents. The agency gets a full relinquishment of the rights of the natural parents before putting the child up for adoption so there are normally no worries about a natural parent later surfacing to try and claim "his or her child."

With agency adoptions, the parents must be at least ten years older than the child to be adopted. The law contains no upper age limits or rules concerning physical or mental disabilities for the prospective parents, but adoption agencies will have their own policies in these areas. Indeed, as birth control and changing societal attitudes toward such concepts as "legitimacy" have reduced the pool of children available for adoption, agencies have become very selective in choosing adoptive parents.

As in stepparent adoptions, a petition must be filed in Superior Court and the adoption must be approved by a judge. If the child is over twelve years of age, his or her consent is necessary. In non-stepparent adoptions, the State of California Department of Social Welfare makes the same type of family background investigations as is undertaken by the County Probation Department in stepparent adoptions. The standards applied in agency adoptions are stricter, however. This is because, unlike the stepparent situation where the new parent is already living in the home and will probably continue to do so with or without the adoption, in the agency situation a child who would otherwise have no relationship with the particular adults is being entrusted to their care.

Most reputable adoption agencies charge high fees ($1,000 or more). Part of this money goes to pay for the careful investigation that is carried out to determine whether the prospective parents are suitable to adopt. Adoption agencies prefer that the adopting parents retain their own lawyer to present the necessary paperwork to the judge. This is silly as the adoption agency does 90 percent of this work and it would not be difficult for the new parents to carry the papers down to the courthouse themselves, saving the $300 or more in attorney fees in the process. If you are in this situation, you might discuss this possibility with the agency.

3. County Adoptions

This is a procedure where children who are in the care of the county are placed for adoption. In some cases the natural parents consent to the adoption, while in others a judge finds that the parents' continued inability to provide a home for the child constitutes an abandonment. Contact the County Social Services Department where you live for more information. Adoptive parents are selected and checked in much the same way as is done with agency adoptions, but the county does its own investigation.

As a result of recent law changes, it is possible to adopt children who have been placed in foster homes by county Juvenile Court authorities (see above). This can only be done after the court makes a finding that the child has been abandoned by his or her natural parents (Civil Code 232). A finding of abandonment is easier to make if a child is in county custody than in the more normal stepparent adoption situation discussed above.[20] All the grounds for finding that a child is free from parental custody and control are listed in Section 232 of the Civil Code, but can be summed up by saying that if the natural parents are unable to take care of their child and don't appear to be able to take care of the child in the future, the child can be freed for adoption.

Therefore, it is now theoretically possible for potential adoptive parents to get on a county list and to adopt children in foster home placement. We say "theoretically possible" because a know-ledgeable professional in the area tells us that there is little chance of adopting a child simply by getting on a county list. This is because judges are often reluctant to find that a child has been abandoned, and because foster parents themselves often want to adopt children freed for adoption. In fact, the law now specifically provides that, in most situations, foster parents are to be given preference over other applicants when it comes to the adoption of their foster children.

There are definite advantages to becoming a foster parent in the hopes that adoption will follow should the child's natural parents not be able to get their act together. The county will often give the new parents financial aid (if they need it) for several years after the adoption. There are no legal costs in this type of adoption, and there is not likely to be much problem with the county Parental Fitness investigation, as the parents have already been approved as foster parents.

There are also disadvantages to travelling this particular road to adoption. Foster children are generally older and therefore have a greater potential for being disturbed as a result of earlier unstable or abusive experiences. Then, too, in many situations the natural parents do rehabilitate themselves sufficiently to regain custody of their children. This can be a devastating blow for the foster parents who have formed deep attachments to the foster child in the anticipation of adoption. Nevertheless, for many this may be the best, and perhaps only, hope of adopting a child.[21]

Note: When the right of a natural parent to the custody and control of a child is terminated by court action, visitation rights may also be terminated in the process, through not necessarily.

---

[20]In the case of *In the Matter of Rose G.*, 57 Cal.App.3d 406 (1976), the court held that where the natural parents had grossly neglected their child and she had been placed in a foster home, six months' failure to visit or contact the child was enough to constitute an abandonment as called for in Civil Code Section 232.

[21]In *Katzoff v. Superior Court*, 54 Cal.App.3d 1079 (1976), foster parents were given the right to appear in court to contest a Social Services Department decision to remove a child from their home.

Note: When the right of a natural parent to the custody and control of a child is terminated by court action, visitation rights may also be terminated in the process, through not necessarily.

4. Independent Adoptions

It is possible in California to adopt a child without going through an adoption agency, and where neither adoptive parent has a relationship with the child. These are sometimes called "private" or "independent" adoptions. When you read about "baby for sale" scandals, this is the type of adoption involved. Although most private adoptions are carried out honestly and fairly, abuses do crop up now and then. Things have been better in recent years as the state has regulated this area a lot more closely.

When a child is located for private adoption, it is essential that you be sure that its mother and father will sign a consent to adoption form. If there is a doubt as to the father, relinquishments should be obtained from anyone who possibly could be the father. Of course, if no one has the foggiest idea who the father is or might be, it is not necessary to get his signature (see Section A of this chapter). Even if a parent will not consent to an adoption, the adoption may still be possible. This is the case if that parent has "abandoned" the child. See California Civil Code Section 232.[22]

"Independent" adoptions also require the filing of a petition with the Superior Court. In this sort of adoption, as with the stepparent adoption, you will probably need an attorney to help, as there is no agency to prepare the paperwork.[23] An attorney with experience in the area may also be helpful in dealing with the State Department of Social Welfare investigator. In this sort of adoption, you can expect a much stricter investigation than in the others. After all, the child is not already in your home, as in the stepparent situation, and there is no reputable agency in the picture as in an agency adoption.

Again, you must be ten years older than the child, but there are no other rules as to mental or physical capability. As with the other types of adoption, you will be asked by the state investigator for your marriage certificate, your final decree of divorce (if there were previous marriages), a certified copy of the adoptive child's birth certificate, the marriage and divorce records of the child's natural parents and whatever else the investigator thinks is relevant.[24]

It is very important that the state investigator recommend that the adoption take place. The discussion about getting this approval in the stepparent adoption section above is also relevant here. Once the state approves the adoption and the court grants it, the child is yours. There is no danger that the case will be re-opened years later or otherwise tampered with, absent a showing of a serious inadequacy in the proceedings, such as forging the consent form of one of the natural parents or failure to notify the father, etc. Once the adoption is approved, the child will be given your last name if you desire and you can have the birth certificate reissued (see Chapter 3).

---

[22]Again, for more information on the legalities of adoption, go to your nearest law library and see *Cal. Practice Volume 11*.

[23]People interested in doing their own paperwork should go to the law library and see *Cal. Forms*.

[24]As we state earlier, you don't need to be married to adopt. It's just easier if you are.

F. Guardianships

1. Temporary Custody of Children

For lots of reasons, minors may live temporarily or permanently with people other than their natural parents. While it may be somewhat unusual for most people other than grandparents or stepparents to take care of someone else's children for a long period of time, you may well find yourself taking in a friend's children during an illness or while they are on vacation. For short periods of time (a few weeks or months), there is no real reason to take any elaborate legal steps, especially if the child's natural parents are reasonably available in case of emergency. However, in case of illness or accident, it would be wise to have something in writing giving you authority to make decisions on behalf of the minor.[25] The following document, which you can draw up yourself, could prove very helpful.

Note to Stepparents: Stepparents who have played the role of a natural parent for years may suddenly find themselves with no authority to seek medical care or enroll their stepchild in school if an inquiry is made as to their legal relationship to the child. If you are a stepparent, it is extremely important that you possess an authorization from your spouse like the one suggested below.

---

[25]Where medical problems arise and there is no authorization signed, get the child to the doctor or hospital as soon as possible. In the meantime, call the police. They will locate (usually by phone) the juvenile judge or referee and get authorization for the medical care by court order. This is usually done in minutes if it is an emergency, with the paperwork being prepared later.

Authorization to Consent to Medical, Surgical, or Dental Examination or Treatment of Minor

I,_____, being the parent, Guardian, or other person entitled to legal custody of _____(name)_____ , _____(birthdate)_____ , a minor child, do hereby authorize _____, into whose care the minor has been entrusted, to consent to any X-ray, examination, anesthetic, medical or surgical diagnosis or treatment and hospital care to be rendered to said minor child under the general or special supervision and upon the advice of a physician and surgeon licensed under the provision of the Medicine Practice Act, or to consent to an X-ray, examination, anesthetic, dental or surgical diagnosis or treatment and hospital care to be rendered to said minor by a dentist licensed under the provisions of the Dental Practice Act.

This authorization is good from _____, 19 _ to _____ 19 _ .

_____
(Parent or Guardian/Date)

_____
(Witness/Date)

(Notarization is not necessary)

2. Long Term Custody of Children

Should you find yourself taking care of children other than your own for an extended period of time, or on a semi-permanent basis, you may want to petition the Superior Court in the county in which you live to make you the legal guardian of the children. Sooner or later, schools, hospitals, banks (if property is involved) and other institutions are all going to ask that you show them some legal authority to make decisions on behalf of children who aren't yours. Obtaining a legal guardianship is a way to handle this problem without going through the much more complicated adoption procedure and without assuming a legal duty to support the children. Under a guardianship, the natural parents still have the duty to provide support for their children, or if they are unable to support, help from Social Security or welfare will be available, depending on the circumstances.

There are no special qualifications to be the guardian of a minor. Normally, the custodians of a child (friends or relatives) simply decide that for practical reasons they need some formal legal authority to make necessary decisions. They file a petition with the Superior Court in the county where they live (assuming that the child is living with them), requesting that a judge appoint them as guardians. The judge will look into the facts of the situation, inquire as to reasons that the natural parents are not taking care of the child, and then, if he (she) approves, will make a legal finding that it is "necessary and convenient" to appoint the petitioners as guardians. If the parents have themselves recommended someone to serve as guardian, either by will or other document, the judge will normally be reluctant to appoint anyone else unless he finds that the people designated by the parents are not qualified to be guardians, or are unwilling to serve.

Filing a petition for a guardianship of a minor is not difficult. You will find a sample petition and instructions in Volume 12 of *Cal. Practice,* which is available at your county law library. The actual forms may be obtained from the Superior Court clerk in your county. As part of the petition, you must list all living relatives of the children in question who live in California. You must also list the location of the parents, wherever they live, unless their address is unknown.[26] In addition, you must officially notify both the parents and the close relatives of the proceeding (see *Cal. Practice Volume 12*).

It is particularly necessary to have a guardianship when the child (or children) you are taking care of has (have) money or valuable property, whether it comes from an inheritance, auto accident judgment, insurance policy or any other source. Banks, insurance companies and the other folks who handle money will demand to see proof of a guardianship before they allow non-parents to handle a minor's money. Where money is involved, a guardian will be required to post a bond. This means that the guardian pays an insurance company to insure against his or her running off with or otherwise misusing the minor's money. The guardian can reimburse himself for the costs of the bond from the minor's property, just as he can reimburse himself for any other reasonable costs resulting from the minor's care, whether they be for room and board, medical bills or whatever. The guardian must keep accurate records and must present these to the court for review at regular intervals.

---

[26]Often guardians get themselves appointed during a time when parents aren't able to take care of their child. Problems can develop later, however, as once the guardianship is set up, the guardian, not the parent, is legally top dog. The parent has the duty to support and the right to visit, but otherwise the guardian is in charge. Also, it may be difficult or impossible for a parent to get the court to end a guardianship and return the child to his/her custody. Parents should think carefully before consenting to a guardianship.

G. Financial Responsibility of Parents for the Acts of Their Children or ('He Broke the Window, Why Should I Have to Pay for It')

Normally, parents are not financially liable for the acts of their children which cause loss to another. This means that if your child is negligent (i.e., trips over his shoelaces and falls on your neighbor's pet begonia plant), you are not legally required to get a new plant or pay for the hospital bills for the old one, even though it might be polite to do so. But did you notice that we say "normally, not "always"? This is because there is a major exception to the general rule. The exception covers acts of "willful misconduct" by the minor. Where willful misconduct is involved, (your child rips up the begonia for the fun of it), the parent(s) or guardian having custody and control of the minor is liable for damages up to $10,000 for each act (see Civil Code 1714.1). If both parents have custody and control, they are *each* liable for the payment of the $10,000 to the damaged party. This means that, if one custodial parent has money (say from an inheritance) and the other doesn't, the damaged party can collect the whole $10,000 from the solvent parent. In theory, the broke party would owe $5,000 to the one that had to pay.[27]

But what is a "willful act" as opposed to a "negligent" one? The law is pretty vague about this, except where a child defaces property with paint or a similar substance. This is usually considered to be "willful misconduct." In other situations, "willful misconduct," or the lack thereof, is pretty much a case by case question. Most accidental or clumsy acts by children won't constitute "willful misconduct," but if the act is semi-delinquent, and especially if the parents knew about the behavior and didn't stop it, liability is likely to be found.[28]

Important: There is one very major exception to these rules. It has to do with guns. Any injury done by a child less than eighteen years with a gun that a parent let the child have, *or left where he could get it,* can cost the parent up to $30,000 for the death or injury of one person or his property, or $60,000 for the deaths of or injuries to more than one person. So, if your guns aren't already secure, let us give you some friendly advice: Get a lock.

Finally, under Education Code 48904, parents are liable (up to $7,500) for the willful misconduct of their children that results in:

• Injury to school employees or other pupils;

• Damage to school property; or

• Damage to personal property belonging to school employees.

In addition, a parent (except those whose children are covered by A.F.D.C.) shall be liable for the reasonable costs of support of a minor if the minor is in the custody of the juvenile court. This is established as being $15 per day.

---

[27]In the case of injury to a person, damages shall be further limited to the medical, dental and hospital expenses incurred by that person. If a parent shares legal custody of a child but not physical custody, and is not exercising actual control over the child when the willful act occurs, that parent cannot be held liable. Robertson v. Wentz, 189 Cal.App.3d 1281 (1986).

H. Emancipation of Children

California has recently adopted an Emancipation of Minors Act (Civil Code Sections 60-70). Under the law, minors under the age of 18 are emancipated if:

• they enter into a valid marriage (see Chapter 1) whether or not the marriage is terminated by a dissolution;

• if they are on active duty with the U.S. military;

• if a court has granted them a declaration of emancipation.

To file an emancipation petition, a minor must be at least 14 years of age, manage his or her own financial affairs, live apart from his or her parent or guardian with that person's "consent or acquiescence," and have the permission of a judge, who after a hearing issues a declaration of emancipation. The declaration can then be filed with the Department of Motor Vehicles, which will issue the minor an indentification card indicating that he or she is emancipated. Once a minor is emancipated, he or she has most of the same rights as an adult, including the right to enter into a binding contract, sue and be sued, work, live separately from his or her parents, etc.

In addition to emancipation under these statutory provisions, a minor may also be emancipated by the fact that he or she is self-supporting and living independently from his or her parents. For details, see Civil Code Section 63.

CHAPTER 8

Children of Former Marriages

A. A Spoonful of Advice

"I don't want Johnny and Sally visiting their father. He smokes marijuana and sets them a terrible example."

"He didn't support the kids, so he can't see them."

"He better get the hell out of here, or I'll call the police."

"All I ask him to do is to visit the kids a couple of times a month. They just don't understand why their father doesn't seem to love them anymore."

"I don't care if she is their mother, she stays out in bars all the time and sleeps with everybody. My kids are not going over there."

"It's those women's groups. They're all lesbians. They're not going to castrate my boy."

"I don't mind the kids visiting their mother, but I won't have them around that creep she lives with."

So it goes, on and on, as people who once loved one another battle over their children. Of course, it doesn't happen every time people separate, but it happens much too often. Every lawyer, psychiatrist, marriage counselor, etc., can tell you dozens of stories like the above. Few other areas of life seem as provocative of paranoia and bitterness. For this reason, and because the legal problems of married people who have children from previous relationships are quite different from those faced by married people generally, we include this separate chapter.

Let's start with an accent on the positive. Fortunately, more and more people are finding ways to handle the problems of raising children after separation in a sane way. What seems to be required is a strong focus on the following facts.

Children need desperately to maintain a friendly, relaxed, loving relationship with both parents. This is true even if you are convinced that your former mate is an idiot.

It is up to you, no matter how hard it is, to help your child maintain a positive relationship with the other parent. This normally means giving your former mate every benefit of the doubt and going a little more than half way when disputes arise. (You're right; it ain't always easy.)

Example: Your former husband fails for two consecutive months to pay you child support even though the court has ordered him to do so. You are justifiably furious. What do you do?

Whether the failure to support is for a good reason, or bad, whether you can work it out in a friendly way or have to go to court (see below), don't cut off his right to see and visit the children, even though you're mad, hurt and desperate for the money. Why? Well, because your action hurts the children more, not less. Also, on a practical level, you are offering your former husband an emotional justification for continuing to fail to support, even though legally he is required to support the children regardless of your behavior.[1] We have noticed in case after case that when children are encouraged to maintain a close relationship with the absent parent, everything, including the arrival of those child support checks, goes more smoothly.

B. Custody of Children

4600—California Civil Code

(a) The Legislature finds and declares that it is the public policy of this state to assure minor children of frequent and continuing contact with both parents after the parents have

---

[1]Civil Code Section 4382: "The existence or enforcement of a duty of support owed by a non-custodial parent for the support of a minor child shall not be affected by a failure or refusal by the custodial parent to implement any rights as to custody or visitation granted by a court to the non-custodial parent."

separated or dissolved their marriage, and to encourage parents to share the rights and responsibilities of child-rearing in order to effect this policy.

In any proceeding where there is at issue the custody of a minor child, the court may, during the pendency of the proceeding or at any time thereafter, make such order for the custody of the child during minority as may seem necessary or proper. If a child is of sufficient age and capacity to reason so as to form an intelligent preference as to custody, the court shall consider and give due weight to the wishes of the child in making an award of custody or modification thereof. In determining the person to whom custody should be awarded under paragraph (2) or (3) of subdivision (b), the court shall consider and give due weight to the nomination of a guardian of the person of the child by a parent under Article 1 (commencing with Section 1500) of Chapter 1 of Part 2 of Division 4 of the Probate Code.

(b) Custody should be awarded in the following order of preference according to the best interests of the child pursuant to Section 4608.[2]

(1) To both parents jointly pursuant to Section 4600.5 or to either parent. In making an order for custody to either parent, the court shall consider, among other factors, which parent is more likely to allow the child or children frequent and continuing contact with the non-custodial parent, and shall not prefer a parent as custodian because of that parent's sex. The court, in its discretion, may require the parents to submit to the court a plan for the implementation of the custody order. When determining child custody in a dissolution action, the court must now take into account whether a parent has a history of abuse against children (i.e., severe physical harm, sexual abuse, etc.). Before considering this question in a given case, the court may require substantial evidence of such history, such as written reports by law enforcement and child protective agencies.

(2) If to neither parent, to the person or persons in whose home the child has been living in a wholesome and stable environment.

(3) To an other person or persons deemed by the court to be suitable and able to provide adequate and proper care and guidance for the child.

(c) Before the court makes any order awarding custody to a person or persons other than a parent, without the consent of the parents, it shall make a finding that an award of custody to a parent would be detrimental to the child and the award to a nonparent is required to serve the best interests of the child. Allegations that parental custody would be detrimental to the child, other than a statement of that ultimate fact, shall not appear in the pleadings. The court may, in its discretion, exclude the public from the hearing on this issue.

Note: Race (either that of a parent or a parent's new spouse) may never be taken into account when determining child custody. Furthermore, a court may not make a custody award on the ground that one parent is economically better able to care for the child than is the other parent.[3]

---

[2]The parents' decision is normally rubber-stamped as part of a divorce or other custody proceeding. Of course, the judge actually makes the order, but when the parents agree, the judge will almost always follow their wishes unless he thinks that the best interests of the child(ren) will be damaged. Unmarried couples with children usually just make their own arrangements. The courts aren't involved unless there is a dispute. See Ihara & Warner, *The Living Together Kit.*

[3]*Burchard v. Garay,* 42 Cal.3d 531 (1986).

Custody is usually decided on the basis of what the parents perceive to be in the best interests of themselves and the child(ren). Recently, more and more parents have been voluntarily choosing joint custody. Indeed, for many families, this is the most sensible alternative, putting the parents on an equal footing and requiring that they deal with each other as sensible adults. In the past, many judges have felt that "joint custody" was not a good idea because it was "inherently unstable." They preferred to grant physical custody to one parent and liberal visitation rights to the other. In part, this was because the old law did not mention "joint custody."

Under the present joint custody law (see above), parents are encouraged to share the rights and responsibilities of child-rearing. This is joint legal custody. To further this end, the law specifically states that preference should be given to both parents jointly. In addition, the law establishes a presumption that joint custody is in the best interest of the child if the parents agree.[4] In fact, when joint custody is granted or denied by the court and either parent requests the reasons for the decision, the judge must state them in the opinion.[5]

Moreover, the new law also provides that if the court decides to award separate custody it should consider which parent is more likely to allow the child frequent and continuing contact with the non-custodial parent. The sex of the parent can no longer be taken as a factor in this determination.

A joint custody award should provide that physical custody be shared in such a way that the child will be sure to have frequent and continuing contact with both parents. This does not necessarily mean that physical custody must be divided equally. Sometimes, in fact, the court will award joint *legal* custody without awarding joint *physical* custody because it may make excellent sense for one parent to provide most of the care and the other most of the money. (Joint physical custody means that each parent will have significant periods of physical custody so that the child has frequent and continuing contact with both parents.)

The court may require a concrete plan from the parents that details how they intend to implement joint custody. In any case, we recommend that whatever agreement is reached be reduced to writing. This need not be a hostile act—a writing is always helpful to refresh the memory should human nature prove true to form and different people remember agreements differently. In addition, should a later dispute arise, a court cannot and will not enforce an oral agreement. This agreement need not be presented to the court unless requested and may be changed from time to time as family needs change. Following are some sample agreements.

Note: Joint Custody Does Not Mean Equal Support: Child custody and support, although obviously related, are different legal obligations. It is perfectly possible (and common) to have a joint custody award with one parent responsible to pay more support than the other. Remember, child support is based on the needs of the child and the ability to pay of the parents, not the physical location of the child.

---

[4]The awarding of joint legal custody over one parent's objection has in fact been approved in one case. *In re Marriage of Wood*, 141 Cal.App.3d 672 (1983).

[5]Civil Code Section 4600.5. The court must also define those situations that require the joint consent of the parents and what the consequences are for failing to obtain it. It must also define each parent's right to the physical control of the child specifically enough to allow the parent deprived of control to implement child snatching or kidnapping laws.

First Sample Joint Custody Agreement

Rebecca Conlon and Lazarus Sandling, having decided to get a divorce, make the following agreement for the purpose of raising their child, Clementine, in a spirit of compromise and cooperation. Both Rebecca and Lazarus agree that they will be guided by the best interests of Clementine and that:

1. Custody of Clementine shall be joint. This means that all major decisions regarding Clementine's physical location, visitation by the non-custodial parent, and any other major decisions, such a those relating to Clementine's health, education, etc., shall be made jointly. For the first year after this agreement is signed, Lazarus shall take care of Clementine during the day on all working days and Rebecca shall take care of Clementine nights and weekends.[6]

2. Support for Clementine shall be provided as specified in the Child Support Stipulation form to be filed with this agreement.

3. If in the future either Lazarus' or Rebecca's income increases to an amount that is more than 30 percent over what is earned by the other, the person with the higher income shall be expected to bear a larger share of the child support, with the exact amount to be worked out at that time, based on the income of both parents and Clementine's needs.

4. Lazarus and Rebecca will make an effort to remain in the area of San Jose, CA., where they presently live, at least until Clementine is in junior high school.

5. Should Lazarus and Rebecca have trouble agreeing to visitation, custody, support or any other problem concerning Clementine, they will jointly agree on a program of counseling to attempt to resolve or compromise their differences. Clementine shall be involved in this process to the maximum amount consistent with her age at the time.

Date: _____   Rebecca Conlon _____

Date: _____   Lazarus Sandling _____

---

[6]The judge will not do this for you, but will normally simply order "that the care, custody and control of the minor child(ren) of the parties, (name) , born_____, 19____, be awarded to petitioner and respondent jointly."

Second Joint Custody Agreement

Sam Matlock and Chris Woodling make this agreement because they are in the process of getting a divorce, but wish to provide for the upbringing and support of their children, Natasha and Jason, in the most responsible and cooperative manner possible. Sam and Chris agree as follows:

1. That until Jason and Natasha are both in school (approximately 3 years) Chris shall have primary responsibility for childcare during the week. Sam shall pay child support of $200 per month per child, as specified in the Child Support Stipulation Form to be filed with this agreement.

2. That Jason and Natasha shall spend most weekends and at least one month during the summer with Sam and that Sam shall be available for babysitting at least two weekday nights;

3. That all major decisions regarding physical location, support, visitation, education, etc., affecting Jason and Natasha shall be made jointly by Sam and Chris, and that Natasha and Jason shall be involved in the decision-making to an extent consistent with their ages at the time;

4. That when both Natasha and Jason are in school, Chris plans to return to her career as a fashion designer at least part-time and that Sam intends to return to school to finish his Ph.D. It is contemplated that during this period of time Chris will earn enough to support the children and Sam will take on a larger share of the childcare duties;

5. Both Sam and Chris are determined to conduct their affairs without recourse to lawyers and courts. If communication becomes difficult, they pledge themselves to participate in a joint program of counseling. If one issue, such as physical custody or amount of support, becomes impossible to compromise, they agree that they will submit the dispute to a binding arbitration.

Date: _____   _____
                             Sam Matlock

Date: _____   _____
                             Chris Woodling

Note: Obviously we can't include all types of agreements here, but we hope this gives you an idea of what is possible. We are often asked what happens if a "joint custody" agreement breaks down and the family can't, despite counseling, etc. communicate well enough to make it work. The answer is the same as for any other custody situation that fails. Either parent can petition the court at any time to have it changed.

Tax Note: Child support is not taxable, but spousal support is. The person paying spousal support can deduct such payments, and the recipient must report it as a taxable income. In some cases, the spouses may be able to save money by juggling these categories, but as of 1984, this has become harder to do. Income tax exemptions are allowed for children, but when the parents are divorced, they cannot both claim the same child as a dependent. The rules for who can claim the child as an exemption also changed in 1984. Now if parents live apart at all times during the last six months of a calendar year, the custodial parent (the parent with physical custody for the majority of the year) will be allowed the dependency exemption. The only exception is if the custodial parent signs a declaration that he or she will not claim the exemption for the taxable year. In a joint custody situation, we assume that the parent having the most physical custody will be entitled to the exemption absent a declaration to the contrary. If parents actually share physical custody fifty-fifty, they should also be able to work out an agreement regarding the dependency exemption. Each parent can deduct the amount expended for a child's medical expenses, regardless of custody.

This 1984 dependency rule does not apply to a decree or agreement executed prior to January 1, 1985, where the custodial parent agreed to release his or her claim to the dependency exemption to the non-custodial parent and the non-custodial parent pays at least $600 of the child support.

For more information, contact the Internal Revenue Service and ask for the I.R.S. publication entitled, "Tax Information For Divorced and Separated Individuals."

C. Visitation of Children

Assuming that one parent is awarded custody, the other is most commonly granted "reasonable rights of visitation," with no attempt to specify times and places. Courts are very supportive of the idea that *both* parents should have as much contact with their children as possible. In fact, if there is no joint custody award, the court is mandated to award custody to the parent who is more likely to allow the parent who doesn't have custody as much time with the children as possible.[7]

4601—California Civil Code

Reasonable visitation rights shall be awarded to a parent unless it is shown that such visitation would be detrimental to the best interests of the child. In the discretion of the court, reasonable visitation rights may be granted to any other person having an interest in the welfare of the child.

---

[7]Custody was in fact changed from one parent to the other when a court found that the custodial parent had frustrated visitation by the non-custodial parent. *In re Marriage of Wood*, 141 Cal.App.3d 672 (1983). And Civil Code Section 4700 allows a parent who incurs extra expense because the other parent thwarts a custody or visitation arrangement to obtain a court order providing for appropriate recompense from the other parent.

Example: Eric and Samantha live with their mother who has custody under a court order stemming from a divorce. Their father wishes to see them most of the time (summers and holidays) that they are not in school. Is this reasonable?

Probably it is, assuming that the children want to spend time with their father.

The non-custodial parent is normally in the more difficult psychological position vis-a-vis the children. He, or she, must necessarily relate to the former spouse to visit with the children, especially when they are small. How easy it often seems to chuck the whole thing and walk away. Well, life isn't made up of easy spaces. Children need both parents. As children get older and get in touch with their own strengths, things often get easier for the non-custodial parent. Opportunities to be a friend, companion and guide commonly develop for the parent who sees the children only occasionally that are seldom experienced by parents who live with their children.

We have noticed that difficulties arising from visitation and custody are particularly likely to arise when parents have differing lifestyles. To a parent who is highly religious and leads an ordered, lights off at ten o'clock sort of existence, allowing the kids to spend the summer with the other parent, who is a drummer in a rock band, may not seem reasonable at all. Of course, the drummer will look at it quite differently. Courts tend to look at reasonableness broadly. We say "tend to" because no two judges are alike and inevitably the particular prejudices of the judge who is hearing a dispute will influence the decision. We would think that a judge would allow the drummer to spend time with his children as long as sensible steps were taken to provide a living environment that wouldn't freak them out. Remember, it is the best interests of the children that must come first.

Important: Normally only criminal activity or conduct that is destructive to oneself (such as uncontrolled use of alcohol, heavy use of drugs, or a history of violent behavior) will be reason to deny visitation. Prostitution, when called to the attention of the court, has been, and still is, a reason to deny visitation. Living in a homosexual relationship used to be almost automatic grounds for denial of visitation but is no longer. Religious differences between parents are also not a reason to deny or limit visitation unless they are clearly shown to be harmful to the children. Even where a parent is obviously unfit to take care of children over a long period, courts normally bend over backwards to allow some contact. Thus, a mother who had attempted suicide several times and had serious alcohol problems might be allowed to visit with her children at a relative's house, as long as another adult was present.

Problems with visitation often develop when parents live long distances apart. This is partly because distance seems to increase paranoia in and of itself, but also because contact with the absent parent becomes more difficult and expensive as the distance increases. Because of the necessities of moving for job, family and other reasons, courts are reluctant to prohibit a parent from removing children from the state where both parents have lived, although this has been done, especially on a temporary basis while a divorce or custody case is pending in court.

Question: *Who has the duty to pay for transportation for the children to visit the absent parent?*

Answer: It depends on circumstances, such as who has more money, who moved away, etc. Try to work out your own compromise. If you can't, a judge will do it for you.

Question: *Does the custodial parent have any sort of duty or obligation to facilitate visitation with the absent parent?*

Answer: Yes, the right of reasonable visitation means that the custodial parent should do those reasonable things to make visitation possible, such as taking the children to the airport or bus station if travel is required and being generally cooperative.

Question: *Can a non-custodial parent refuse to pay child support if the custodial parent interferes with his or her court-ordered visitation rights?*

Answer: No. A parent owing support must continue payments regardless of how the custodial parent behaves with respect to visitation. However, the non-custodial parent can get his or her visitation rights enforced by the court and can request compensation for money spent in attempting to exercise his or her visitation rights.

Question: *What happens if children are visiting an out-of-state parent and that parent tries to keep them by going to court where he (she) lives to try changing custody?*

Answer: The second state will respect the custody and visitation orders of the first state. In other words, they will not cooperate in childnapping. There is an exception to this rule, however. If the judge in the state where the children are visiting is convinced that their returning to the other parent would jeopardize their safety, he (she) might let them stay. It is a very unusual finding, however, so there is usually no reason to be paranoid about letting the kids visit out-of-state.[8]

D. Modification of Custody and Visitation Orders

What happens when misunderstandings do arise concerning custody or visitation arrangements? What should you do when you feel, and your former spouse feels, that there is an insoluable dispute? The conventional legal answer used to be to get a lawyer and go back to court to demand that a judge agree with whatever you want to happen. Custody and visitation can be changed by a court on the petition of either parent at any time. Thus, a father who has been denied the right to take his children camping for a month in the summer and to see them every other weekend during the rest of the year probably could get a court order specifying that he be able to see the children at these times. As a practical matter, however, courts do not like to tamper with existing custody and support arrangements unless there has been a significant change in the circumstances that existed when the original arrangements were made.

---

[8]Every state has adopted the Uniform Child Custody Jurisdiction Act, requiring second states to respect the custody and visitation orders of the first state, with the exception discussed above. A federal law, the Parental Kidnapping Prevention Act also requires second states to respect the orders of first states, and contains a federal parent locator system to track down kidnappers on a national basis. If your spouse was supposed to return the kids (or snatches them up when it's not his or her turn for a visit) don't go and "steal" your kids back. You could be arrested for kidnapping even though you have a valid order giving you custody; go and get the court to enforce your order. If your kids have been removed from the United States, the U.C.C.J.A. still applies, and the United States is considering signing on to an international treaty (the Hague Convention on Civil Aspects of International Child Abduction) which would help locate kidnapped children removed from the U.S. If you are involved in an intrastate, interstate or international custody dispute or kidnapping, see a lawyer (Chapter 12). See also Chapter 11(D) on domestic emergencies.

Further, in our opinion, running to court to alter existing arrangements is often an unwise way to proceed. Our reasons for saying this include the following:

• Court proceedings are expensive. Why waste money on the legal system that could be used to benefit the children? You might be surprised if you knew how many court battles last only as long as the money holds out.

• Lawyers and court proceedings almost always increase paranoia and bitterness. Lawyers get paid to fight. It's unrealistic to expect a peaceful solution by hiring an army (even a small one) and going to war. Even if you win, you are inviting future battles.

• Judges have no particular training in handling domestic disputes. The conventional, and perhaps not completely fair, definition of a judge is "a lawyer who knows a politician." Because court calendars are crowded and time is short, you often aren't even able to get the judge to pay much attention to your dispute.

Fortunately, we are not alone in our opinion. Many people, including a majority of the legislature, understand that a courtroom is not a conducive setting to work out disputes concerning family matters, so we now have what is known as The Family Conciliation Court Law[9], which provides for free or inexpensive counseling to those couples who wish it in all larger counties. Often this is provided for by a department called Family Court Services. The idea is to try to help save your marriage. At the very least, counselors can help make your dissolution easier and more successful. If one party to a dissolution wants counseling, they fill out the counseling statement that comes as part of the packet of dissolution forms.

In addition to the marital conciliation service offered in the larger counties, mandatory mediation services are utilized in all counties in cases where there is a contested child custody or visitation dispute (see Chapter 10, Step 12). As described in Civil Code Section 4607:

The purpose of such mediation proceeding shall be to reduce acrimony which may exist between the parties and to develop an agreement assuring the child or children close and continuing contact with both parents after marriage is dissolved.

In many counties, conciliation and mediation services are provided by the same office; in some they are organized separately.[10]

Even if the parents believe that the problems are so deep and persistent that the only solution is for a judge to tell them what to do, they still have the opportunity to work out their dispute first. Whenever anyone files formal papers where there appears to be a dispute about visitation or custody rights, both parties will automatically be referred to a "Court Mediator." This will happen in the context of a divorce or other separation proceeding, a request for modification of an existing order, or a new proceeding in the case where the parents never married.[11]

---

[9]Code of Civil Procedure Section 1740.

[10]When the mediator makes a recommendation to the court, in the event that agreement is not reached, either side may require the mediator to explain the reasons for the recommendation and face cross-examination in court. *McLaughlin v. Superior Court*, 140 Cal.App.3d 473 (1983).

[11]In a case where the parents never married, the only way to get into family court is with a paternity suit. Thus, if custody is in dispute, and the parents want the court—or mediator—to assist them, one parent must file a petition for paternity (to which the other may concede), even if there is no disagreement about paternity.

The mediator is a professional counselor, sometimes a member of the staff of the Family Conciliation Court. Mediation sessions are confidential and private and are most often conducted with the exclusion of lawyers.

The efforts of the mediator are directed towards helping the parties come to an agreement after explaining all the possible variations of a visitation schedule that would make sense in the individual situation. After an agreement is reached, it is then reported to the judge and, in most cases, adopted as the judge's order.

In the relatively few cases where mediation does not result in an agreement, the mediator makes recommendations to the judge which, in most cases, are followed to the letter.

Example: Joe and Josie can't agree on the times and places that Joe should visit their two infant children, Cleo and Claude. In the original divorce order, nothing was said beyond the fact that Joe should have "reasonable rights of visitation."

After talking to both Joe and Josie and considering their individual problems, a mediator might persuade them to agree or make a recommendation as follows:

1. Every other weekend, starting at 6:00 p.m. Friday and ending at 8:00 p.m. Sunday, Joe will pick up and return the children to Josie's home.

2. Two weeks at Christmas vacation.

3. One week at Spring vacation.

4. July and August.

Some parents whose custody status was originally determined prior to the advent of the joint custody law (1980) may now be tempted to seek a court modification to attain a joint custody status. After all, the law now clearly states that this form of custody is preferred. And, the change in the law constitutes a significant change in circumstances. If both parents agree to this sort of modification, there should be no problem. However, if the custodial parent wishes to preserve the current arrangement, and this arrangement appears to have worked out from the child's standpoint (e.g., the child appears to be emotionally stable and doing well in school), the mediator will be relunctant to recommend (and the court to grant) a change, even though the statute seems to indicate that this would be appropriate. The reason for this is simple: The court's first duty is to the best interests of the child, and those interests are usually furthered by the greatest possible stability under the circumstances.

Stepparent Visitation Note: A court has the power to award visitation rights to a stepparent if that person and a child's natural parent get a divorce. This means if Ben, who has two children by a prior marriage, marries Sally, and then Ben and Sally divorce, a court can award Sally the right to visit Ben's two children. Civil Code Section 4351.5.

Grandparent Visitation Note: Courts may also grant visitation rights to a child's grandparents when the parents get a divorce, unless both parents are opposed to it. If the parents disagree about grandparent visitation rights, the issue will be referred to mediation. Civil Code Section 4351.5.

E. Contesting Custody of Children

Full scale custody fights where one parent wishes to get physical custody of the children from the other tend to be long, expensive and nasty. Normally, it is unwise to start this sort of proceeding unless there are overwhelming reasons to do so—the only such reasons we know being that the children are being actively harmed by their present living situation. The non-custodial parent frequently asks:

"If my former wife lives with someone else without being married, can I get custody away from her?"

"If my former husband drinks too much, can I get a custody change?"

"I have an arrest record for marijuana use; does this mean my kids can be taken away?"

"My son is nine years old and wants to live with me. Will the court follow his wishes?"

"Is it actually possible for a father to get custody of young children?"

The answer to all of these questions is, "It depends." In spite of what your next door neighbor, your best friend, or the former legal secretary that your cousin knows told you, the law does not say that smoking grass, living with a homosexual[12] or heterosexual lover, drinking or keeping an alligator in the garage will result in a loss of child custody. In fact, taken alone, each of these probably will not. Ultimately, it is up to each individual judge to determine who shall get custody. He or she will look at the whole situation and at the best interests of the children. In doing this, the judge will necessarily apply his or her own standards (prejudices).

---

[12]Gay people used to do very poorly in California when they tried to get custody of their children while living in a gay relationship. However, recent legal decisions, most notably *Jullion v. Jullion,* Alameda County Superior Court, April 1978, have held that lesbianism has no bearing on child custody. A good source for more information is *A Legal Guide for Lesbian/Gay Couples,* by Curry and Clifford. Order information is included in the back of this book.

However, just like the case of visitation disputes, all custody disputes fall under the juris-diction of the Family Conciliation Court and Mediation Services (see Section C). Now the judge will review an agreement of the parties, or, if no agreement was reached, a report and recommen-dation by the mediator. To repeat, the new law affords ample opportunities to the disputing parties to resolve their disputes regarding custody and visitation rights before the matter ever comes in front of a judge. In the great majority of cases, the judge will accept and adopt the agreement of the parties or recommendations by the mediator as the judge's order.

F. Problems with Child Support

This is a heavy area of the law. Our society (or most of it) has little sympathy for the non-supporting parent. As we stated in Chapter 7(C), both parents of children have a legal obligation to support them until age 18, unless there has been a court order (as part of a divorce or other action) specifying that one parent must bear all, or most of, the burden.[13] Child support debts are not treated as being equal to other debts. They are your most important obligation. If you fail to pay them when reasonably able to do so, you can, and probably will, be fined and put in jail.[14]

In most cases, there will have been a court order setting a child support amount as part of a divorce action. In fact, it is possible to obtain a temporary child support order upon the filing for dissolution without first going to court (Civil Code Section 4357.5). How to obtain one is covered in *How To Do Your Own Divorce in California*, Sherman (Nolo Press). This law applies to all dependent minor children, no matter when a child support order was originally entered.[15]

1. An Overview of the Agnos Child Support Standards Act

Here is an outline of how the California law (Agnos Act) that determines how child support obligations are to be computed. For detailed guidance in computing child support obligations and seeking a modification of support under the new act (called the "Agnos Child Support Standards Act of 1984"), consult *How to Modify and Collect Child Support in California*, by Matthews, Siegel and Willis (Nolo Press).

---

[13]The parents themselves cannot contract away their support obligation. (See Civil Code Sections 196.5 and 7012.)

[14]In Chapter 17 of *Billpayers' Rights*, Warner and Elias, Nolo Press, we discuss child support debts in detail.

[15]A child who is living at home and attending high school full-time is entitled to support until he or she graduates or turns 19, whichever occurs first. A parent's duty to support a child beyond the age of majority only applies when the child is disabled from supporting himself through employment. Thus, a court of appeals ruled that a parent does not have an obligation to support an adult child who is in college. *Jones v. Jones*, 179 Cal.App.3d 1011 (1986).

The basic purpose of the Act is to impose child support obligations on both parents that will, at a minimum, assure the child the same level of support as his benefits would be under the Aid to Families With Dependent Children welfare program. Also, to the extent that parents can afford a larger amount of support, the new legislation encourages the courts to order it.

The first step in computing child support obligations is to determine the income available to each parent for the payment of such support (termed the parent's "annual net disposable income").[16] This income is to be computed by using an official form provided by the California Judicial Council called the Income and Expense Declaration and available from your County Clerk. The form permits a number of automatic deductions to be taken (e.g., income tax, social security, health insurance deductions, mandatory union dues) and also allows for for certain deductions in the event of hardship.

After each parent's annual net disposable income is toted up, the joint result is multiplied by 18% for one child, 27% for two children, 36% for three children, 40% for four children, 44% for five children, and an additional 4% for each additional child up to ten. If the result is less than the AFDC standard for that number of children, the child support shall be set at the lower amount. If the result is greater than the AFDC standards, then the child support minimum will be set at the AFDC level, although the judge does have the discretion to set the actual support obligation at a higher level.[17] Let's consider an example.

Assume that Jill and Ted Cuellar have two minor children, Marie and Tommy. Jill files for a dissolution. Because Jill and Ted cannot agree on a fair child support level, they turn to the Agnos standards. They fill out the income and expense determination forms provided by the Court Clerk and determine that they have a combined net disposable income of $20,000. Because they have two children, they multiply this sum by 27%. The result is $5,400. They divide this sum by 12 to reach the monthly amount, or $450. They next determine that the AFDC standard for two children is also $450 per month. In this case, Jill and Ted's combined support obligation to Marie and Tommy will be set at $450. If Ted and Jill had a higher net disposable income, their minimum obligation would still be $450 (although the court has the discretion to award a higher amount, which they normally do by reference to a supplementary county schedule, discussed below). If their income was less, on the other hand, their obligation would be lower.

Once the overall support obligation to the children is computed, the next step is to figure out what each parent's portion of this obligation will be. This depends on the proportion of the total income that each parent's separate income represents. For instance, if one parent's income is two-thirds of the total, while the other parent's income is one-third, their respective obligations would be equal to these proportions.

To return to the Cuellar family, if Ted's income were two-thirds of the total $20,000 and Jill's were one-third, Ted would be responsible for two-thirds of the $450 obligation, or $300, while Jill's obligation would be one-third of the total, or $150. Similarly, if Ted and Jill had an equal net disposable income, each parent would be assigned one-half of the support obligation, or $225 each.

16"Income" includes not only wages or salary, but also rents and profits from property, interest and dividends from investments, spousal support from other marriages, etc.

17The AFDC standards are found in tables included with the Judicial Council forms.

Once the parent's respective obligation is computed, it is necessary to next decide who actually has to part with the cash. In situations where one parent has sole physical custody, this determination is easy—the non-custodial parent pays the custodial parent. If Jill has custody of Marie and Tommy, for example, Ted would pay Jill (Civil Code Section 4722).

In the event parents share joint physical custody, however, things are not quite so easy. Suppose, for example, that Ted and Marie spend one-half of the their time with Jill and one-half with Ted. If Jill and Ted had an equal income, there would be no child support payment. But what if Ted's income is two-thirds of the total, while Jill's is one-third? In this situation, Ted might have to pay Jill all or some of the $150 difference between her obligation and his. Just how much this would be would depend on how much Jill would save as a result of Ted's substantial periods of custody (Civil Code Section 4727).

The Agnos law permits divorcing or divorced parents who have not applied for public assistance or assigned their support rights to the county to agree to a support arrangement that provides a lesser support obligation than the mandatory minimum. However, the courts are instructed not to approve such agreements unless the parties are aware of the mandatory minimums and state that their children will be adequately supported. The agreement form, termed a "Stipulation to Establish or Modify Child Support," is produced by the Judicial Council and available at the County Clerk's office. It requires the parties to have reviewed a booklet on the law published by the Judicial Council and available at the County Clerk's office (Civil Code Section 4728).

Turning once more to Jill and Ted, assume that Jill has sole custody of Tommy and Marie while Ted has two-thirds of the combined net disposable income and thus a $300 minimum support obligation. Ted and Jill agree that Ted will only pay $175 a month support but assume certain daily obligations connected with the children's school and extra-curricular activities, buy their clothes and take care of doctor bills. The court may approve this agreement if Ted and Jill sign the stipulation form providing that they both understand their rights and duties under the child support laws, have reviewed the Judicial Council booklet, and will adequately support their children.

This entire discussion so far has focused on the minimum child support standards that must be satisfied in both original dissolutions and modification proceedings. However, the law is not satisfied with children only receiving the minimum. Under the Agnos Act, courts are required to consider whether parents can afford to pay a higher amount of support.

In deciding whether an additional amount is warranted, the courts will refer to county-mandated support schedules prepared especially for this purpose. You can get the child support schedule in force in your county from the Superior Court Clerk.

Note: Low-income parents who have previously negotiated payment amounts with a district attorney's office can expect to have these raised. This is true even though the D.A. operates under criminal law standards which basically hold that no one can be jailed or fined for failure to pay child support unless they have the ability to do so. In other words, if you can only possibly afford $50 per month per child because you have a very low income, the D.A. can't succeed in a criminal prosecution against you for not paying more. However—and this is the most important part—because the legislature has significantly raised the minimum they consider to be acceptable, you can be sure that the District Attorney's offices will demand more too.

Important: We were recently asked, "What if one parent (the mother, let's say) is rich in her own right? Will the court still order the father to pay support, assuming that the mother has custody and the father is not wealthy?" Yes, but as the child support act takes into consideration the income of both parents, the parent without custody will end up paying less. Of course, if an absent parent doesn't pay support and the parent with custody simply doesn't care and doesn't do anything about the non-support, no one else will raise a fuss either. The exception to this rule occurs if the custodial parent is receiving welfare, in which case the D.A. will want to have a conversation with the non-supporting parent.

2. Changing Amount of Child Support

Often, no sooner is a child support order entered as part of a divorce then the facts change and the amount to be paid becomes either unrealistically high or low. Loss of a high-paying job, for example, could make it impossible for the father of two children to pay the mother $500 per month for the support of each child. In this situation, conventional wisdom would say that the father should get a lawyer and file an action to modify the child support. But it may be just as wise, if not wiser (and certainly cheaper), for the father to modify child support without a lawyer. A full discussion of circumstances which warrant a change in child support, the process of requesting the judge to modify an order, including an explanation of how to fill out the forms, and a discussion of when a lawyer's participation is advisable, is contained in *How to Modify and Collect Child Support in California*, Matthews, Siegel and Willis (Nolo Press).

Child support can be changed at any time, assuming there has been a change in circumstances, or assuming that the child support modification is being sought under the simplified modification procedure discussed later in this section.

For purposes of modifying a child support order issued prior to July 1, 1985 (the effective date of the Agnos Child Support Standards Act), the existence of the Act itself constitutes a changed circumstance (Civil Code Section 4730). This means that to the extent that parents have stipulated before July 1985 to a support obligation less than the minimum, no change in circumstances need be established to apply to court for an upwards modification (Civil Code Section 4728(b)).

As we indicated, it is possible to obtain a modification of a child support order without a lawyer. Under a simplified modification procedure (Civil Code Section 4700), a parent may petition the court once a year (more often in case of emergencies) to award a 10% change in support (either up or down) for each year that has passed since the last obligation was set. This procedure is specifically designed to be used without a lawyer and can be brought without showing a change in circumstances. If the second parent does not respond to the petitioner's preprinted, fill-in-the-blanks forms, the change can be obtained without either having to appear in court or having the other spouse sign any papers.

Perhaps the most significant benefits of this new simplified procedure will be felt by people who have not requested a modification of their child support for a number of years. This is because they are eligible to request a 10% change for each year since the previous child support order without having to show any change in their (or their spouse's) financial circumstances.

Example: Albert and Mary were divorced three years ago. Both were working—Albert making $2,000 per month and Mary $1,500 per month. As part of their dissolution, the court ordered Albert to pay Mary $400 per month child support for their one child. In the last three years, both Albert and Mary have had several pay raises. In this situation, Mary is eligible to use the simplified procedure to ask for a 30% ($120) increase in child support. She can do this herself, without a lawyer, and it will be routinely approved unless Albert contests it. He would probably be unwise to contest if his income has increased significantly.

Warning: The Agnos Child Support Standards Act (discussed at the beginning of Section F, above) provides that it's provisions shall apply to all applications for modification. This apparently means that both parents will need to fill out an income and expense statement before the court will even consider their simple petition. Concisely put, the simplified procedure is less simple than it used to be.

Disregarding the conventional "get everything buttoned down in court" wisdom, many parents simply make custody modification agreements informally amongst themselves. Where people enjoy a fair degree of trust and are able to communicate, we have seen this approach work well. If you and your former spouse do decide to agree on a different child support arrangement than what is contained in the court order stemming from your divorce, be sure to write it down.

Voluntary Support Modification Agreement[18]

John Amaro of 100 South Street, El Monte, California, and Sally Burton of 57 San Pablo Avenue, Redding, California, make the following agreement as regards the support of their two minor children, Anne Amaro and Roger Amaro:

1. That because John Amaro has suffered a serious illness which has reduced his income by 80 percent, it is agreed that the $1,000 per month child support ordered in the divorce action between parties is too high.

2. In order to avoid an expensive court proceeding to lower child support, and because John Amaro's health problems should improve in the next six months, it is agreed that John Amaro will pay to Sally Burton the sum of $225 per month for the support of Anne and Roger Amaro, commencing May 1, 19___, and terminating with the payment of November 1, 19___, and that all additional amounts of support for this time period are forever given up by Sally Burton.

3. It is further agreed the full monthly amount of support ordered as part of the divorce proceedings ($1,000) will be paid on the first of each month, commencing December 1, 19___.

_____   _____
Date   John Amaro

_____   _____
Date   Sally Burton

(Notarization is not necessary, but is a good idea.)

---

[18]You will need to modify this agreement to fit your circumstances. If you wish to present the agreement to a judge and have it formally approved, contact the Court Clerk of the court that issued the divorce decree. To cover the possible future deterioration of your relationship with your ex-spouse, we recommend that you obtain such court approval when feasible. However, we also remind you that the judge will probably want to see an income and expense statement from both parents before she acts.

3. Failure to Support

Few things are more frustrating to the parent with the day-to-day responsibilities of raising children than the failure of the other parent to pay child support, especially when he or she is financially able to do so. As noted above, we hesitate to advise you to seek redress in lawyers and courts, but failure to pay child support may be one time when you have no choice if you have tried persuasion and it has failed. Of course, there is a difference between habitual and deliberate failure to pay support, and missing a payment or two where there is some legitimate reason for the delinquency. There is little point in hauling someone into court who is doing the best he or she can.

Important: We were recently asked about back support. Can it be collected later, or does the obligation simply disappear if the parent with custody doesn't move to collect the money immediately? Unpaid child support doesn't go away; it can be collected later. If, for example, a man disappears for a few years, and then reappears and gets a job, his former spouse can demand all the money unpaid while he was gone. As of January 1, 1986, this can even be done after the child turns 18.[19] For this reason, a modification of child support should always be obtained if payments cannot be made for some reason. See *How to Modify and Collect Child Support in California,* Matthews, Siegel and Willis, Nolo Press.

4. How Are Delinquent Child Support Orders Enforced?

Basically, delinquent child support orders are enforced in four ways:

a. By a legal action brought under the divorce to hold the non-supporting parent in "contempt of court." This sort of action is filed by a private attorney on behalf of the parent with custody and is civil in nature, although a judge can sentence a non-supporting parent to jail for a short time, if he or she has willfully violated an existing support order (is in "contempt of court"). In situations where the parent is one or more months behind in child support payments, the judge also has the power to order the non-supporting parent's employer to deduct money directly from the parent's paycheck to cover child support obligations.[20] Also, income tax returns may be intercepted, as may any other money owed to the paying parent by a state agency (e.g., lottery winnings). In addition, the judge is now required to order the non-supporting parent to pay the custodial parent's attorney fees. This attorney may demand some money from the parent instituting the action before the action is filed, especially if collection from the non-supporting parent appears doubtful.

b. In situations where people are poor, including most of those where welfare is involved, private attorneys are normally not interested. Here most actions are brought by county district attorneys under Welfare and Institutions Code Section 11350 for child-support arrearages (and

---

[19]Civil Code Section 4708.

[20]Back and future child support can now be easily collected directly from a paying spouse's California employer or provider of benefits if 1) the paying spouse falls one month or more behind in his or her obligations and 2) the recipient spouse uses a simple do-it-yourself procedure to obtain a wage assignment order from the court. This procedure is explained in *How to Modify and Collect Child Support in California* by Matthews, Siegel and Willis (Nolo Press).

future support if the custodial parent is receiving welfare for children under the Aid to Families with Dependent Children (AFDC) program). In this situation, it makes no difference whether there is a divorce or not. Remember, even without a court order, both parents have a legal duty to support their children if they are able.

c. Failure to pay child support when parents live in different states presents special problems. The Revised Uniform Reciprocal Enforcement of Support Act (RURESA) was enacted to improve enforcement of support orders when the parties live in different states. Collections in these situations used to be primarily handled by the district attorney. The law was recently amended so that private lawyers may represent the custodial parent, and although there is no specific requirement that the delinquent parent pay attorney's fees, there is a good argument for it. We hope the fact that private lawyers may now advocate on behalf of a child who is not receiving support may encourage more frequent enforcement of these claims, which are often given low priority by the local district attorney. Often, the first problem is to locate the absent parent. Under RURESA, there is now a central computer in Washington, D.C., which is used to find parents who skip out on their support obligations. This computer has income tax and social security information, making it more difficult for a parent to avoid support short of fabricating an entirely new identity or leaving the country.

Once a non-supporting parent is located, the district attorney in the county where the custodial parent lives gets in touch with the district attorney in the county where the non-supporting parent lives. Normally, a citation letter is sent to the non-supporting parent requesting that he or she come in to the Family Support Division of the district attorney's office and agree to a payment schedule. If this procedure doesn't result in prompt payments, criminal prosecution follows.

d. A parent can also obtain a judgment in another state for the amount of support due and enforce that judgment directly in California.[21]

Warning: Non-custodial parents should be prepared to be shocked by how much they are ordered to pay. Gone are the days when $50 a month was considered adequate. Children are expensive, and an attempt is normally made to collect as much as the traffic will bear. By arguing, pointing out other obligations and the necessity of going to the grocery store now and again, a parent can sometimes get payments lowered slightly, but don't count on it. All indications are that state and national authorities are making a major effort to squeeze more money from parents who are not supporting as part of a national campaign to cut welfare payments.

Note for Parents Who Are Sued By the District Attorney for Child Support: When the district attorney brings an action against you for child support, and/or to establish your paternity, and you can't afford an attorney, you may be entitled to a free attorney appointed by the court. Further, if you are asked to sign a judgment which orders you to pay a certain amount of child support, you may be entitled to consult with an attorney free of charge to see whether the judgment is proper.

When agreeing to any particular amount of support, be sure that you will be able to pay it. The district attorney likes to get large judgments and may try to pressure you to pay more than you're able.

If you are in doubt, don't sign the agreement. Tell the judge in court what your situation is and how much you can realistically pay.

---

[21]*Liebow v. Superior Court,* 120 Cal.App.3d 573 (1981).

5. Miscellaneous Support Considerations

In addition to the child support paid for the day-to-day living expenses for the children, some parents make arangements for other financial matters which come up when raising kids. For example, if either parent has health insurance available to him or her, often the parents will include a provision requiring that parent to maintain the kids on the insurance. If both have insurance, they will both want to maintain the kids; if neither has insurance, they may make an arrangement to buy some and share the costs. Other miscellaneous support considerations include paying the cost of private education for children not yet in college and/or arranging the cost of the children's higher education, paying for any extraordinary medical care not covered by the insurance and naming the children as beneficiaries on life insurance policies.

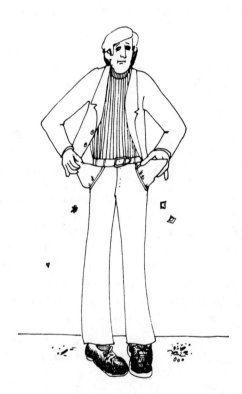

G. What Happens When One Parent Has Remarried?

There is no reason from a legal point of view to include this section. The visitation and support rules discussed above apply equally, whether or not one or both parents remarry. However, practical experience tells us that problems are particularly likely to develop or surface at this time.

A subsequent marriage often works to mellow the person marrying. Marriage is usually an exciting time—one when a person feels successful. It is easy to feel forgiving to a former mate at such a time. But just as this is a moment when the remarrying parent may relax, the remarriage is likely to threaten the other parent, especially if he or she is not leading a full life. While at a conscious level this person may want his or her former mate to be happy, at another, the reaction may be "not too happy." But enough peasant wisdom. Let's review a few facts:

• The law as regards support, visitation or custody does not change because one or both parents remarry.

• The natural parents still nave the duty to support. The people they marry have no such duty.

• It takes a formal adoption before someone who is not a natural parent has a legal duty to support. A child cannot be adopted without the consent of both natural parents, unless the child has been abandoned (see Chapter 7).

• Courts consider it reasonable and normally beneficial for children to visit with a parent and the parent's new spouse and family, absent any particular circumstances that might upset the child.

Important: A child may be temporarily upset if a parent remarries because of a fear of losing the affection of the parent to the new spouse. This understandable feeling can be compounded if the new spouse has children. This is not a reason to try to deny visitation, but to encourage it. A parent who considers petitioning a court to limit visitation by a parent who has remarried should examine his or her own motives carefully.

But what happens if the wife of a shoe clerk gets a divorce and then marries a wealthy dentist and goes with her two children to live with the dentist in a situation where the new husband is generous and shares his material possessions with the children as if they were his own? Does this change the shoe clerk's duty to support? Legally, no. However, if the clerk can show hardship, it might be easier to obtain a downward modification of the amount. Suppose, on the other hand, that the clerk remarries into money that is made available to him as community property or as a gift? It might then be possible for the wife to obtain an increase. But, while the court may consider an actual increase of available income from remarriage as a factor in a support modification hearing, the court is not permitted to either consider a new spouse's ability to earn or any income of that spouse that is not actually available to the spouse having the duty to support.

This entire area can become quite complex. If you face a situation where the income of a new spouse becomes the potential subject of a child-support dispute, you would do well to consult an attorney. See Chapter 12 for how to do this.

Note on Children's Names (see Chapter 3): Often the parent with custody of the child, especially a mother who has remarried, will want to have the child use the last name of her new husband. This can be done in two ways:

1. By the new husband formally adopting the child.[22]

2. By a court-approved name change.[23]

When an adoption take place, the adopting parent is responsible for all child support obligations, and the natural parent is off the hook. However, a simple name change does not involve the duty to support.

---

[22]For a full discussion, see *How to Adopt Your Stepchild*, by Frank Zagone, Nolo Press. Order information in the back of this book.

[23]All the forms and instructions for doing this are contained in *How To Change Your Name*, Loeb and Brown, Nolo Press. See back of this book for ordering information.

CHAPTER 9

Divorce—
Spousal Support

∞

A. Introduction

Alimony, or spousal support as it's now known, is probably the most misunderstood aspect of a marital dissolution. All too frequently, when divorces are mentioned in the media we hear only of the huge alimony which the husband has to pay his wife for the rest of her life. What we are not told about are the majority of circumstances where either no spousal support is ordered, or the amount ordered is a pittance. In short, spousal support is not the automatic award it used to be, and when it is granted, it is often limited to a short period of time. Even when spousal support is granted for a set period, it normally ends at remarriage.[1]

Note: If spousal support is not granted as part of a divorce proceeding, it cannot be granted later. However, if it is granted initially, and there is no written agreement to the contrary, it can be modified in the future if circumstances or need or ability to pay should change. In some situations, one spouse will ask for a token amount of alimony—perhaps $1 per month—in order to have the legal right to ask for more later if it's needed.

---

[1]Spousal support may also be reduced if a person receiving it cohabits with (lives with) a person of the opposite sex. Civil Code Section 4801.5 says, "Except as otherwise agreed by the parties in writing, there shall be a rebuttable presumption affecting the burden of proof, of decreased need for support.

B. What Determines Whether Spousal Support Is Awarded and in What Amounts?

A kind of mystery surrounds the question of when spousal support is ordered and in what amount. One person may be ordered to pay $300 or more a month in spousal support payment, only to find out that friend who has a much higher income escaped this obligation altogether.

Fortunately, as is the case with most mysteries, this one has a solution of sorts. When deciding whether or not to award spousal support, and if so, in what amount, the court is required by Civil Code Section 4801 to consider these factors:

• Age or health of each party;

• Earning capacity of each party;

• Degree to which earning capacity of a spouse was diminished by attention to domestic duties;

• Needs of each party;

• Obligations and assets of each party (including separate property);

• Duration of marriage;

• Ability of supported spouse to work without an adverse effect on children;

• Time required for supported spouse to become self-supporting;

• Standard of living of parties;

• The cost of a life insurance policy on the life of a supporting spouse;

• Any other factors which justice and fairness require to be considered.

In considering these factors, the court must take into account 1) the impairment of the supported spouse's earning capacity caused by devotion of time to domestic duties, 2) the extent to which the supported spouse contributed to the other spouse's education, training or license, and 3) the supported spouse's marketable skills (if any) and what training or education might be needed to make the spouse self-supporting.

Okay, now you know the factors a court uses to decide spousal support questions. But are you more enlightened? Probably not. With all these factors (variables) for setting the amount and duration of spousal support, it is clearly difficult to predict what the result might be in any one case. About the only statement which can be made with any confidence is that each case is different from every other when it comes to settling the spousal support question.

Nevertheless, there are several general principles which will help guide you to at least a ball park estimate:

• In setting the actual dollar amount of support, most courts use pre-computed guidelines like the one shown directly below.

• Most courts will do their best to assure a continuity in the standard of living for both parties, assuming a marriage of five years or more.

• Most courts will require some spousal support if there are minor children below school age.

• Most courts will deny spousal support where the marriage lasted less than five years and no *minor children* are involved.

Guidelines For Duration of Spousal Support
After Dissolution or Legal Separation

Length of Marriage	Duration of Support
Under 12 years	It is presumed that spousal support shall terminate after a period equivalent to one-half the duration of the marriage.
12 to 25 years	There is no presumption for termination; factors to be considered (whether or not it shall terminate): supported spouse's education, training, work experience, health and age; supporting spouse's ability to pay support; supported spouse's eligibility for social security.[2]
Over 25 years	It is presumed that permanent spousal support shall not terminate unless supported spouse remarries.

1. Presence or absence of preschool children to be considered if supporting spouse has income above minimum.

2. Special consideration to be given to the ill health of either spouse.

3. After 25 years of marriage, the supported spouse (usually wife) is presumed to require spousal support.

4. Duration of temporary spousal support payment should be taken into account.

Amount of Spousal Support

If the *net* earnings of one spouse are $300 to $600, *maximum* support to the other spouse is one-third of that income.

If the *net* earnings of one spouse are over $600, *maximum* support to the other spouse shall not exceed 40 percent of that amount.

If there is both spousal and child support, the combined order should not exceed 50 percent of the supporting spouse's net income.

No spousal support shall be provided to any spouse who, following dissolution, has income sufficient to maintain his or her standard of living.

Counties have adopted spousal support schedules similar to the child support schedules discussed in Chapter 8. When making temporary awards (while the divorce action is pending), the court virtually always follows the schedules. When making final awards, the court uses the schedules as a guideline, but is prohibited from making an award based solely on the schedules.

---

[2]Current Social Security Regulations (42 U.S.C. 402b) provide that a supported spouse divorced after ten years of marriage is entitled to dependent's social security benefits.

C. A Spousal Support Example

We've thrown a lot of general principles at you; now let's look at some specific examples.

Nick and Kate have been married for seven years. They have two children aged 3 and 6. Nick is a computer engineer employed by Peach Computer and earns a net income of $3,000 per month. Kate is a special education teacher who quit teaching when the first child was born and who has worked only occasionally as a substitute since. Kate is the owner of $10,000 worth of stocks left to her in trust by her grandmother. Nick has a vintage Mercedes automobile which he owned before the marriage and which is now worth about $20,000. The only other asset is a community property home which Nick and Kate received as a wedding present and which is now worth $100,000. Nick and Kate have agreed that Kate will live in the family home and have physical custody of the two minor children (legal custody is to be joint). Nick has agreed to pay $800 a month for child support but doesn't want to pay spousal support.

Using the principals which we outlined earlier, a court might reason as follows:

"Let's see, Nick has greater earning capacity than Kate. Kate will need to stay home and care for a three-year-old, at least until the age of six, unless she can arrange and pay for childcare. Kate has the house with no mortgage payment and some ability to teach, but her earning capacity is reduced because of her six year absence from the job market. Each spouse has some separate assets, but they are not of particularly large value. Each person is healthy. The marriage was of moderate duration.

Nick brings home $3,000 a month. The spousal support schedule indicates support should last for three-and-one-half years, and would be as high as $700, since the additional $800 of child support makes $1,500, or 50 percent of Nick's net income.

"I think I'll grant spousal support for three years, since after that time the youngest child will be in school. Because of Kate's use of a mortgage-free house, I'll limit spousal support to $300, for total support obligation of $1,100."

The judge's thinking might change if any one of the variables changed. For example, if Kate had a large mortgage payment to meet on the house, the spousal support might go up significantly. If Kate were immediately employable as an Emergency Room Physician at $50,000 a year, on the other hand, there would probably not be any spousal support awarded at all. The result would be the same if Nick were only making $700 a month as a teacher's aide or there were *no* minor children.

The moral? *When it comes to spousal support, each case stands alone.*

D. Connecting Spousal Support to the Division of the Marital Estate

In a few situations, spousal support may prove to be an important part of your property settlement agreement, even though a court would not have ordered it in a contested use. Sound confusing? It's not really. Now and then a community estate is large and tied up in assets that would be hard to sell or which one or the other spouse wants to keep. For example, suppose you wanted to keep the family home but your spouse claimed $50,000 as her share of your pension plan. Rather than sell the home or borrow in the commercial market, you both might prefer for you to pay sizeable spousal support payments over the next five or ten years, even though your wife has a good job of her own. This would allow you to pay off your obligation to the community estate over time. Because spousal support is tax free to the payor and easy to enforce if not paid, it may be advantageous to both spouses to forego a strict equality in community property division in exchange for a spousal support order. In order for spousal support payments to be fully deductible by the payor, an award must meet the following requirements:

• The payment must be in cash;

• No payment may be made after the death of the the recipient;

• Payments cannot be made to people in the same household (i.e., you and your ex must live apart);

• There can be no agreement between the parties that the payments not be deducted (or included);

> • The payments can not be disguised child support (there are more rules on this);

> • The payments must be pursuant to a written marital settlement or separation agreement; and

> • If the payments total more than $15,000 per year, they must be paid in three consecutive years following the separation, though they need not be paid for 36 months (e.g., annual payment in excess of $15,000 would be fully deductable if paid from December 1, 1987 to January 31, 1989).

Tax Note: To the extent you believe that tax considerations are important in your situation, we suggest you see an accountant or the I.R.S. regulations for more details. This is especially important if you anticipate that your spousal support payments will exceed $15,000 a year.

E. Effect of a Spouse's Education or Training on Spousal Support

In Chapter 9, we discussed the new method for handling the cost of one spouse's education or training in the event of a later dissolution. Basically, this involves requiring the spouse receiving the education to pay back the community estate for community funds expended on the education. In addition, when fixing spousal support, the court must consider the extent to which one spouse contributed to the other's education or training, or obtaining of a license.

Assume, for example, that Ellen works to put Jerry through law school. Years later, when Jerry and Ellen divorce and Ellen asks for a large sum in spousal support, the court must consider the extent to which Ellen's contribution to Jerry's larger earning capacity entitles her to a larger cut of his salary. While the statute does not provide any specific guidelines, it is probable that the courts will use spousal support as a supplement to the rules discussed in Chapter 4 to make sure that a spouse who has worked to advance the education or training of the other spouse is not left out in the cold when the community is divided by a dissolution degree.

F. Enforcement of Spousal Support

In recent years the legislature has recognized that enforcing spousal support orders is as important a public priority as enforcing child-support orders. Accordingly, the method discussed in Chapter 8, Section F(3)(a) for collecting child support is also available to enforce spousal support orders. Basically this method involves obtaining a contempt order or an order attaching the defaulting spouse's wages or income tax refunds. How to enforce Spousal Support is covered in *How to Modify and Collect Child Support in California,* by Matthews, Siegel and Willis (Nolo Press).

G. Continued Health Care Coverage

Although health care is not technically spousal support, it is one of the economic advantages of marriage and where divorced spouses suffer great losses. Under federal law, if your former spouse's employer offers group health insurance to his or her employees, the employer must make available to you (as the employee's ex spouse) the health insurance at the group rate for a period of 36 months following final decree of the divorce. But don't delay. You have only 60 days from the day the divorce becomes final to notify the health plan administrator that you want their plan.[3]

---

[3]This law applies to widows and widowers as well. For a thorough discussion of other laws effecting older people, see *Sourcebook for Older Americans*, Matthews, Nolo Press.

CHAPTER 10

Divorce—
The Mechanics
of Getting One[1]

⊂⊃

A. Getting Clear

Even the nicest marriages sometimes come to an end. And endings are always hard. No matter how sensitive, caring and giving each of you is, there are likely to be some difficult moments. The loss of an important part of your life can't help but affect you in powerful ways. Our society almost requires that we look at divorce as failure—after all, aren't we supposed to stay married until "death do us part"?

Our experience is that separation offers a chance for positive change and that, while the actual divorce process is commonly scary and miserable, most people are glad they did it a short time later. We are not divorce advocates, but we are open to the idea that spending one's life with more than one person can be a good alternative to the traditional pattern.

Unfortunately, all of us have been trained to think of our legal (dispute resolution) system as a place little more civilized than a battlefield where we should bite, kick and scratch our way to "victory." Put these feelings about courts and lawyers together with the understandable feelings of hostility and resentment that can occur at the end of a relationship, and you have plenty of fuel for

---

[1]Yes, we know that the word "divorce" has been replaced by "dissolution" in California, but since everyone still uses "divorce," we will too, at least some of the time.

an enormous fire[2]—unfortunately, it's a fire that may scorch you as well as people you love if you let it get started. It's all too easy to let your feelings of loss—anger, hostility, guilt, resentment—manifest themselves in bitter arguments over who gets the silver service, children or house. Whether you get on top of these arguments or they get on top of you can be the critical point determining whether your divorce is decent or horrible. Often the truth is that you are not really arguing about the property, or even the children—you are simply using them as excuses (pawns) to get at your mate.

It is essential that you take time to cool off before you start dealing with legalities. Simply let the highly charged atmosphere that often accompanies separation mellow out a bit. It's crazy to let the emotional pressures of a moment (usually a bad one) rush you into making decisions which will profoundly affect your future lives. You may need a little outside help to be able to relate to one another positively—if so, divorce (separation) counseling is widely available and we highly recommend it, especially where children are involved. The idea of counseling at this point is not to get back together, but to separate decently. As our friend Ed Sherman often says, "Relate to one another positively when you can, and not at all when you can't."

Here are the basic things that must be talked about and agreed upon when you are thinking about divorce:

• Whether or not your marriage should be ended. Many people wish to try a trial separation before deciding for sure. See Chapter 2. Others will want to see someone from the Family Conciliation Court [see B(8) below].

• Who is to have custody of the children? We talk about the possibility of joint custody in Chapter 8.

• How is visitation with the children to be handled? This can be particularly important if a long distance is involved. See Chapter 8.

• How are the children to be supported? Often one parent will pay the other (custodial parent) an amount for support which must take into consideration the ability to pay as well as the needs of the children. See Chapter 8.

• Will one spouse pay the other anything for spousal support? In many situations, spousal support is no longer appropriate; in others, it's essential. See Chapter 4.

• How will the community property and bills accumulated during the marriage be divided? See Chapter 4.

B. A Short Survey of California Divorce Law

California is a "no-fault" divorce state. As we noted, technically the very term "divorce" has been replaced by "dissolution." The idea behind "no-fault" is simple—a court shouldn't be in the position of encouraging couples to drag each other through all their past bitterness and broken expectations. No-fault divorce has been a valuable reform and has worked exceedingly well. But we

---

[2]In fact, one of our friends knows a lawyer who represented a woman in a hotly-contested divorce; the "enormous fire" occurred when the husband burned down part of the lawyer's office. No doubt the husband was all fired up and wanted to share the experience.

at Nolo Press applaud the recent trend of the courts divesting themselves of their role as the principle forum for the resolution of domestic affairs.[3] The notion that an antiquated, expensive and time-consuming court system that forces couples into antagonistic, adversary roles does anything to promote domestic tranquility or to arrive at a fair and just solution is frankly beyond our belief. People's domestic relationships and disputes should be removed from court altogether. The proper place to resolve them is through a system of mediation and arbitration administered by people who have knowledge and experience in the area of domestic relations, rather than ex-lawyers who were given a black robe as a prize for knowing the right politician.

1. Grounds for Divorce

To be eligible for a divorce in California you must state one of the following two grounds (Civil Code Section 4506):

• "Irreconcilable differences which have caused the irremediable breakdown of the marriage."

• "Incurable insanity."

In practice, everyone files under the first ground. The courts are not interested in an itemization of what the "irreconcilable differences" are. Your statement that they exist is enough.

2. Grounds To Oppose a Divorce

Is it possible for a person to oppose his/her spouse's request for a divorce because he/she thinks that the irreconcilable differences are not so bad and that the marriage is capable of being patched up? No. Let us repeat—the court will not consider evidence as to the existence or non-existence of the "irreconcilable differences." If one person wants out, that's enough.

3. The Contested Divorce

Even though California has a no-fault divorce system under which all community property is to be divided equally, most counties have guidelines for the award of spousal support and there is a strong trend toward awarding joint custody of children. There are still contested dissolutions with

---

[3]See discussion of the role of the Family Conciliation Court and Mediation Services in Chapter 8(C).

lawyers who charge $150-$200 an hour battling it out. In our experience, this is just plain silly. Couples who mediate their disputes (see Chapter 12) should be able to avoid a court contest even if there are serious unresolved disputes. Nevertheless, those who do contest their dissolutions should realize that this process often involves all sorts of paperwork (interrogatories, depositions, etc.) and court appearances and depending on the case, can drag on and on. Of necessity, the information in the rest of this chapter applies primarily to uncontested dissolutions.

4. Residency

To file for a divorce either you *or* your spouse must have lived in California for a least six months and in the county you choose to file in for three months just prior to filing your papers.

5. Cost

If you do your own divorce, your total out-of-pocket cost should be about $150. This includes court filing fees, service of process by a paid process server, if necessary, the cost of the *How To Do Your Own Divorce in California* book, etc.

Attorney fees vary from a rock bottom of $250 to many thousands of dollars, depending on who you are, who the attorney is, and what your case is like (see Chapter 12). Unfortunately, attorneys often make people paranoid and their presence in a case often results in small disputes being escalated into big ones.

Another good alternative is "divorce typing services," who also often refer to themselves as independent paralegals. These are non-lawyers trained to do all the paperwork for you while you make the big decisions. (See the inside back cover of this book for a list.) The cost of this service if $75-$200, not counting filing fees, and it can be an excellent approach in uncontested cases.

6. How Long Does It Take?

An uncontested dissolution can be gotten in six months. The time is counted from the day that the person filing the divorce has the other person served with papers. A contested dissolution can take a year or two.

7. First Papers

There are a number of forms that must be filed in proper sequence to get a dissolution. These are clearly set out in *How To Do Your Own Divorce in California* by Charles Sherman (Nolo Press) along with all the necessary instructions on how to fill them out, and won't be repeated here. The petitioner (the person initiating the divorce) starts by filing a Petition and Summons. The purpose of the Petition is to set out the broad outlines of the issues to be decided, including what is to happen to the children (custody and support) and a list of the property. If the petitioner and the other spouse ("respondent") have already worked out the details of their property division and have made custody and support arrangements (see Sections C, D, and E below), the respondent normally files no papers in response to the petition. This allows the matter to proceed quickly as an uncontested default. If the respondent and the petitioner have come to no agreements and there are important areas of dispute, we recommend mediation (see Chapter 12). If this fails to produce agreement, the respondent must file an Answer within thirty days of the day he or she was served with the Petition in order to have the right to appear in court. Contested cases are most often handled by lawyers.

8. Family Conciliation Court

Most large counties in California maintain Family Conciliation Court services. The state is in the business of nurturing and protecting the marriage institution and it doesn't like to give up without a fight. Although the purpose of Conciliation Court is to try and save your marriage, they can also help you dissolve it in an easier, more peaceful fashion by working out some of the problems and terms of your separation. If it doesn't work out, you can go back to the legal action, and all you will have lost is time. An initial consultation is free and any subsequent charges are reasonable. For information and the necessary form to initiate this procedure (the "confidential counseling statement"), contact the Conciliation Court in your county. If they aren't separately listed, ask the County Clerk for information.

9. Serving Your Papers

After the Petition and Summons have been filed, they must be given to (served on) the respondent. This can be easy, since in most situations the respondent voluntarily accepts them. However, if the respondent avoids service, you may have to hire a professional process server. If the respondent is missing, service can be accomplished by newspaper publication. It is possible to serve people in the military, but special rules are involved, which are discussed in *How To Do Your Own Divorce in California.*

10. Arranging for a Court Hearing

Thirty days after the papers have been served and a "proof of service" form has been returned to the court, a court hearing may be scheduled. Again, we are assuming that this is a default situation (one spouse is missing or refused to participate, or both spouses have worked out and agreed to the terms of their divorce). The form you file is called a "Request for Default."

11. Paperwork Prior to Court

Where there are no children, property, or request for spousal support, preparing the papers to take with you to court consists of little more than filling in your names and a few dates on a form entitled Judgment of Dissolution of Marriage. In this situation, if you have been married less than five years, you will probably qualify for a Summary Dissolution and not have to go to court at all (see Section F, below). This is called a Declaration for Default or Uncontested Declaration. In general, it works very nicely, especially where there are no children. As to whether it will work for you, see Step 14 below). However, if you have property or minor children, or one person wants spousal support, you must do a little more paperwork, even if you and your spouse are in complete agreement. Again, all of this is set out in *How To Do Your Own Divorce in California*. If at the time of your regular dissolution there is significant property, you will want to tell the judge how you want to divide it in writing. There are two different ways to proceed with a written agreement:

• The relatively simple Stipulated (Agreed Upon) Judgment; and

• The more detailed Marital Settlement Agreement (see the sample in Chapter 4).

Once you have agreed on the details, neither of these is difficult to prepare.

12. Mediation

If you and your spouse have a dispute about child custody or visitation, Civil Code Section 4607 requires that you be referred to Court Mediation prior to a hearing before a judge. This very sensible requirement results in the parties making their own custody or visitation agreement in over 80 percent of the cases. Only the few cases where there is no agreement now go before a judge.

13. The Court Hearing

After the "Request for Default" and some other technical paperwork is taken care of, you can request a court hearing.[4] Your case will be heard on the "default" calendar within a a few weeks and will normally be grouped with several others of the same type. Only the petitioner shows up in court, the defaulting respondent does not. The hearing is usually little more than a formality. The petitioner explains to the judge that the residency requirements (see B3 above) have been met

---

[4]In many counties, court hearings have been done away with for regular dissolutions as well as for summary dissolutions. Instead, your case will be presented to the judge in writing, by affidavit, without anyone needing to appear.

and that "during the course of the marriage, certain irreconcilable differences have led to the irre-mediable breakdown of the marriage." If there is property and debts, the petitioner explains to the judge the proposed details on division, and in the case of children, a proposal as to custody, support, visitation, etc. This is also the appropriate time to waive or request spousal support and for women who choose to take their husbands' names to request that the judge restore them their former name if they so desire.

The court hearing usually takes less than five minutes. If there are no minor children and little or no property, there is very little to say. *How To Do Your Own Divorce in California* contains a complete outline of what to say and when to say it. Tens of thousands of people have represented themselves successfully in dissolution proceedings and have gained a measure of self-respect from being able to deal with the court system on their own.

14. Dissolution By Affidavit (A Substitute for a Court Hearing)

In some circumstances, couples who agree to the terms of their regular dissolution may proceed by affidavit and without a court appearance.[5] This law actually sets out the circumstances under which a couple could be ordered into court by the judge who reviews the affidavit. These include a determination that chances of reconciliation are reasonably positive, the proposed child support order is less than adequate, or a personal appearance would be "in the interests of justice."

This procedure is not the same as the Summary Dissolution (see Section C of this chapter). Because it is so new, and because it is being used in different ways in different counties, it is not possible to explain the exact mechanics of the proceedings. And because it is so new, we have no prediction as to what use the judges and other court personnel will put this new law. Our recommendation is to ask the County Clerk in your county if it is available, and if so, if it fits your situation. Meanwhile, use another method explained in this chapter.

---

[5]Civil Code Section 4511.

15. Judgment of Divorce

Following the hearing, judgment that the parties are entitled to a dissolution is entered. The judgment sets out orders for child support, custody, visitation, spousal support (alimony), property division and any requested name change. It does not end your marriage. You must wait six months from the day the respondent was served with papers or "appeared" in the case for the judgment to become final. The judgment form itself specifies the exact date that your marital status will be terminated (i.e., the divorce is final). Remember: You are not divorced until the marital termination date entered on the front of your judgment. However, if this presents a particular difficulty, the court does have the authority to move the date up.

Each judgment dissolving a marriage is required by Civil Code Section 4352 to contain the following notice:

Please review your will, insurance policies, retirement benefit plans and other matters that you may want to change in view of the dissolution of your marriage. Ending your marriage may automatically change a disposition made by your will to your former spouse.

Again, let us say as loud as we can—you are not divorced until the Court Clerk gives you a properly executed and stamped Final Judgment. You would be amazed at the number of people wandering around California who think that they are divorced, but who are still married because they forgot these final details.

C. The Summary Dissolution

The summary dissolution procedure in California is a greatly simplified divorce process that requires only two forms and no court appearance. It still takes six months to get a final judgment by this method, however. The drawback is that it is very narrowly restricted. It can only be used by couples who fulfill the following requirements:

1. They have been married no longer than five years;

2. They have no children together and the wife, to her knowledge, is not pregnant;

3. They own no real property;[6]

4. All community property is worth less than $13,000 and all separate property of either spouse is worth less than $13,000 and the community debts are less than $4,000 (automobiles and auto debts are excluded from these amounts);[7]

5. They have prepared and signed an agreement which states how property and debts are to be divided and have actually transferred the assets and titles;

6. They have read and understood a booklet entitled "Summary Dissolution Information"

---

[6]A couple may own a lease on their family home so long as it does not contain an option to purchase or extend for more than one year from the date of filing.

[7]It may be possible for the spouses to make their own property division—that is, transfer community property worth more than $13,000 to each person as separate property prior to filing an action.

prepared by the state and available from the Court Clerk;

7. Either of the spouses meets the California resident requirement (6 months in California and 3 months in one county just prior to filing) and alleges that "irreconcilable differences have caused the irremediable breakdown of the marriage."

8. They must waive all rights to spousal support and appeal.

For more detailed information, the booklet mentioned in item 6 above is available at all Superior Court Clerk's offices and should be obtained if you are considering this method. It is also reproduced in *How To Do Your Own Divorce in California,* with the forms and instructions on how to fill them out.

This procedure is still too new to gauge what effect it will have on the dissolution business. Although it is billed as the Summary Dissolution law, it could almost be as aptly titled the Trial Marriage law, since it may well have the practical effect of enticing all those undecided couples, who were avoiding the marriage institution because of the paranoia-strewn and labyrinthine way out, into taking their vows.

It is encouraging to see the legislature finally move towards a simplification of our cumbersome divorce law. While the new procedure is still way too narrow in scope, it is a step in the right direction.

Disadvantages: Either spouse can frustrate the summary divorce proceedings at any time during the six-month period from the time the papers are served until a final judgment is entered, by simply revoking the whole action. If this happens, the other person has to start over with the longer procedure. As divorce is often a time when people play emotional games with each other ("I will revoke the whole thing if you don't stand on your head"), you want to be sure that both people are serious about going through with the summary dissolution action before you start.

CHAPTER 11

Domestic Emergencies

There are times when one person needs immediate court protection against another person's behavior which has arisen in the context of a domestic relationship. The most common type of domestic emergency involves violence, which is defined as emotional, physical or sexual abuse inflicted upon a person by another member of the household. The relationship may be that of spouses, lovers, parent and child, siblings, etc. Victims of domestic violence are in need of immediate court intervention to get the abuser out of the house and other places where the victims routinely go (work, school, day care, etc.).

Other types of domestic emergencies include when:

• A spouse and children are left by the other spouse with absolutely no money;

• A spouse threatens to try to take all the community property or to stop paying the mortgage on the house; or

• A parent tries to snatch the children and remove them from the state.

The various types of court relief available to a domestic emergency victim are outlined in this chapter. Due to space limitations, however, we are unable to give you specific step by step instructions on how to get this relief. Hopefully, knowing what your rights are will at least lead you to the next step, which is to obtain assistance in enforcing them.[1]

---

[1]In a domestic violence situation the court clerk should help you file your papers correctly. Other assistance can either come from a lawyer or from one of the form typing services listed on the inside of the back cover (assuming they handle domestic emergencies).

A. The Domestic Violence Prevention Act

It is tragic that many couples who once blissfully bonded together (formally or informally) come to kick, beat, sexually assault, harass, and even kill each other. FBI statistics reflect this shattering reality by indicating that a woman is abused every 18 seconds. There are an estimated 28 million battered women in the United States—more than half the married women in the country. Although family abuse is certainly not a recent phenomenon, public recognition and concern over the seriousness of the problem is. In response to mounting pressure for some kind of legal relief for the victims of these acts of domestic violence, the California legislature enacted the Domestic Violence Prevention Act (DVPA).[2]

1. What Types of Orders Can the Court Grant under the DVPA?

The purposes of the DVPA are to prevent a recurrence of domestic violence in situations where it has occurred and to assure a period of separation for the persons involved. To facilitate these goals, a court can grant a Temporary Restraining Order (TRO) "ex parte" (only one party telling her side of the story). The TRO can:

• Legally restrain the abuser from "contacting, molesting, attacking, striking, threatening, sexually assaulting, battering, or disturbing the peace" of the other household members specified in the order;

• Order the abuser to leave the home, regardless of whether he is the legal owner or renter, and not return to the home unless it is necessary to recover clothing and personal effects;[3]

• Order the abuser to keep away from certain places, things, or people; and

• Determine temporary child custody and visitation rights.[4]

In addition, the court has the authority in a TRO to:

• Restrain the abuser from disposing of real or personal property;[5] and

• Determine the temporary use of real or personal property and payment of certain kinds of debts.

Once the court issues a TRO, it will schedule a hearing at which both sides can express their views. After this hearing, the court is authorized to make orders that will continue in effect for an indefinite time, including:

• All of the six "ex-parte" orders listed above;

• Child custody and visitation rights in the case of a nonmarital relationship;

• An order for child support if the abuser is the father;

---

[2]Code of Civil Procedure Section 541.

[3]This part of the order can be made when the actual or threatened harm is either emotional or physical in nature, and regardless of whether the relationship was marital or nonmarital.

[4]Not available in the case of nonmarital relationship between parties.

[5]Not available in the case of nonmarital relationship between parties.

• An order that the abuser pay to any household member for any loss (like wages) or out-of-pocket expenses (medical costs, temporary housing) incurred because of the domestic violence;

• An order requiring all household members to participate in counseling where the parties agree, intend or continue to live with each other; and

• An order for the payment of attorenys' fees and costs to the prevailing party.

The court may issue these more permanent orders without first issuing a TRO where one party sets a hearing and formally notifies the other of the day, time, location and issues so that each has an opportunity to present his of her views.

2. Who Can Get Orders Prohibiting Domestic Violence?

The person who requests the court order (the "plaintiff") must have:

• lived with, or have lived in the same household with, the abuser until very recently; or

• been a party to a pending proceeding under the Uniform Parentage Act.

Also, the plaintiff must:

• be related to the abuser by blood, marriage, or adoption; or

• have been formerly married to him[6]; or

• if not related to him in these ways, there must have been a sexual relationship.[7]

Thus, unmarried couples are covered, but unrelated roommates who have had a fight can't obtain these orders, unless they have been sexually intimate. The plaintiff does not have to live in the household with the abuser if she left to avoid abuse. Nor is the plaintiff required to file for divorce or legal separation as a prerequisite to obtaining relief in the event the couple is married.

---

[6]Although every law we discuss is gender neutral, the overwhelming majority of situations are those in which women are abused by men. Therefore, throughout we identify the abuser/defendant as "he" and the victim/plaintiff as "she."

[7]The law actually provides that either the plaintiff or the defendant must have had a sexual relationship with someone now living in the household. For example, the plaintiff could be a grandmother and the defendant could be a former lover of her daughter who is living with her now.

3. How Long Does It Take?

Ex parte orders are usually issued immediately upon filing the "Application and Declaration," "Order to Show Cause," and "Temporary Restraining Order" with the County Clerk's office in the Superior Court. At the time the temporary restraining order is granted ex parte, the judge will set up a hearing within 20 days so that the other person can tell his side of the story. The exact procedure for obtaining the judge's signature and hearing varies from county to county. The county clerks are the best source to find out this information.

Any temporary restraining order granted at this hearing can last up to 1 year unless the court shortens or lengthens the time or unless both parties agree to an extension.

4. What About the Forms?

Your local County Clerk's office sells a complete set of forms for filing orders with step-by-step instructions. The cost is about $4. As we mentioned, we don't have space to further instruct you in the steps necessary to obtain a TRO. For actions brought under the DVPA, however, the clerk will provide you with a complete set of instructions and perhaps some advise as well. Free advise on how to fill out the forms may also be available through the family support unit of your local District Attorney's office.

5. Serving the Papers

After the temporary restraining order has been signed by the judge, you will need to have it served on (i.e. delivered to) the defendant (abuser), along with the "Application and Declaration" and the clerk's instruction booklet, at least two days before the date the hearing has been scheduled by the judge. The service must be done by someone over 18 years old; it cannot be done by you or any other household member named in the TRO. Whoever serves the defendant must complete the Proof of Service form and must file it with the court.

You also should deliver the order to every law enforcement agency within the jurisdiction so that it can be enforced. To be safe, this means an immediate personal delivery to the local, county, and state police and sheriff departments where you live. It may also mean the law enforcement departments which have jurisdiction over the schools, child care centers, places of employment and anywhere else from which the defendant has been ordered to stay away.

Important: Service on the defendant and proof of that service are vitally important in this situation because the point of the whole process is to ensure enforcement and prevent further acts of violence. The county sheriff's department regularly serves people and so if you can't find anyone or are unsure how to proceed, contact the sheriff's department in your county. It may cost you $25-$50.

6. What Happens if the Defendant Violates the Order?

If the abuser-defendant knowingly and willfully violates the court order, he has committed a misdemeanor punishable by a fine of not more than $1000 or imprisonment in the county jail for not more than six months.[8] If the abuser-defendant meets certain criteria, however, he may be diverted to a counseling program.[9] "Diverted" means that instead of going through the criminal court process, the defendant participates in a rehabilitation program. This will usually occur when the abuser-defendant:

• has no conviction for any offense involving violence within the last seven years;

• has never had any probation or parole for any offense revoked; and

• has not already been diverted within the previous five years because of acts of domestic violence.

When a violation of an order occurs, the victim must inform the police so that they may arrest the abuser. A criminal hearing is then held to determine if the abuser-defendant should be diverted (upon the recommendation of the District Attorney) and if so, whether he consents to counseling and waives his right to a trial. He may or may not be required to pay for the counseling depending on his individual financial situation. The counseling period cannot be less than six months or longer than two years.

If the abuser-defendant completes the counseling program satisfactorily, the arrest and charges will be sealed, which means they are treated as if they never occurred.[10] On the other hand, if the court rules that the abuser-defendant doesn't qualify to be diverted, or if diversion is recommended but the abuser-defendant fails to go along with the program, criminal proceedings go forward.

The diversionary program is new in California, although it has been in existence with varying success in other states. In theory, it provides the abuser with an opportunity to change his behavior while avoiding the taint of having been a defendant in a criminal case. In practice, we must wait to see if this diversionary program breaks the cycle of violence.

Important: It is a mistake to think that a piece of paper which says you are protected from violence is the same as real physical protection. As anyone who has worked in the domestic relations field knows, a court order will not stop a fist, a knife, or a bullet in a situation where a person has gone completely nuts. Or, to put the matter in slightly different words, if a spouse or former spouse is crazy enough to want to commit physical abuse (and risk the penalties), the existence of a restraining order (with the reasonably mild penalties for violating it) aren't likely to stop him. If there is a real fear for safety, a good lock, or better yet, a confidential change in physical location, are likely to be of more immediate help than a restraining order (see Section C).

Penal Code 12028.5 provides that a sheriff or police officer may, at the scene of an incident of domestic violence involving a threat to human life or a physical assault, take temporary custody of any firearm in plain sight or discovered in the course of a search consented to by one of the

---

[8]Penal Code Section 273.6.

[9]Penal Code Section 1000.6.

[10]Moreover, any record that indicates that a person participated in such a program cannot be used against him for purposes of employment, benefit, license or certificate or in any action or proceeding.

occupants of the residence. A gun or other firearm so seized cannot be released for at least 48 hours (but is required to be released within 72 hours).

B. Spousal Rape

The essential guilt of rape consists in the outrage to the person and feelings of the victim of the rape. Any sexual penetration, however slight, is sufficient to complete the crime.[11]

Society is beginning to change its notion of rape from that of a sexual act to that of a violent act. As in so many other instances where there is an evolution in societal values, laws concerning rape have been amended to reflect the change. For example, in many states, cross-examination of a rape victim on her previous sexual history is forbidden, and definitions of rape have been modified to be gender neutral so that both males and females can be victims of rape.

In California, spousal rape is now a crime.[12] Previously, courts and legislatures were reluctant to deviate from the common law precedent established in antiquity that a husband is immune from the crime of raping his wife. But in the wake of growing concern over the large number of the married women in this country subjected to abuse by their husbands, and in the recognition that rape is a violent act, the crime of rape in California is now defined to include:

• the act of sexual intercourse when a wife resists, but her resistance is overcome by force or violence; or

• the act of sexual intercourse when a wife is afraid to resist because of her husband's threats of great and immediate bodily harm.

There can be no arrest or prosecution on a charge of spousal rape, however, unless the violation is reported to the proper authorities within 90 days. This 90-day reporting requirement appears to have been included because of the fear on the part of the lawmaker that charges of rape would be used months later as a weapon in court proceedings arising from a dissolution petition.

C. Battered Women Shelters

The laws that we have just described are far reaching when compared to the lack of any protections just a few years ago. They provide relatively simple procedures a woman can follow either with or without an attorney with the hope of preventing further violence to her and her family. But the steps she must follow still involve a court procedure and any court process is almost by definition too slow for immediate relief in an emergency.

Many times a woman and her children are in immediate physical danger and wisdom dictates that they remove themselves from the physical presence of the abuser (or potential abuser) as quickly as possible. In the past, a primary reason women have failed to do this is that they have had no place to run. Consequently, California has enacted legislation that provides funding for shelters for women and children in this situation. The locations of the shelters are not made public in order to protect the victims and staff. Battered Women Shelters unfortunately pass in and out of

---

[11]Penal Code Section 263.

[12]Penal Code Section 262.

existence frequently. To locate a Battered Women's Shelter or program near you call, WOMAN, Inc., located in San Francisco, at 415-864-4722. WOMAN, Inc. maintains an up-to-date list of shelters and programs throughout the state.

Note: The police have an obligation[13] to provide a written notice to victims of domestic violence that informs them:

• how to obtain information about available shelters;

• how to obtain information about other domestic violence services in the community;

• that the victim has the right to press the district attorney to file a criminal complaint against the abuser[14]; and

• that the victim has the right to petition the civil court for various protective orders.

D. Domestic Emergencies Not Involving Violence

There are a number of potential situations affecting divorcing husbands and wives that do not involve violence but that still give rise to the need for emergency orders from a judge before the actual trial of the divorce or before a marital settlement agreement has been drafted. First we list the most common emergencies and then discuss the procedures which are available to the affected spouse.

---

[13]Penal Code Section 13701.

[14]When a person "presses charges" against another, they are really requesting that the district attorney file the charges. In California, as in most states, only the district attorney, city attorney, and state attorney general can actually file criminal charges against a person.

Common Non-violent Domestic Emergencies

1. **Child-snatching within state**—You have come home from work to find that your spouse has left and taken the children to another part of the state.

2. **Child-snatching to another state**—You and your spouse had worked out a custody and visitation schedule, but over the weekend when she had the kids, she left the state and threatened that you'll never see the kids again;

3. **Left high and dry**- You don't work outside the home (and didn't during the marriage); now that you've separated, he refuses to assist in supporting you and you have no other source of income;

4. **Children need support**—Although you are able to meet most of the children's financial needs, you cannot meet them all. Your spouse, from whom you're separated, refuses to provide any assistance;

5. **Assets need protection**—Your spouse left last night; you have good reason to believe that she will empty out all of the community bank accounts and cash in all or virtually all of the other community assets;

6. **Foreclosure of home is threatened**—Your spouse left about three weeks ago and refuses to contribute anything toward the mortgage or other monthly bills. You're afraid the bank is going to begin foreclosure proceedings pretty soon;

Even if your situation is not exactly the same as one of these just listed, if you're experiencing a definite domestic emergency of some type you may be a prime candidate for an ex parte or other type of temporary order. In this section, as with the last, we give you an overview of when these orders can be obtained, but don't detail how to handle these procedures yourself. Again, hopefully, our information will help you to better understand your options and to seek assistance when appropriate.

Form Note: Each of the forms used in these procedures has been officially issued by the California Judicial Council. When we refer to a form by name, we also give you the form's judicial council number (e.g., Application and Supporting Declaration, 1285.20). Knowing both the name and number of the form you need can be helpful when you are trying to obtain it from the court clerk's office.

1. **Child-snatching within state** (Situation 1), **Child-snatching to another state** (Situation 2),[15] and **Assets need protection** (Situation 5).

Ex parte orders (See section A(1) above) can be sought in each of these three situations. It may also be appropriate to seek ex-parte relief when **Foreclosure of home is threatened** (situation 6). Here's a brief description of how to seek ex-parte orders in these situations.

• Fill out 3 forms—"Application and Supporting Declaration" (1285.20), "Temporary Restraining Order" (1285.05) and "Order to Show Cause" (1285). These forms are available from the court clerk.

• Deliver these filled out forms to the judge for his signature. In situation 6 (**Foreclosure of home is threatened**) you should notify the other side before applying for an ex-parte order.

---

[15]See also Section F below.

A telephone call is enough, but make sure you let the judge know that you made the call (whether or not you got through). Situations 1, 2 and 5 do not need this prior notice, as they fall within exceptions to the notice requirement.[16] On the other hand, we suggest you provide the notice if you reasonably can.

• Once the judge signs the papers, you have been granted a temporary order which will last only a few weeks. The court has also issued an order as part of your temporary order requiring your spouse to attend a hearing within 20 days at which the issues you raised in your ex-parte appearance may be addressed by both sides.

• After the judge signs the papers, you must file the originals with the court clerk, who will stamp the copies and give them back to you. You will propably have to pay a $14 filing fee. (If you cannot afford this, ask the court where you can find the forms for waiver of the fees.) Make sure you also have a blank "Responsive Declaration to Order to Show Cause or Notice of Motion" (1285.40), which is available from the court clerk.

• Have the sheriff or another disinterested adult (anyone over the age of 18 who is not you) serve the papers (i.e., deliver them to the other party), including the blank "Responsive Declaration." Make sure you keep a copy of these papers for your own files. The papers will have to be served at least 15 days before the hearing (unless the judge specified a shorter time, which is common in these types of cases—if he did, it will say so in the papers). The ex parte order does not take effect until it is properly served. If your spouse has taken off with the kids and you don't know where she's gone, you may need to hire a private investigator to start looking. Have whoever served your spouse fill out a Proof of Service and file it with the court clerk before the hearing date.

• Once your spouse has been properly served with the papers, you have an enforceable order. If your spouse violates the order before the hearing, you can ask the court to hold him in contempt of court, and depending on the violation, ask to have him thrown in jail. (If you're having trouble serving your spouse and the 15 day deadline runs out, go back to the judge and have him change the hearing date. Make sure you tell the judge the problem you're having.) At the hearing, the judge will decide whether to make the ex parte order effective for the duration of your divorce proceeding. Argue vigourously for this. Chances are if your spouse has done something fairly nasty and the judge fears he'll or she'll do it again, the judge will make the order permanent.

2. Left high and dry (Situation 3), **Children need support** (Situation 4) and **Foreclosure of home is threatened** (Situation 6).[17]

Here's how you generally proceed in these situations.

1. Fill out the proper forms—"Order to Show Cause" (1285) and "Application for Order and Supporting Declaration" (1285.20). If your request is for support, payment of debts or any other financial issue, you'll need to fill out an "Income and Expense Declaration" with its attachments

---

[16]You don't have to attempt giving notice to the other side when it would be futile to do so, unduly burdensome under the circumstances, or when it would defeat the very purpose of the order.

[17]Only you can decide how much of an emergency there is with your debts. If the bank is threatening foreclosure there are a whole lot of steps it must take before the actual foreclosure can occur and so you may be able to get away with a non-ex parte order.

(1285.50, 1285.50a and 1285.50b). It's also a good idea to ask the court clerk if you need to bring anything else to the hearing. Some counties require pay stubs, tax returns, etc.[18]

If your request is to keep your spouse from emptying the bank accounts or taking other community property (situation 5), you'll need a "Property Declaration" (1285.55). If you're requesting custody, you'll need a "Uniform Child Custody Jurisdiction Act (UCCJA) Declaration" (MC-150).

2. Next, call the court clerk to obtain a hearing date, which you have to indicate on the "Order to Show Cause." If you want the hearing in fewer than 20 days, you'll have to get the judge to check off section 3a on the "Order to Show Cause." This is a good idea if foreclosure proceedings are threatening or if you're in need of immediate financial help.

3. As with the ex parte order, the "Order to Show Cause" must be signed by the judge before being served on your spouse. You don't, however, need to notify your spouse here because the judge is just ordering her to appear in the courtroom and tell her story.

4. File the papers—follow step 4 under ex parte orders.

5. Serve the papers—you need the sheriff of other adult over the age of 18 (excluding yourself) to deliver them to your spouse at least 15 days before the hearing (unless the judge signed section 3a—then the judge will tell you by when the papers need to be served). If your spouse has previously filed papers in this case, you can mail him (or his attorney) the papers. But they must be mailed at least 20 days before the hearing. (Mailing won't work if section 3a is checked.) Whether you serve in person or by mail, you also need to serve a blank "Responsive Declaration" (1285.40) and a blank "Income and Expense Declaration" with attachments (1285.50, 1285.50a and 1285.50b), "Property Declaration" (1285.55) or "UCCJA Declaration" (MC-150) if you filed a completed one.[19] Make sure the Proof of Service is filled out and filed with the court before the hearing.

6. Show up at the court on the day of the hearing. Get there a little early so you can locate the correct courtroom. Ask the clerk if you have trouble finding it. Be prepared to thoroughly tell your side and to explain to the judge why you need what you are requesting.

Note: Keep in mind that you can combine all your issues (if you have more than one) and set all the hearings at the same time. If you get an ex parte order (and therefore have a date set for a hearing on making it permanent), and then your spouse sets a hearing on who is going to make the car payments, call the court clerk to have him move one of the hearings so they are set for the same day.

---

[18]Complete instructions for filling out the income and expense declaration forms are contained in *How to Modify And Collect Child Support in California,* Mathews, Siegel and Willis (Nolo Press).

[19]The purpose of providing your spouse with these blank forms is to get his or her version of the facts and issues raised in the forms into the court record.

E. Expedited Child Support Orders

This is a relatively new procedure where a parent (or the district attorney in the case where neither parent is suporting a child) files 4 forms with the court and serves them on the other parent. If the other parent does not object within 30 days, there becomes an enforceable child support order for the amount set by the Agnos standard (see chapter 8) without there ever having been a court hearing.

1. What Forms?

•Application for Expedited Child Support Order (1297);

•Income and Expense Declaration with attachments (1285.50, 1285.50a and 1285.50b);

•Minimum Child Support Worksheet (1285.25); and

•Expedited Child Support Order (1297.20).

Note: Detailed instructions on how to fill out the "Income and Expense Declaration" and the "Minimum Child Support Worksheet" are found in *How to Modify and Collect Child Support in California*, Matthews, Siegel & Willis, Nolo Press.

2. What Do You Do After You File These at the Courthouse?

Before filing these forms, make sure you have 2 extra copies of each—one for serving and one for yourself. Also get 3 blank "Responses to Application for Expedited Child Support Order and Notice of Hearing" (1297.10) and 3 blank "Income and Expense Declarations" with attachments. One set of what you filed along with the 3 blank "Responses" and the 3 blank "Income and Expense Declarations" must be served on your spouse. Have either the sheriff or any other adult over 18 (but not yourself) do the serving.

3. What Happens After the Papers are Served?

Your spouse has 2 choices. First, he may do nothing; in that case, you will have an enforceable child support order which becomes effective 30 days after the papers were served. Second, he may file a response (within 30 days of being served with the papers), setting forth his objections and asking the court for a hearing. He is then obligated to serve you with notice of the hearing at least 15 days before it is scheduled.

4. What If Your Spouse Sets a Hearing?

If your spouse sets a hearing, both you and your spouse must go and bring your most recently filed state income tax returns.[20] (Whoever doesn't bring the tax returns, loses.) At the hearing, the judge will ask questions about income, earnings, expenses and debts, and then decide if and how much child support should be awarded. If your spouse sets the hearing on a day which you can't make, call the court clerk and try to get it changed. Your reason for not being able to make the meeting must be substantial, however, not just that you're "busy."

F. Interstate (and International) Child Custody Disputes

We have all seen the missing kids on the milk cartons and shopping bags; many of these kids have been taken from one parent by the other who then goes into hiding with the child. These problems are even more compounded when the child is taken out of California.

If you are involved in an interstate or international child custody dispute, we advise you to get an attorney (chapter 12). These disputes commonly give rise to questions involving a precise knowledge of federal laws and procedures, and the rules governing jurisdictional conflicts between states. Even international law may be involved when national borders are crossed. As with previous sections, we only provide an overview of what's involved.

In response to a growing number of interstate disputes which lead to conflicting custody decrees (one parent was awarded custody by one state; the other parent was awarded custody by a different state), every state (including the District of Columbia, Guam and Puerto Rico) has adopted the Uniform Child Custody Jurisdiction Act (UCCJA). This law limits the circumstances under which a court can make—or modify—a custody award. In addition, a federal law, the Parental Kidnapping Prevention Act (PKPA), was enacted by Congress to address the same concerns.

---

[20]You may also have to produce your federal returns under proposed legislation that is expected to be signed into law effective January 1, 1988.

The UCCJA requires that a state meet at least one of the following four tests before the courts of that state can make an initial custody award. These tests are (in order of preference[21]):

1. The state is the child's home state—this means that the child has resided in the state for a least 6 consecutive months, or was residing in the state for 6 consecutive months but is now absent because of a parent's removal or retention;

2. There are significant connections with and substantial evidence in the state regarding the child's care, protection, training and personal relationsips;

3. The child is physically present in the state at the time the action is filed and either has been abandoned or is in danger of being abused or neglected if she or he returns to the other parent; or

4. No other state can meet one of the above 3 tests, or another state can meet at least one of the tests but its courts have declined to make a custody award when provided an opportunity to do so.

If a state cannot meet one of these tests, even if the child is present in the state, the courts of that state cannot make a custody award. Also, a parent who has wrongfully removed or retained a child in order to create a "home state" or "significant connections" will be denied custody.

In the event more than one state can meet one or more of the above tests, the law contemplates that only the courts in one of these states should make a custody award. This means obviously that once a court makes an initial award in a state that meets one of these tests, courts of another qualified state cannot make the initial award. And,when a parent goes to a second state (e.g., Oregon) and tries to modify an existing order issued by a different state (e.g., California), the Oregon court should refuse to hear the case and instead enforce the original California decree.

Summary of How Judges Decide Interstate Custody Disputes

- judges don't make custody awards unless one of the four "tests" can be met.

- judges look to see if another state has already made a custody award.

- judges look to see if another state has a hearing pending before it.

- judges look to see if another state meets a higher test.

Here are some examples of how the UCCJA and PKPA work:

Example 1: Sam and Diane met and married in Missouri. They moved to California where their child (Sam Jr.) was born. Sam, Diane and Junior lived in California until Junior was 10. At that time, Sam took Junior to Missouri in an effort to divorce Diane and raise Junior himself. When Sam goes to court in Missouri and requests custody of Junior, his request will be denied because California is Junior's "home state," the state with which Junior has "significant connections" and Sam removed Junior from California in an effort to creates "home state" jurisdiction in Missouri. (In this situation, Diane should go to court in California and request custody.)

---

[21]This means that the first test is considered to be stronger than the second test, and so on. If there is a conflict between the courts of two states regarding a custody award, the courts of the state meeting the stronger test is usually accorded priority or preference.

Example 2: Let's stick with Sam, Diane and Junior. This time, Sam and Diane married in Missouri, and Junior was born and raised (his early years) there as well. Round about Junior's 8th birthday, Diane's company transfers her to California and so the family moves. After 3 months, she's transferred back and so Diane, Sam and Junior load up the U-Haul and go back to Missouri. Diane misses California and so she grabs Junior and heads back west. California will deny her request for custody because the "significant connections" are with Missouri and because Diane wrongfully took Junior out of Missouri. No state is the "home state" because Junior hasn't lived continuously in any one state for six months. (Here, Sam should go to court in Missouri and request custody.)

Example 3: Let's leave Sam, Diane and Junior for a while. Sandy and Pat have been married for 6 years; they have one child (Chris). They've lived their entire time together in New York, though Pat is originally from California. Times turn tough for Sandy and Pat, and Sandy gets abusive with Pat and Chris. Pat flees to California with Chris and requests exclusive custody. California should grant Pat's request because Chris is in California and in danger of being abused if returned to New York. In this case, Pat's removal of Chris from New York is not wrongful.

Example 4: Lana the lion tamer and Clarence the clown are members of the Munrab & Yeliab traveling circus. They've been married 5 years and have two kids. Lana is getting tired of Clarence's lack of seriousness; Clarence thinks Lana spends too much time with the big cats. They decide to divorce, and Lana quits Munrab & Yeliab to go to work for its competitor, Lingring Sisters. While Lingring is in California, Lana (who is able to establish California residency) goes to court and requests custody of the kids. Because there is no "home state" nor any state with "significant connections," California should make a custody determination.

Example 5: Remember Sam, Diane and Junior? Well, suppose Diane's transfer to California works out, but after 6 months in California Sam gets really tired of the ocean and misses the Cardinals baseball team so he moves back to Missouri. Either California or Missouri could make a custody decision (no matter where Junior is)—California is the "home state" and Missouri has "significant connections." The law contemplates that California would be the right place because "home state" ranks first, but there is no guarantee. This may be a matter of who gets to court first.

What if your spouse takes the kids and leaves or threatens to leave the country? The UCCJA is by its own terms applicable in international disputes. This means that California (or any other state) will recognize and enforce properly made decrees from other countries and will refuse to make a custody award where a child has been snatched and brought to the U.S. unless the child is in danger. In return, some other nations are beginning to recognize U.S. awarded custody orders. There is also a procedure whereby a parent who lives in the U.S. and has a valid custody order can deliver to the U.S. State Department-Passport Issuance Office a copy of the custody order; the State Department will then either revoke any passport already issued for the child, or make sure that no passport is issued for the child in the event one is requested by someone other than the custodial parent.

These procedures, however, are often insufficient to prevent international child snatching episodes. There is an international treaty (the Hague Convention on Civil Aspects of International Child Abduction) which has been introduced into Congress in the hope that the U.S. will sign on and help put an end to our children being battered around liked ping-pong balls.

CHAPTER 12

Lawyers

Lawyers were once dry fellows in English villages who could read, write and had a fireproof box to store important records. No more. They have multiplied like rabbits and spread stridently across the land until they control courts, legislatures, executive branches of government, consulting companies, public and private lobbies, groups, etc., ad infinitum. How this happened is a story we don't have time to tell here. As you already know, we live in a sick society, a part of whose sickness is its lawyer-fixation (domination). Why, hardly a day goes by when the news doesn't feature several lawyers parading back and forth volubly promoting one or another cause— usually, it seems, their own. Not only do we accept the presence of a lot of lawyers in our midst (more than any other nation in the world), but we feed them uncommonly well. Just getting the esquire after one's name seems to automatically entitle one to eat at the top end of the trough.

So what else is new, and what does all this have to do with finding and using lawyers? Very little, except to remind you that lawyers are everywhere and to suggest that they didn't come to run this country without all of our help. We hire, appoint, elect and continue to tolerate them. By getting this book and reading this far, you have made a small personal declaration of independence. You could have bought the same information at $75-$150 per hour at any lawyer's office. All around you there are individuals, and here and there groups, discovering the same thing. If you enjoy knowing more about the procedures and rules that surround you, consider seeking some of these people out.[1] Consider, too, learning how to look up legal information on your own. We are happy to report that many people are doing this, and *Legal Research: How to Find and Understand the Law,* by Steve Elias, is one of our most successful books.

---

[1] Nolo Press has published the *People's Law Review,* which contains much information on self-help law resources, groups, skills etc. See the back of this book for order information.

Unfortunately, however, there are still times when you need a lawyer. Indeed, we point many of them out in the book. As the movement toward liberating law from lawyers and breaking their monopoly over it, and us, is still in its infancy, there are many areas of the law where the information or skill you need is available no place but at the lawyer's office. Also, there are times when you will be dealing with persons and institutions (banks and insurance companies are good examples) who are themselves so used to dealing with and through lawyers that they won't pay attention to anyone else.

If you do decide to relate to a lawyer, don't do it casually—put some time and effort into deciding who you are going to talk to and what you hope to achieve. There is a glut of lawyers these days; California has tens of thousands more than it needs (many are hunting for clients just like you right now), so you can get away with being choosey. Also, remember—and this is important—it is your problem (life) that is being worked on, not the lawyer's. You are a damned fool if you don't make it clear from the start that the lawyer is there to help and advise you, but that you plan to make the major decisions yourself.

A. What Lawyers Can Do for You

There are several basic ways a lawyer can help you. Let's look at these in more detail.

1. Consultation and Advice

The lawyer can listen to the details of your situation, analyze it for you, and advise you on your position and best plan of action. Ideally, he or she will give you more than just conclusions; he or she will educate you about your whole situation and the alternatives available from which you can make your own choices. This kind of service is the least expensive since it only involves an office call and a little time. A charge of more than $50-$75 for a consultation might be considered excessive. Find out the fee *before* you go in. Incidentally, of all the things lawyers can do for you, this may be the most worthwhile. Talk is relatively cheap and may allow you to avoid more serious (expensive) problems later.

2. Negotiation

The lawyer can use his or her special talents, knowledge and experience to help you negotiate with another person, agency or corporation. In case of serious problems, he (she) may be able to do this more successfully than you, especially if you are at odds with someone who is used to dealing with lawyers. Without spending much of his (her) own time, he (she) can often accomplish a lot through a letter or phone call. Receiving a message on an attorney's letterhead is, in itself, sobering to some people. A lawyer can sometimes possess considerable skill as a negotiator. Also, if bad turns to worse, a lawyer can often bluff by threatening legal action. You can then decide at a later time whether to pursue it. But remember, lawyers make money when disputes are prolonged and have an often unconscious motive to escalate little fights into big ones. Remember, too, that you may be a pretty good negotiator yourself if you understand all the facts involved in the dispute.

3. Mediation

This developing area of legal practice involves helping people arrive at the solutions to their own disputes with the help of a lawyer mediator.[2] Mediation works especially well in domestic disputes and we believe it is a far superior approach than fighting in court. Unfortunately, many lawyers have little use for this innovative technique and others don't know much about it. Essentially, mediation around issues of property division, spousal support, or child custody or support consists of having the divorcing spouses sit down with someone who has a thorough knowledge of domestic law and talking until a solution satisfactory to both is reached. Assuming this occurs, the agreed-upon solution is then reduced to writing and presented to a judge. No hassle takes place in court.

There are a number of slightly different ways mediation is practiced, some of which also involve psychologists, social workers, etc., but all are based at arriving at a non-coerced solution and avoiding the traditional adversary court system. The best description of mediation we know about is contained in a book by Joan Blades called *Mediate Your Divorce* (Prentice-Hall).

4. Law Suits

In some rare instances, you may have a case that should go to court. Having a lawyer handle a court case is very expensive, except where the lawyer will represent you on a contingency fee arrangement (he or she only gets paid if you win the case) or where the other side may be required to pay your lawyer's fees under a contract or statute.[3] Unfortunately, the archaic language, forms and courtroom procedures make it difficult for nonlawyers to represent themselves except in Small

---

[2]Please distinguish private mediation practiced by lawyers, which we discuss here, from the court-sponsored mediation of child custody disputes which is discussed in Chapters 8 and 10.

[3]Lawyers are prohibited from representing clients in divorce cases on a contingency fee basis. And while statutes provide that one spouse should pay all (or some) of the other spouse's legal fees, remember that many marriages break down because of lack of money, so don't count on this.

Claims Court.[4] Access to courts for a reasonable cost is a major area where reform is needed. If you hire a lawyer to represent you in court, be sure you know what you are paying for.

5. Checking Your Work

There may be times when you have done your own legal work (i.e., prepared divorce, adoption or bankruptcy papers) and you simply want someone with more experience to check them. You should be able to find a lawyer to do this, but you may have to shop around a bit. Simply ask lawyers what their attitude toward helping you do your own thing is and what they charge. If you get someone who is willing to help, but obviously has a lot of doubts about what you are doing, keep calling. Try and fix an agreeable hourly fee in advance.

B. When You Are Entitled to a Lawyer for Free

In addition to requiring assigned lawyers for the defense of criminal or juvenile delinquency proceedings, our legislature and courts require counsel for indigent people in the following two domestic situations:

1. A male defendant in a paternity proceeding brought by the state;

2. The parents of a child, and the child, where the state wishes to assert some kind of control over the child.

Each court determines whether a person qualifies as an indigent for purposes of free attorneys, but if your income is anywhere near what you would be receiving from welfare or unemployment insurance, you would certainly qualify.

In addition to appointed counsel, most counties have a legal aid program which is available to the poor for advice, consultation, and sometimes representation.

Note: Lawyers representing parties in a dissolution proceeding are entitled to payment from the "community estate." Until recently, lawyers would have to wait until after the divorce to collect their fees (unless, of course, they were paid "up front"). Now, however, a lawyer may apply to the court for payment during the course of the proceeding and may require either of the parties involved to pay the fees, depending on their individual circumstances.

The most important effect of this change is that a poor person will find it easier to hire a lawyer so long as their spouse *or* the community property is able to meet the attorney's fees.

---

[4]We highly recommend Small Claims Court for small disputes. *Everybody's Guide to Small Claims Court,* Warner, Nolo Press, is an excellent guide to filing your papers, presenting your case and collecting when you win. Unfortunately, for those of you who are owed back child support, the small claims court cannot be used to collect it. *In re Marriage of Lackey* 143 Cal.App.3d 698 (1983).

C. Finding a Lawyer

Finding a lawyer who charges reasonable prices and whom you feel can be trusted is not always an easy task. There is always the realistic fear that by just picking a name out of the telephone book you may get someone unsympathetic or perhaps an attorney who will charge too much. You should realize that you are not the only one who feels a little scared and intimidated. Here are some suggestions:

1. Paralegal "Typing Service" Assistance

For those who want to do their own divorce, but don't want to do their own paperwork, nonlawyer independent paralegals offer a good alternative. See the back of this book for a list. The cost of this service is normally $75-$200, depending on the complexity of the particular action.

2. Legal Aid

If you are poor, you may qualify for free help from your legal aid office (often called legal services or legal assistance). Check your yellow pages under Attorneys for their location, or ask your County Clerk.

3. Group Legal Practices

A new but rapidly growing aspect of California law practice is the Group Legal Practice program. Many groups, including unions, employers and consumer action groups, are offering plans to their members whereby they can get legal assistance for rates which are substantially lower than offered by most private practitioners. Some of these plans are good, some mediocre, and a few are not worth much, but most are better than nothing.

4. Private Attorneys

If you don't know an attorney that can be trusted and can't get a reliable recommendation from a friend, you have a problem. While you might be lucky and randomly pick an attorney who matches your needs perfectly, you might just as easily wind up paying too much for too little. Here are some suggestions that should make your search a little easier:

• Referral panels set up by local bar associations. Lawyers are initially screened on their expertise in domestic matters. There is usually a small fee for an initial consultation. You may get a good referral from these panels, but be sure to question the lawyer whose name you are given about his or her qualifications and sympathy to your concerns. One reason lawyers list their names on referral panels is that they don't have enough business.

• Consult the ads in the classified section of the newspaper under "Attorneys." This will give you a good idea as to price and range of services offered.

• Shop around by calling different law offices and stating your problem. Ask them how much it would cost for a visit. Try to talk to a lawyer personally to attempt to get an idea of how friendly and sympathetic he is to your concerns. Offices that use the word "Legal Clinic" in their title often specialize in the mass production of simple types of cases (bankruptcy, divorce, debt problems, etc.) at reasonable prices.

• Remember, lawyers whose offices and life styles are reasonably simple are more likely to help you for less money than lawyers who feel naked unless wearing a $1,000 outfit. You should be able to find an attorney willing to discuss your problems for $50-$100.

TABLE OF CONTENTS

■ BUSINESS AND FINANCE

How To Form Your Own Corporation
By attorney Mancuso. Provides all the forms, Bylaws, Articles, minutes of meeting, stock certificates and instructions necessary to form your small profit corporation. Includes a thorough discussion of the practical and legal aspects of incorporation, including the tax consequences.

California Edition	$24.95
Texas Edition	$21.95
New York Edition	$19.95
Florida Edition	$19.95

The Non-Profit Corporation Handbook
By attorney Mancuso. Includes all the forms, Bylaws, Articles, minutes, and instructions you need to form a non-profit corporation. Step-by-step instructions on how to choose a name, draft Articles and Bylaws, attain favorable tax status. Thorough information on federal tax exemptions, which groups outside of California will find particularly useful.

California only	$24.95

The California Professional Corporation Handbook
By attorneys Mancuso and Honigsberg. In California a number of professions must fulfill special requirements when forming a corporation. Among them are lawyers, dentists, doctors and other health professionals, accountants and certain social workers. This book contains detailed information on the special requirements of every profession and all the forms and instructions necessary to form a professional corporation.

California only	$29.95

Marketing Without Advertising
By Phillips and Rasberry. A creative and practical guide that shows small business people how to avoid wasting money on advertising. The authors, experienced business consultants, show how to implement an ongoing marketing plan to tell potential and current customers that yours is a quality business worth trusting, recommending and coming back to.

National Edition	$14.00

Billpayers' Rights
By attorney Warner. Complete information on bankruptcy, student loans, wage attachments, dealing with bill collectors and collection agencies, credit cards, car repossessions, homesteads, child support and much more.

California only	$12.95

Bankruptcy: Do-It-Yourself
By attorney Kosel. Tells you exactly what bankruptcy is all about and how it affects your credit rating, property and debts, with complete details on property you can keep under the state and federal exempt property rules. Shows you step-by-step how to do it yourself; comes with all necessary forms and instructions.

National Edition	$15.95

The Partnership Book
By attorneys Clifford and Warner. When two or more people join to start a small business, one of the most basic needs is to establish a solid, legal partnership agreement. This book supplies a number of sample agreements which you can use as is. Buy-out clauses, unequal sharing of assets, and limited partnerships are all discussed in detail.

National Edition	$18.95

Chapter 13: The Federal Plan to Repay Your Debts
By attorney Kosel. This book allows an individual to develop and carry out a feasible plan to pay most of his/her debts over a three-year period. Chapter 13 is an alternative to straight bankruptcy and yet it still means the end of creditor harassment, wage attachments and other collection efforts. Comes complete with all necessary forms and worksheets.

National Edition	$14.95

Small Time Operator
By Kamoroff, C.P.A.. Shows you how to start and operate your small business, keep your books, pay your taxes and stay out of trouble. Comes complete with a year's supply of ledgers and worksheets designed especially for small businesses, and contains invaluable information on permits, licenses, financing, loans, insurance, bank accounts, etc. Published by Bell Springs.

National Edition	$10.95

Start-Up Money: How to Finance Your Small Business
By Business Consultant McKeever. For anyone about to start a business or revamp an existing one, this book shows how to write a business plan, draft a loan package and find sources of small business finance.

National Edition	$12.95

The Independent Paralegal's Handbook: How to Provide Legal Services Without Going to Jail
By attorney Warner. More and more nonlawyers are opening legal typing services to help people prepare their own papers for divorce, bankruptcy, incorporation, eviction, etc. Called independent paralegals, these legal pioneers pose much the same challenge to the legal establishment as midwives do to conventional medicine. Written by Nolo Press co-founder Ralph Warner, who established one of the first divorce typing services in 1973, this controversial book is sure to become the bible of the new movement aimed at delivering routine legal services to the public at a reasonable price.

National Edition	$12.95

Getting Started as an Independent Paralegal (two audio cassette tapes)

By attorney Warner. In these two audiotapes, about three hours in all, Ralph Warner explains how to set up and run an independent paralegal business and how to market your services. He also discusses in detail how to avoid charges of unauthorized practice of law.
National 1st Edition $24.95

■ *ESTATE PLANNING, WILLS & PROBATE*

Plan Your Estate: Wills, Probate Avoidance, Trusts and Taxes

By attorney Clifford. Comprehensive information on making a will, alternatives to probate, planning to limit inheritance and estate taxes, living trusts, and providing for family and friends.
California Edition $15.95

Nolo's Simple Will Book

By attorney Clifford. This book will show you how to draft a will without a lawyer in any state except Louisiana. Covers all the basics, including what to do about children, whom you can designate to carry out your wishes, and how to comply with the technical legal requirements of each state. Includes examples and many alternative clauses from which to choose.
National Edition $14.95

WillWriter—a software/book package

By Legisoft. Use your computer to prepare and update your own valid will. A manual provides help in areas such as tax planning and probate avoidance. Runs on the Apple II family, IBM PC and compatibles, Commodore, Macintosh).
National Edition $49.95
Commodore Edition $39.95

How to Probate an Estate

By Nissley. Forms and instructions necessary to settle a California resident's estate after death. This book deals with joint tenancy and community property transfers as well as showing you how to actually probate an estate, step-by-step. The book is aimed at the executor, administrator or family member who will have the actual responsibility to settle the estate.
California Edition $24.95

■ *FAMILY AND FRIENDS*

How to Do Your Own Divorce

By attorney Sherman. This is the original "do-your-own-law" book. It contains tear-out copies of all the court forms required for an uncontested dissolution, as well as instructions for certain special forms.
California Edition $14.95
Texas Edition $12.95

A Legal Guide for Lesbian/Gay Couples

By attorneys Curry and Clifford. Here is a book that deals specifically with legal matters of lesbian and gay couples: raising children (custody, support, living with a lover), buying property together, wills, etc. and comes complete with sample contracts and agreements.
National Edition $17.95

The Living Together Kit

By attorneys Ihara and Warner. A legal guide for unmarried couples with information about buying or sharing property, the Marvin decision, paternity statements, medical emergencies and tax consequences. Contains a sample will and Living Together Contract.
National Edition $14.95

California Marriage and Divorce Law

By attorneys Ihara and Warner. This book contains invaluable information for married couples and those considering marriage or remarriage on community and separate property, names, debts, children, buying a house, etc. Includes prenuptial contracts, a simple will, probate avoidance information and an explanation of gift and inheritance taxes. Discusses "secret marriage" and "common law" marriage.
California only $15.95

Social Security, Medicare & Pensions: A Sourcebook for Older Americans

By attorney Matthews & Berman. The most comprehensive resource tool on the income, rights and benefits of Americans over 55.Includes detailed information on social security, retirement rights, Medicare, Medicaid, supplemental security income, private pensions, age discrimination, as well as a thorough explanation of social security legislation.
National Edition $14.95

How to Modify & Collect Child Support in California

By attorneys Matthews, Segal and Willis. California court awards for child support have radically increased in the last two years. This book contains the forms and instructions to obtain the benefits of this change without a lawyer and collect support directly from a person's wages or benefits, if necessary.
California only $17.95

How to Adopt Your Stepchild

By Zagone. Shows you how to prepare all the legal forms; includes information on how to get the consent of the natural parent and how to conduct an "abandonment" proceeding. Discusses appearing in court and making changes in birth certificates.
California only $19.95

The Power of Attorney Book

By attorney Clifford. Covers the process which allows you to arrange for someone else to protect your rights and property should you become incapable of doing so. Discusses the advantages and drawbacks and gives complete instructions for establishing a power of attorney yourself.
National Edition $15.95

How to Change Your Name

By attorneys Loeb and Brown. Changing one's name is a very simple procedure. Using this book, you can file the necessary papers yourself, saving $200 to $300 in attorney's fees. Comes complete with all forms and instructions for the court petition method or this simpler usage method.
California only $14.95

Your Family Records: How to Preserve Personal, Financial and Legal History

By Pladsen and attorney Clifford. Helps you organize and record all sorts of items that will affect you and your family when death or disability occur, e.g., where to find your will and deed to the house. Includes information about probate avoidance, joint ownership of property and genealogical research. Space is provided for financial and legal records.
National Edition $14.95

■ *LANDLORD/TENANT*

Tenants' Rights

By attorneys Moskovitz, Warner and Sherman. Discusses everything tenants need to know in order to protect themselves: getting deposits returned, breaking a lease, getting repairs made, using Small Claims Court, dealing with an unscrupulous landlord, forming a tenants' organization, etc. Sample Fair-to-Tenants lease, rental agreements, and unlawful detainer answer forms.
California Edition $14.95

The Landlord's Law Book: Rights and Responsibilities

By attorneys Brown and Warner. Now, for the first time, there is an accessible, easy to understand law book written specifically for landlords. Covers the areas of discrimination, insurance, tenants' privacy, leases, security deposits, rent control, liability, and rent withholding.
California only $24.95

The Landlord's Law Book: Evictions

By attorney Brown. This is the most comprehensive manual available on how to do each step of an eviction, and the only one to deal with rent control cities and contested evictions including how to represent yourself in court if necessary. All the required forms, with directions on how to complete and file them, are included. Vol. 1 covers Rights and Responsibilities.
California only $24.95

Landlording

By Robinson (Express Press). Written for the conscientious landlord or landlady, this comprehensive guide discusses maintenance and repairs, getting good tenants, how to avoid evictions, record keeping and taxes.
National Edition $17.95

■ *REAL ESTATE*

All About Escrow

(Express Press) By Gadow. This book gives you a good understanding of what your escrow officer should be doing for you. Includes advice about inspections, financing, condominiums and cooperatives.
National Edition $12.95

The Deeds Book

By attorney Randolph. Adding or removing a name from a deed, giving up interest in community property at divorce, putting a house in joint tenancy to avoid probate, all these transactions require a change in the way title to real estate is held. This book shows you how to choose the right deed, fill it out and record it.
California Edition $15.95

Homebuyers: Lambs to the Slaughter

By attorney Bashinsky (Menasha Ridge Press). Written by a lawyer/broker, this book describes how sellers, agents, lenders and lawyers are out to fleece you, the buyer, and advises how to protect your interests.
National Edition $12.95

For Sale By Owner

By Devine. The average California home sold for $130,000 in 1986. That meant the average seller paid $7800 in broker's commissions. This book will show you how to sell your own home and save the money. All the background information and legal technicalities are included to help you do the job yourself and with confidence.
California Edition $24.95

Homestead Your House

By attorney Warner. Under the California Homestead Act, you can file a Declaration of Homestead and thus protect your home from being sold to satisfy most debts. This book explains this simple and inexpensive procedure and includes all the forms and instructions. Contains information on exemptions for mobile homes and houseboats.
California only $8.95

■ *COPYRIGHTS & PATENTS*

Legal Care for Your Software

By attorney Remer. Shows the software programmer how to protect his/her work through the use of trade secret, trademark, copyright, patent and, most especially, contractual laws and agreements. This book is full of forms and instructions that give programmers the hands-on information they need.
International Edition $24.95

Intellectual Property Law Dictionary

By attorney Elias. "Intellectual Property" includes ideas, creations and inventions. The Dictionary is designed for inventors, authors, programmers, journalists, scientists and business people who must understand how the law affects the ownership and control of new ideas and technologies. Divided into sections on: Trade Secrets, Copyrights, Trademarks, Patents and Contracts. More than a dictionary, it places terms in context as well as defines them.
National Edition $17.95

How to Copyright Software

By attorney Salone. Shows the serious programmer or software developer how to protect his or her programs through the legal device of copyright.
International Edition $24.95

Patent It Yourself

By attorney Pressman. Complete instructions on how to do a patent search and file for a patent in the U.S. Also covers how to choose the appropriate form of protection (copyright, trademark, trade secret, etc.), how to evaluate salability of inventions, patent prosecution, marketing, use of the patent, foreign filing, licensing, etc. Tear-out forms are included
National Edition $24.95

Inventor's Notebook

By Fred Grissom and attorney David Pressman. The best protection for your patent is adequate records. The Inventor's Notebook provides forms, instructions, references to relevant areas of patent law, a bibliography of legal and non-legal aids, and more. It helps you document the activities that are normally part of successful independent inventing.
National 1st Edition $19.95

■ RESEARCHING THE LAW

California Civil Code

(West Publishing) Statutes covering a wide variety of topics, rights and duties in the landlord/tenant relationship, marriage and divorce, contracts, transfers of real estate, consumer credit, power of attorney, and trusts.
California only $17.00

California Code of Civil Procedure

(West Publishing) Statutes governing most judicial and administrative procedures: unlawful detainer (eviction) proceedings, small claims actions, homestead procedures, wage garnishments, recording of liens, statutes of limitation, court procedures, arbitration, and appeals.
California only $17.00

Legal Research:
How to Find and Understand the Law

By attorney Elias. A hands-on guide to unraveling the mysteries of the law library. For paralegals, law students, consumer activists, legal secretaries, business and media people. Shows exactly how to find laws relating to specific cases or legal questions, interpret statutes and regulations, find and research cases, understand case citations and Shepardize them.
National Edition $14.95

■ RULES AND TOOLS

Collecting Court Judgments

By Ginny Scott. Winning a court judgment is only half the battle. This book covers skip tracing (how to find someone who owes you money), how to get paid while keeping good will, how to use collection agencies, and how to find out what property is available to satisfy your debt.
California 1st Edition $19.95

Make Your Own Contract

By attorney Elias. Provides tear-out contracts, with instructions, for non-commercial use. Covers lending money, selling or leasing personal property (e.g., cars, boats), leasing and storing items (with friends, neighbors), doing home repairs, and making deposits to hold personal property pending final payment. Includes an appendix listing all the contracts found in Nolo books.
National Edition $12.95

The Criminal Records Book

By attorney Siegel. Takes you step-by-step through the procedures available to get your records sealed, destroyed or changed. Detailed discussion on your criminal record what it is, how it can harm you, how to correct inaccuracies, marijuana possession records and juvenile court records.
California only $14.95

The People's Law Review

Edited by Warner. This is the first compendium of people's law resources ever published. Contains articles on mediation and the new "non-adversary" mediation centers, information on self-help law programs and centers (for tenants, artists, battered women, the disabled, etc.); and articles dealing with many common legal problems which show people how to do-it-themselves.
National Edition $8.95

Everybody's Guide to Small Claims Court

By attorney Warner. Guides you step-by-step through the Small Claims procedure, providing practical information on how to evaluate your case, file and serve papers, prepare and present your case, and, most important, how to collect when you win. Separate chapters focus on common situations (landlord-tenant, automobile sales and repair, etc.).
National Edition $10.95
California Edition $14.95

Fight Your Ticket

By attorney Brown. A comprehensive manual on how to fight your traffic ticket. Radar, drunk driving, preparing for court, arguing your case to a judge, cross-examining witnesses are all covered.
California only $16.95

How to Become a United States Citizen

By Sally Abel. Detailed explanation of the naturalization process. Includes step-by-step instructions from filing for naturalization to the final oath of allegiance. Includes a study guide on U.S. history and government. Text is written in both English and Spanish.
National Edition $9.95

Draft, Registration and The Law

By attorney Johnson. How it works, what to do, advice and strategies.
California only $9.95

Murder on the Air

By Ralph Warner and Toni Ihara. An unconventional murder mystery set in Berkeley, California. When a noted environmentalist and anti-nuclear activist is killed at a local radio station, the Berkeley violent crime squad swings into action. James Rivers, an unplugged lawyer, and Sara Tamura, Berkeley's first female murder squad detective, lead the chase. The action is fast, furious and fun. $5.95

29 Reasons Not to Go to Law School

By attorneys Ihara and Warner, with contributions by fellow lawyers and illustrations by Mari Stein. A humorous and irreverent look at the dubious pleasures of going to law school. 2nd Ed. $6.95

ORDER FORM

Quantity	Title	Unit Price	Total

Prices subject to change

Subtotal _____

Tax (CA only): San Mateo, LA, & Bart Counties 6 1/2%
Santa Clara & Alameda 7%
All others 6%

Tax _____

Postage & Handling

No. of Books	Postage & Handling
1	$1.50
2-3	$2.00
4-5	$2.50
Over 5	add 5% of total before tax

Postage & Handling _____

Total _____

Please allow 3-5 weeks for delivery.
For faster service, add $1 for UPS delivery (no P.O. boxes, please).

Name _____

Address _____

_____

☐ VISA   ☐ Mastercard

_____ Exp. _____

Signature _____

Phone (   ) _____

☐ Please send me a catalogue

ORDERS: Credit card information or a check may be sent to NOLO Press, 950 Parker St., Berkeley CA 94710

Use your credit card and our **800 lines** for faster service:

ORDERS ONLY (M-F 9-5 Pacific Time):

US: 800-992-NOLO
Outside (415) area **CA: 800-445-NOLO**
Inside (415) area **CA: (415) 549-1976**

For general information call: **(415) 549-1976**

Libraries contact: NOLO PRESS DISTRIBUTION, Box 544 , Occidental CA 95465
(800) 822-8382 in California
(800) 433-6656 outside California

About the Authors

TONI IHARA

Toni was educated at the University of California at Santa Barbara and Berkeley, and is a graduate of the School of law at the University of California at Davis. She is the co-author of *Protect Your Home with a Declaration of Homestead* and *The Living Together Kit*, as well as *29 Reasons Not to go to Law School*.

RALPH WARNER

Ralph graduated from the Boalt School of Law at the University of California, Berkeley. As a pioneer of the self-help law movement he has authored a number of books aimed at giving people the knowledge necessary to solve their own legal problems, including the much-acclaimed *California Tenants' Handbook* and *Everybody's Guide to Small Claims Court* as well as *The People's Law Review*.

STEPHEN R. ELIAS

Steve received a law degree from Hastings College of Law in 1969. He practiced in California, New York, Vermont and again in California until 1981 when he decided to make a full time career of helping non-lawyers understand the law. Steve is the author of Nolo's *Intellectual Property Law Dictionary* and editor of *Patent It Yourself* by David Pressman and *How to Copyright Software* by M.J. Salone. Steve has also authored or co-authored five other Nolo Press books. At present Steve is working on a book about trademarks and business names.